CLIFFS

SAT II WRITING

Subject Test

PREPARATION GUIDE

by

Allan Casson

Series Editor
Jerry Bobrow

Cliffs Notes
INCORPORATED
LINCOLN, NEBRASKA   68501

ISBN 0-8220-2325-3

FIRST EDITION

CONTENTS

PART III: INTRODUCTION TO THE ESSAY EXAM

PART IV: FIVE FULL-LENGTH PRACTICE TESTS

PREFACE

When you're studying for the SAT II Writing Subject Test, keep in mind that the multiple-choice section of the exam (Part B) accounts for two thirds of the test time and two thirds of your overall score. Consequently, you should probably budget your study time similarly.

It is easier to prepare for the multiple-choice section of the exam than for the essay section. The knowledge you need to answer the multiple-choice questions is identified specifically and is covered thoroughly in this book in the Introduction to the Multiple-Choice Exam, the Grammar and Usage Review, and the complete explanations following each practice exam.

It is more difficult to prepare for the essay section of the exam (Part A) because that section tests writing and thinking skills acquired over all the years you've been in school. It is quite possible, however, to sharpen those skills and to direct them toward writing the types of essays required by this exam. The Grammar and Usage Review will help you to accomplish this goal by pointing out mechanical errors you should certainly avoid in your essays. The Introduction to the Essay Exam will help you to understand the basis on which readers score your essay. This section will also show you student essays scoring from high to low to give you a good idea of the kind of writing you must produce to score well. Since the best way to learn to write is by writing, using the Essay Topics and having them scored and commented on by a knowledgeable friend will make you comfortable with writing such essays under timed conditions.

FORMAT OF A RECENT
SAT II WRITING SUBJECT TEST

Part A	Essay	1 Question
20 minutes	Personal-analytical essay on a general topic	

Part B	Multiple-Choice	60 Questions
40 minutes	Identifying Sentence Errors (usage)	20 questions
	Improving Sentences (sentence correction)	18 questions
	Improving Paragraphs (revision in context)	12 questions
	Identifying Sentence Errors (usage)	10 questions

Total time: 1 hour

The essay counts one third of the final score; the multiple-choice questions count two thirds of the final score.

ANSWERS TO YOUR QUESTIONS ABOUT THE EXAM

What College Board publications should I consult?

Anyone planning to take the SAT II Writing test should read carefully the section of *The Official Guide to SAT II: Subject Tests* that deals with this exam. This book gives a list of the common writing problems that are tested in the multiple-choice section, examples and explanations of each of the three kinds of multiple-choice questions, and a complete sample exam with answers. It also includes one example of a writing sample topic and twelve student essays on that topic. These illustrate the six possible scores on the essay in the writing section. A scoring guide explains the qualities of each of the six essay scores.

When should I study this book?

If you're not confident about your abilities in the multiple-choice section, start to study the material about that section of the exam right away. The careful study of the grammar and style instruction in this book can noticeably improve your score.

Your success on the writing sample will be determined by your native ability, the luck of the topic, and above all, the instruction and experience in writing that you've had. While no preparation guide can begin to replace what you've discovered in your high school English classes, you can increase your confidence and your score by carefully using the materials provided here and by practicing the types of essays the exam will require you to write.

What should I study on the night before the exam?

Since the exam is really testing all your years of English study, if you need to study on the eve of the exam, you're probably in trouble. It's likely that you'll do better if you relax the night before. Watch television and get a good night's sleep. If you're so compulsive that you feel you must study on any night before an exam, look over the grammar section and reread the general advice about the writing sample. Since taking multiple-choice exams is pretty boring, don't take a lot of sample exams the night before so that the real thing will seem a little fresher to you.

Do I write the essay in pen or pencil?

Pencil. Take at least two to the exam. If you're nervous about losing things, take three or four.

What should I take to the exam?

Take your Admission Ticket, pencils, watch, and an accepted form of identification with your picture on it.

Where can I get sample exams to use to study for the SAT II Writing test?

There are three good sources. One is the *Official Guide to the SAT II: Subject Tests* published by the College Board. The second is one of the older editions of *Ten SATs,* which you might come across in a store selling used books. The old SAT included the Test of Standard Written English, which used thirty-five of the Identifying Sentence Errors questions and fifteen of the Improving Sentences questions but did not include the Improving Paragraphs questions.

The third source is this book. Many of the exams in commercially published study guides (not this one, of course) are uneven and include questions on problems that will not appear on the exam. Questions written by nonprofessionals are often either too easy or too hard.

Part I:
Introduction to the Multiple-Choice Exam

THE MULTIPLE-CHOICE QUESTIONS

There are three kinds of questions in the multiple-choice section of the SAT II Writing test: Identifying Sentence Errors (sometimes called usage) questions, Improving Sentences (sentence correction) questions, and Improving Paragraphs (also called revision in context) questions. A typical exam will have twenty Identifying Sentence Errors questions, followed by eighteen Improving Sentences questions, followed by twelve Improving Paragraphs questions, which consist of two sets of six questions based on two passages of student writing. Finally, there are an additional ten Identifying Sentence Errors questions. The exact number of questions of each type may vary slightly; the total number of questions may be one or two fewer than sixty.

IDENTIFYING SENTENCE ERRORS QUESTIONS (USAGE)

In this section, each question is a single, complete sentence of fewer than thirty words (and usually fewer than twenty-five) with four underlined words or phrases lettered A, B, C, and D. A fifth choice (E) is for no error. The sentence may be correct (no error), or there may be a usage error in one of the underlined words or phrases.

The following are examples of the Identifying Sentence Errors (usage) questions, with an explanation of the answers. Some of these explanations suggest ways to change the sentences to make them correct. *In this section of the exam, however, remember that you don't need to correct the sentence; you only need to identify the underlined section that contains an error.*

Directions: The following sentences may contain one error of grammar, usage, diction, or idiom. No sentence will contain more than one error, and some have no error. If there is an error, it will be underlined and have a letter beneath it. Sections of the sentence that are not underlined cannot be changed. In selecting your answer, observe the requirements of standard written English.

If there is an error, choose the one underlined part that must be changed to correct the sentence. If there is no error, choose (E).

EXAMPLE:

The film tell the story of a cavalry captain and his wife
       A   B
who try to rebuild their lives after the Civil War. No error
    C   D   E

Correct answer: A

1. The greatest strength of the American political system is each
                                                            A
   voter's right to determine which way they will vote. No error
                    B   C   D   E

The singular *is* agrees with the singular *strength.* The plural *they,* however, does not agree with the singular *each voter.* The right answer is (C).

2. Like Faulkner, Eudora Welty's stories <u>give the reader</u> a sense
     <u>   </u>
          A   B

<u>of what</u> life in the South <u>must have been like</u> in the thirties.
   C   D

<u>No error</u>
  E

The problem in this sentence is at the beginning. As it now stands, the comparison is not Faulkner and Welty (two authors) or Faulkner's stories and Welty's fiction (two works), but Faulkner and Welty's stories (a writer and a writer's works). The corrected sentence would read *Like Faulkner's* or *Like those of Faulkner* or *Like the stories of Faulkner*.

3. The workers at the American embassy in Moscow

   <u>have been affected</u> in some way by radio waves, <u>but there is no</u>
          A   B

   certainty about <u>just what</u> <u>the effects have been.</u> <u>No error</u>
                   C   D   E

This is a sentence with no error. Don't hesitate to choose (E) when you can't find a usage error that you are sure about. About one in five questions in this section of the exam will have no error.

4. Unaffected <u>by neither hunger nor cold</u>, Scott covered up to
                       A

   twenty miles <u>on each of the days</u> that the weather
                       B

   <u>permitted him</u> to <u>travel at all.</u> <u>No error</u>
        C   D   E

The error here is (A), a double negative, since *Unaffected* and *neither* are both negatives. To correct the usage, change *Unaffected* to *Affected* or *neither . . . nor* to *either . . . or.*

5. The governor $\underset{A}{\underline{\text{hopes}}}$ $\underset{B}{\underline{\text{to increase and redistribute}}}$ tax money,

   $\underset{C}{\underline{\text{raising}}}$ the expenditure on education and $\underset{D}{\underline{\text{equalizing them}}}$

   throughout the state. $\underset{E}{\underline{\text{No error}}}$

There are no errors in (A), (B), or (C), but there is an error of agreement in (D). The plural pronoun *them* refers to the singular *expenditure.* The corrected sentence would have either *expenditures* and *them* or *expenditure* and *it.*

6. The trustees of the fund $\underset{A}{\underline{\text{which determine}}}$ the awarding of the

   grants $\underset{B}{\underline{\text{are planning}}}$ $\underset{C}{\underline{\text{to meet}}}$ in Washington, $\underset{D}{\underline{\text{not New York.}}}$

   $\underset{E}{\underline{\text{No error}}}$

The error here is the choice of the pronoun *which* in (A). Since the trustees are men and women, the correct pronoun is *who.*

7. The increase in the number $\underset{A}{\underline{\text{of predators}}}$ that

   $\underset{B}{\underline{\text{carry infectious diseases}}}$ to the herds of zebra and gnu $\underset{C}{\underline{\text{are a}}}$

   serious concern $\underset{D}{\underline{\text{to the park rangers.}}}$ $\underset{E}{\underline{\text{No error}}}$

This is another error of agreement. The subject of the sentence is the singular noun *increase,* and its verb, although widely separated from it, is the plural *are.* It should read *the increase . . . is.*

IMPROVING SENTENCES QUESTIONS
(SENTENCE CORRECTION)

This question type presents a single sentence with all or part of it underlined. The five lettered choices present five possible versions of the underlined part. The rest of the sentence that is not underlined cannot be changed and must be used to determine which of the five answers is the best. The first choice (A) repeats the original version, while the next four make changes. Sometimes the original sentence is better than the four proposed alternatives. The following are examples of this question type with an explanation of the right answer.

Directions: The following questions test correctness and effective expression. In selecting the answer, pay attention to grammar, diction, sentence structure, and punctuation.

In the following questions, part or all of each sentence is underlined. The (A) answer repeats the underlined portion of the original sentence, while the next four offer alternatives. Choose the answer that best expresses the meaning of the original sentence and at the same time is grammatically correct and stylistically superior. The correct choice should be clear, unambiguous, and concise.

EXAMPLE:

The forecaster predicted rain and the sky was clear.

(A) rain and the sky was clear
(B) rain but the sky was clear
(C) rain the sky was clear
(D) rain, but the sky was clear
(E) rain being as the sky was clear

Correct answer: D

---

1. When she was only five, Janet's mother married for the third time.

   (A) When she was only five, Janet's mother married for the third time.
   (B) When only five, Janet's mother married for the third time.
   (C) When Janet was only five, her mother married for the third time.
   (D) When Janet's mother married for the third time, she was only five.
   (E) Janet's mother married, when Janet was only five, for the third time.

   The major problem in this sentence is the uncertainty about whom the *when she was only five* clause modifies, five-year-old Janet or her mother. In (A) and (D), the *she* appears to refer to the mother, while (B), although the pronoun is missing, also seems to make the marrying mother five years old. Both (C) and (E) remove the ambiguity. In the choice between these two sentences, (C) is preferable, since (E) places the phrase *for the third time* awkwardly away from the verb *married,* which it modifies.

2. After he graduated from college, his parents gave him a new car, ten thousand dollars, and sent him on a trip around the world.

   (A) After he graduated from college, his parents gave him a new car, ten thousand dollars, and sent him on
   (B) After graduating from college, his parents gave him a new car, ten thousand dollars, and
   (C) After he had graduated from college, his parents gave him a new car, ten thousand dollars, and
   (D) After he had graduated from college, his parents gave him a new car, ten thousand dollars, and sent him on
   (E) After graduating from college, his parents gave him a new car, ten thousand dollars, and sent him on

   There are two problems in the original sentence, parallelism and verb tense. The verb *gave* begins a series with nouns as objects (*car, dollars*), but the third part of the series (*and sent him on*) interrupts the series. Choices (B) and (C) correct this error by making *trip* a third object of *gave*. But (B) can't be right because it begins with a dangling participle; it appears that the parents are graduating from college. Choice (C) correctly uses the past perfect tense (*had graduated*) to place the action of graduating before the past action of the verb *gave*.

3. <u>When one reaches the first plateau, it</u> does not guarantee that you will complete the climb to the summit.

   (A) When one reaches the first plateau, it
   (B) Because one reaches the first plateau, it
   (C) One's reaching the first plateau
   (D) That you have reached the first plateau
   (E) Reaching the first plateau

There is an inconsistency in the pronouns in this sentence. The part that can't be changed uses *you,* but the underlined section uses *one*. A right answer will either use *you* or get rid of the pronoun altogether. (A), (B), and (C) can't be right, but (D) and (E) are grammatical. In this case, (E) is preferable because it is shorter.

4. <u>To prune a rose is more dangerous than pruning an azalea.</u>

   (A) To prune a rose is more dangerous than pruning an azalea.
   (B) To prune a rose is more dangerous than azalea pruning.
   (C) Pruning a rose is more dangerous than pruning an azalea.
   (D) It is more dangerous to prune a rose than it is to prune an azalea.
   (E) Pruning a rose is more dangerous than to prune an azalea.

The object here is to make the verbs on either side of the *than* parallel. You can use two infinitives (*to prune, to prune*) or two gerunds (*pruning, pruning*) but not one of each as in (A), (B), and (E). Choice (D) has the correct verb parallels but is much more wordy. The right choice is (C).

5. When swimming for Northwestern, <u>Debbie Holm set records</u>
   <u>that lasted for ten years</u>.

   (A) Debbie Holm set records that lasted for ten years
   (B) the records Debbie Holm set lasted ten years
   (C) ten-year records were set by Debbie Holm
   (D) the records of Debbie Holm lasted ten years
   (E) Debbie Holm's records lasted ten years

The phrase that begins this sentence has an understood but
unwritten subject, the person who was swimming at Northwestern.
The phrase will dangle unless this subject follows the comma. Only
(A) puts the understood subject immediately after this phrase.
Choices (B), (C), (D), and (E) all make it look as if the *records* were
the swimmers.

IMPROVING PARAGRAPHS QUESTIONS
(REVISION IN CONTEXT)

In this section of the exam, there are two sets of questions based
on a short sample of student writing. As a rule, the selection is three
paragraphs and about three hundred words long. There are six or
seven questions on each passage. One or two of these will ask you to
combine two or three sentences. One may ask you to recognize and
correct a usage error. Others will deal with a variety of topics that
arise from the selection. There may be questions on sentence
structure, on transitions from sentence to sentence or paragraph to
paragraph, on the organization of the passage or a paragraph, on
logic, on clarity, on rhetorical strategy, or on verbosity. The
following is a set of Improving Paragraphs questions based on two
paragraphs from a student essay.

<u>Directions</u>: The following passages are early drafts of student
essays. Some parts of them need to be revised.

Read the selections carefully and answer the questions that
follow. There will be questions about sentence structure, diction,
and usage in individual sentences or parts of sentences. Other
questions will deal with the whole essay or paragraphs and ask you

to decide about organization, development, and appropriate language. Choose the answer that follows the requirements of standard written English and most effectively expresses the intended meanings.

(1) Is a man or a woman more likely to ask questions? (2) I think it depends on what the circumstances are and on who is around when a time to ask questions comes along. (3) In my family, my mother and I ask more questions than my brother or my father when all our family is together. (4) My father would never ask for directions when we're in the car, and this is when he is not sure of the way. (5) My mother would stop right away to ask, unless she was in an unsafe neighborhood.

(6) My brother tells me that he asks questions in school, and when he is at work after school, he doesn't. (7) It is because he thinks his boss will think he doesn't know his job. (8) He won't ask any questions at all. (9) At work he will ask questions only to his friend, Eddie. (10) Based on the actions of my brother and my father, men are more likely to not ask when they don't know something because they think it will hurt their image as able to do things well. (11) Women are more practical and will not drive around not knowing where you are.

1. Which of the following is the best version of the underlined portion of sentence 2 (reproduced below)?

   I think it depends <u>on what the circumstances are and on who is around when a time to ask questions comes along.</u>

   (A) (As it is now)
   (B) on the circumstances
   (C) on what the circumstances are and who is around at the time
   (D) on the circumstances and who is around when a time to ask questions comes along
   (E) on what the circumstances and the situation are for asking questions

Since the word *circumstances* really includes *who is around* or *situation*, there is no need to say more than what is said in (B). All of the other choices are, by comparison, wordy.

2. Which of the following is the best version of the underlined portion of sentence 4 (reproduced below)?

My father would never ask for directions when we're in the car, and this is when he is not sure of the way.

(A) (As it is now)
(B) car, and at a time when he is not sure
(C) car, even if he is not sure
(D) car, when he may not be sure
(E) car, because he is not sure

This section of the exam is likely to ask a question that depends on the careful choice of the right connective. Here, the use of *even if* (C) is both concise and fully expressive.

3. Which of the following is the best way to revise and combine sentences 7, 8, and 9 (reproduced below)?

It is because he thinks his boss will think he doesn't know his job. He won't ask any questions at all. At work he will ask questions only to his friend, Eddie.

(A) Because he thinks his boss will think he doesn't know his job, he won't ask any questions at work unless he asks questions to his only friend, Eddie.
(B) At work, he will ask only his friend Eddie questions so his boss won't think he doesn't know his job.
(C) He won't ask any questions at work at all, unless he asks his friend Eddie, because he thinks his boss will think he doesn't know his job.
(D) Because he doesn't want his boss to think he doesn't know his job, he won't ask any questions at all at work, but he will ask his friend Eddie questions.
(E) He will ask his friend at work, Eddie, questions, but not his boss, who will think he doesn't know his job.

In questions requiring sentence combining, try to avoid the repetition of words or phrases, like *ask* and *questions* here. Choices (A) and (D) repeat both words, and (C) repeats *ask.* The word order of the first clause of (E) is awkward. The best choice is (B)—the shortest and clearest version.

4. Which of the following phrases should follow *"Based on the actions of my brother and my father"* in sentence 10?

   (A) men are more likely (as it is now)
   (B) it is more likely that men
   (C) my opinion is that men are more likely
   (D) men, unlike women are more likely
   (E) men are probably more likely

The problem in this sentence is that the opening phrase will dangle unless it is followed by something that is *"based on . . ."* The writer's opinion, not men, is based on the actions of her father and brother; the right answer here is (C).

5. The writer of this passage employs all of the following EXCEPT

   (A) development of a contrast
   (B) employment of specific examples
   (C) chronological organization
   (D) raising and answering a question
   (E) reference to personal opinions

The writer contrasts men and women, using examples from her family. The passage opens with a question which the rest of the two paragraphs attempts to answer. Sentence 10, for example, is a personal opinion. The correct answer here is (C); the passage does not use a chronological organization.

ANSWER SHEET FOR SAMPLE MULTIPLE-CHOICE EXAM

The following pages present a sample exam of fifteen questions, with five questions of each of the three question types. Try to complete the exam in fifteen minutes and use your results to see with which of the question types you have difficulty and what kinds of grammatical errors you are likely to overlook. The answers and explanations are on pages 23–25.

Identifying Sentence Errors

1 Ⓐ Ⓑ Ⓒ Ⓓ Ⓔ
2 Ⓐ Ⓑ Ⓒ Ⓓ Ⓔ
3 Ⓐ Ⓑ Ⓒ Ⓓ Ⓔ
4 Ⓐ Ⓑ Ⓒ Ⓓ Ⓔ
5 Ⓐ Ⓑ Ⓒ Ⓓ Ⓔ

Improving Sentences

6 Ⓐ Ⓑ Ⓒ Ⓓ Ⓔ
7 Ⓐ Ⓑ Ⓒ Ⓓ Ⓔ
8 Ⓐ Ⓑ Ⓒ Ⓓ Ⓔ
9 Ⓐ Ⓑ Ⓒ Ⓓ Ⓔ
10 Ⓐ Ⓑ Ⓒ Ⓓ Ⓔ

Improving Paragraphs

11 Ⓐ Ⓑ Ⓒ Ⓓ Ⓔ
12 Ⓐ Ⓑ Ⓒ Ⓓ Ⓔ
13 Ⓐ Ⓑ Ⓒ Ⓓ Ⓔ
14 Ⓐ Ⓑ Ⓒ Ⓓ Ⓔ
15 Ⓐ Ⓑ Ⓒ Ⓓ Ⓔ

SAMPLE MULTIPLE-CHOICE EXAM

IDENTIFYING SENTENCE ERRORS

1. The prosecutor <u>feared</u> the showing of a teleplay
   A

   <u>based on the defendant's life</u> would make <u>it</u> impossible
   B   C

   <u>in selecting</u> a jury. <u>No error</u>
   D   E

2. <u>There are</u> among the scientists <u>who have seen</u> the pictures
   A   B

   <u>sent from</u> Jupiter unanimous agreement <u>about the success</u> of
   C   D

   the telescope. <u>No error</u>
   E

3. The popularity <u>of many recent films</u> <u>is due</u> <u>not to their</u>
   A   B   C

   sentiment or morality, <u>but to their</u> violence. <u>No error</u>
   D   E

4. Many historians <u>believe</u> the Kennedy-Nixon election
   A

   <u>was decided by</u> the television debate <u>in which</u> <u>he appeared</u>
   B   C   D

   unshaven and humorless. <u>No error</u>
   E

5. Because the volcanoes on the island of Hawaii <u>are more active</u>
   A

   <u>than other islands,</u> <u>it</u> is the center <u>for geological studies.</u>
   B   C   D

   <u>No error</u>
   E

17

IMPROVING SENTENCES

6. Four financial analysts prepare a summary of stock market activity <u>each week, and it is broadcast by them</u> on public radio.

   (A) each week, and it is broadcast by them
   (B) each week, and then it is broadcast
   (C) each week and it is broadcast by them
   (D) each week, and they broadcast it
   (E) broadcasting each week

7. Reacting to a false report of dangerous pesticides, <u>the cranberry harvest of 1959 went unsold to the nation's consumers.</u>

   (A) the cranberry harvest of 1959 went unsold to the nation's consumers
   (B) the cranberry harvest of 1959 was not bought by the nation's consumers
   (C) the nation's consumers refused to buy the cranberry harvest of 1959
   (D) the nation's consumers do not buy the cranberry harvest in 1959
   (E) the 1959 harvest of cranberries was not bought by the nation's consumers

8. Carlos Fuentes sees Columbus's arrival in America <u>not as a cultural catastrophe, but as a seminal event</u> in a tragic and triumphant history.

   (A) not as a cultural catastrophe, but as a seminal event
   (B) not as a cultural catastrophe, but it is a seminal event
   (C) not as a cultural catastrophe, as a seminal event
   (D) as a seminal event, not as a cultural catastrophe
   (E) was not a cultural catastrophe, but it was a seminal event

9. According to the critics, the MTV awards ceremony <u>was tasteless, according to</u> the audience, it was better than ever.

   (A) was tasteless, according to
   (B) was tasteless according to
   (C) was tasteless, and according to
   (D) was tasteless, but according to
   (E) was tasteless but to

10. Weaver's policy allowed a slave to earn cash <u>if they were able to produce</u> more than the average expected output each week.

   (A) if they were able to produce
   (B) if they produced
   (C) if they overproduced
   (D) by producing
   (E) producing

IMPROVING PARAGRAPHS

(1) Many people think that they have insomnia. (2) If they haven't had eight hours of sleep, they think they have insomnia. (3) There is no evidence to support the common belief that you have to have eight hours of sleep every night. (4) Some people sleep as little as two hours a night. (5) They wake up the next morning, and they feel fine. (6) Some people need only five hours of sleep. (7) Some people must have more than eight hours of sleep to feel refreshed. (8) It is harder to keep track of time in a dark room than in the daylight. (9) It is easy to overestimate how long you have been awake or underestimate how long you have been asleep.

11. As an introduction to the content of the paragraph as a whole, which of the following is the best version of the first sentence?

   (A) Many people think that they have insomnia. (as it is)
   (B) Many people have insomnia.
   (C) Many people think they have insomnia, but they may be mistaken.
   (D) Why do so many people think that they have insomnia?
   (E) Is less than eight hours of sleep a sign of insomnia, as many believe?

12. Which of the following is the best way to combine sentences 1 and 2 (reproduced below)?

Many people think that they have insomnia. If they haven't had eight hours of sleep, they think they have insomnia.

(A) Many people think that they have insomnia; if they haven't had eight hours of sleep, they think they have insomnia.
(B) If they haven't had eight hours of sleep, there are many people who think they have insomnia.
(C) Many people haven't had eight hours of sleep, and they think they have insomnia.
(D) Many people, when they haven't had eight hours of sleep, think they have insomnia.
(E) Many people who haven't had eight hours of sleep are the ones who think they have insomnia.

13. Which of the following is the best version of the underlined parts of sentences 4 and 5 (reproduced below)?

Some people sleep as little as two hours a <u>night. They wake up the next morning, and they feel fine.</u>

(A) night; they wake up the next morning, and they feel fine
(B) night, waking up the next morning and they feel fine
(C) night, and they feel fine waking up the next morning
(D) night, but they wake up the next morning and feel fine
(E) night yet wake up the next morning feeling fine

14. All of the following pairs of sentences would probably be improved by being combined EXCEPT

(A) 1 and 2
(B) 2 and 3
(C) 4 and 5
(D) 6 and 7
(E) 8 and 9

15. Which of the following would be the best replacement of sentences 8 and 9 (reproduced below) to make the conclusion of the paragraph more coherent?

It is harder to keep track of time in a dark room than in the daylight. It is easy to overestimate how long you have been awake or underestimate how long you have been asleep.

(A) Because the number of hours asleep is difficult to estimate, many people have slept more than they think and do not really need more.

(B) It is harder to keep track of time in a dark room than in the daylight; it is easy to overestimate how long you have been awake or underestimate how long you have been asleep.

(C) Because it hard to keep track of time in the dark, people cannot really tell how long they have been asleep.

(D) Insomniacs cannot really tell how long they have slept.

(E) Insomniacs are more likely to overestimate their sleeplessness than to underestimate it.

ANSWERS TO THE
SAMPLE MULTIPLE-CHOICE EXAM

IDENTIFYING SENTENCE ERRORS

1. (D) The error is the unidiomatic use of *in selecting* (a preposition followed by a gerund) instead of *to select* (an infinitive) after *impossible.*

2. (A) The phrase *There are* uses a plural verb. When we finally reach the subject of this verb, it is the singular *agreement,* producing (no pun intended) agreement error.

3. (E) There is no error in this sentence. The singular *is* agrees with the singular *popularity,* while the phrases *not to their* and *but to their* are correctly parallel.

4. (D) The error is the ambiguous pronoun *he.* A reader has no way of knowing whether the antecedent of this pronoun is Kennedy or Nixon.

5. (B) The comparison here is illogical. The sentence compares the more active volcanoes to other islands, not to volcanoes on the other islands. The correct sentence would read *more active than those on other islands.*

IMPROVING SENTENCES

6. (D) The first clause of the sentence uses a verb in the active voice (*prepare*), but the second clause uses a passive (*is broadcast*). Choice (D) uses active verbs in both parts of the sentence, while (A), (B), and (C) keep the passive. (C) is also a run-on sentence. (E) is briefer, but it loses some of the meaning of the sentence.

7. (C) The participle that begins this sentence dangles; that is, it is placed to modify *the cranberry harvest,* but it should be next to *consumers.* It is the consumers, not the harvest, who reacted. (D) avoids the dangling participle but changes the past tense of the verb to the present.

8. (A) The original version of the sentence is correct. The correlative conjunctions *not . . . but* should be followed by parallel constructions. There are parallelism errors in (B) and (E). (C) loses the contrast pointed by the use of *but.* (D) changes the meaning by separating *seminal event* from the phrase that completes it, *in a tragic and triumphant history.*

9. (D) There are two independent clauses here. They can be two separate sentences or one sentence with either a semicolon or a conjunction and a comma. Choices (A) and (B) leave the conjunction out, and (E) leaves out the comma. The punctuation is correct in (C) and (D), but (D) is a better choice, since the two halves of the sentence contrast, and *but* denotes a contrary idea to follow.

10. (D) The error in (A), (B), and (C) is an agreement error; *slave* is singular, but the pronoun in all three is the plural *they.* (D) solves the problem by omitting the pronoun. The original meaning is unclear if the preposition *by* is dropped.

IMPROVING PARAGRAPHS

11. (C) As it stands, the first sentence raises questions about the content of the paragraph. Does it mean that they do have insomnia or that they only think they do? Most of the paragraph—which is desperately in need of revision—is about the difficulty in determining what insomnia is and why it is hard to define. Of the five possibilities, (C) does the best job of preparing a reader for the rest of the paragraph. (B) misleads the reader, and (D) and (E) ask questions the paragraph will not answer.

12. (D) When combining sentences, try to consolidate words that are repeated once or twice. Here, the redundant phrase is *they think that they have insomnia.* Choice (B) adds the unneeded *there are* and uses *they* twice. (C) uses *they* twice, and (E) adds the wordy *are the ones who.*

13. (E) As in 12, avoid the repetition of words. Here, the pronoun *they* is unnecessary in (A), (B), (C), and (D). Since the sentences imply a contrast, the conjunctions *yet* or *but* are better than the *and.*

14. (B) All of these pairs could be combined except (B). Combining these sentences would greatly improve the writing.

15. (C) The paragraph has moved from the varied number of hours of sleep people require to a slightly different topic, the difficulty of determining how long one has slept. Choices (A), (D), and (E) add new information not included in the original sentences. (B) is as wordy and unpointed as the original. (C) is at least more concise and attempts to relate the idea to the difficulty of deciding what insomnia is, the notion hidden beneath the wordy writing of the paragraph.

ANSWERS TO YOUR QUESTIONS ABOUT THE MULTIPLE-CHOICE EXAM

Should I guess on questions I'm not sure about?

First, be sure to answer as many questions as you can. Avoid losing points by spending too much time on one question or on one section of the test. Don't be afraid to guess if you can eliminate two or three of the five choices. You get no credit for an unanswered question and lose a quarter of a point for each wrong answer. But if you have reduced your options to two or three instead of five, your chances are one in two or one in three, while your loss, if you choose incorrectly is one fourth.

When a question seems hopeless, don't waste time on it. Skip it (and skip the space on the answer sheet) and go on.

One system that some students find useful is to cross out answers (on the test, not on the answer sheet) they are sure are wrong, like this:

(A̸)
(B)?
(C̸)
(D)?
(E̸)

The question marks indicate possible answers. If you go on and come back to this question later, you'll waste no time considering the wrong answers you've eliminated already. If you plan to use this or a similar system, practice it several times before you take the exam. Don't waste time on your system that could be better spent answering the questions on the test.

Are there trick questions in the multiple-choice section?

There are no trick questions, although some are more difficult than others. The whole point of the SAT II Writing exam is to test as widely, accurately, and fairly as possible. If you know the materials in this book—or in any up-to-date book about standard written English—you should find nothing on the exam with which you are not already familiar.

Is it advisable to answer the multiple-choice questions in the order in which they appear on the test?

Do them in whatever order makes it easiest for you. If you find the Identifying Sentence Error questions easier than the other two types, you may want to complete questions 1 through 20 and 51 through 60 before you begin the Improving Sentences and Improving Paragraphs sets. But if you do skip around, be sure you're using the right circles on the answer sheet, and be sure to go back and complete the questions you jumped over. Make the most of the forty minutes you have to complete as many questions as possible.

What if a multiple-choice question seems too easy?

Be glad it's too easy rather than too hard. Don't assume that because an answer seems obvious to you, there must be some trap. In every set of questions, there are a few *very* easy questions and a few very hard ones. Don't throw away the chance to get the easy points by trying to second guess the exam. If a question reads

<u>I don't got no money,</u> but <u>I am</u> a <u>happy</u> <u>man.</u> <u>No error</u>
          A   B   C   D   E

choose letter (A) and go on to the next question.

What if I've had five answers in a row of (C) and I'm pretty sure the sixth is (C), although (B) is a possibility? What letter do I choose?

Choose (C). You've probably made a mistake or two in the five (C) choices in a row. *Don't* play games with the letter patterns of your answers. Choose the answer that you think is right regardless of the letter of the answer before or after. This exam is about style and usage, not about code breaking.

What if I don't finish all of the questions?

You can still get a high score on the test. Not all test takers finish. If you're having trouble finishing practice tests in forty minutes, keep in mind that there are usually ten Improving Sentences (single-sentence, usage-error) questions at the end of the exam, and if you're running short of time, you should complete these questions before you begin a set of questions that requires you to read the three-paragraph student essay in the Improving Paragraphs section or the five different possible versions of a sentence in the Improving Sentences part of the exam.

If you find yourself out of time before you've finished, don't randomly fill in the blank spaces on your answer sheet. With each wrong answer counting minus .25, the law of averages is against you.

How much of my final grade does the multiple-choice section determine?

In the final composite score, the multiple-choice results count two-thirds and the writing sample one-third, reflecting the forty-minute/twenty-minute time division of the exam.

What is the score given for a right answer, a wrong answer, and no answer at all?

In determining your raw score, a right answer is one point, no answer is zero, and a wrong answer is minus .25. On a sixty-question, multiple-choice exam, the raw score could range from minus 15 (all wrong) to 60 (all right). The scores reported to you and the colleges will convert this raw score to a scale of 20 to 80. You'll also get a converted score for your writing sample on the 20 to 80 scale and a score for the whole exam using the 200 to 800 scale.

You can convert your raw score (the number of right answers less the number of wrong answers multiplied by .25) to an *approximate* scaled multiple-choice score using the following table. (To determine your composite score, multiple-choice and essay, see page 147.)

Multiple-Choice Raw Score	Approximate Scaled Score
51–60	67–80
41–50	56–66
31–40	47–55
21–30	39–46
11–20	32–38
1–10	23–31

GRAMMAR AND USAGE
ON THE MULTIPLE-CHOICE EXAM

The writers of the SAT II Writing test make no secret of what points of grammar and style will be tested in the multiple-choice sections. Using the list of writing problems printed in *The Official Guide to SAT II: Subject Tests,* the sample exam in that book, and the sample exam on the old SAT Test of Standard Written English, we can formulate a list of the nearly thirty writing faults that are most likely to appear on the exam. All of them won't turn up on the exam you take, but you can be absolutely sure that more than twenty of them will—and possibly as many as twenty-five. Some of them will appear more than once (verb agreement, for example) and some in both the Identifying Sentence Errors and the Improving Sentences sections. The following chart lists the twenty-eight writing faults most likely to be on the exam. The second column gives a very simple sentence to illustrate the fault (on the exam, unfortunately, the errors won't be nearly so easy to see), with the error in italics. The third column refers to the Sample Exam printed in the *Official Guide to SAT II: Subject Tests.* The question numbered here tests for the recognition of this writing problem. The other number, which gives a page reference, directs you to the page of the Grammar and Usage Review in this book where the discussion of this error begins.

Type of Error	Example	Question Number/ Discussion Page
1. Noun agreement error	*France and Italy* are *a country* in Europe.	16/p. 50
2. Subject-verb agreement error	The *students* of English *is taking* the test.	6, 11, 55/p. 47
3. Pronoun agreement error	*Jack* was late, so we left without *them*.	2, 8, 18, 25, 51/p. 49
4. Unclear pronoun reference	*Jane, June, and Joan* applied, and *she* got the job.	p. 85
5. Missing specific pronoun antecedent	Dave ate too fast *which* made him sick.	30/p. 85
6. Change of pronoun subjects	*One* needs a calculator, and *you* should bring two pens.	p. 75
7. Wrong pronoun	She is the judge *which* sentenced the felon.	7/p. 92
8. Adjective/adverb error	His writing is *carelessly* because he writes too *rapid*.	20/p. 38
9. Comparative adjective error	Of the *seven* swimmers, she is the *stronger*.	5/p. 39
10. Misplaced modifier	We saw the boy and *his mother in a Batman costume*.	24/p. 70
11. Dangling modifier	*Flowing from the mountain top*, *he* drank from the stream.	24/p. 67
12. Double negative	There is *hardly no* coffee left in the pot.	3/p. 90
13. Illogical comparison	In California, the *sun* rises *later than New York*.	13, 58/p. 91
14. Verb tense sequence error	He *rang* the bell, *opened* the door, and *enters* the house.	52/p. 58
15. Verb tense error	Last week she *buys* a new car.	p. 58

Type of Error	Example	Question Number/ Discussion Page
16. Change of voice of verb	He *runs* a mile daily, and weights *are lifted* by him.	p. 74
17. Verb form error	He has *brung* a bottle of wine.	49/p. 55
18. Sentence fragment	*Having three sisters, two of them doctors.*	21, 35/p. 89
19. Comma splice	She has three *sisters, two of them are doctors.*	22, 27, 31/p. 105
20. Fused (or run-on) sentences	She has three *sisters two of them are doctors.*	p. 105
21. Parallelism error	He is studying *biology, physics, and how to swim.*	26, 29, 32, 34/p. 75
22. Coordination error	Ames wrote only about Boston, *and* he was never there.	p. 113
23. Subordination error	Wilson sets many of his novels in Galway, *and he was born there.*	p. 113
24. Diction error	He will be *relapsed* from prison in June.	15/p.95
25. Idiom error: gerund-infinitive confusion	I am eager *in seeing* the film. He is incapable *to answer* the question.	19, 53, 57/p. 96
26. Idiom error: choice of preposition	They are in support *to* the idea.	14/p. 95
27. Idiom error: choice of conjunction	He is as subtle *than* a fox.	1, 10/p. 95
28. Wordiness	Because *of the fact that* he failed to give *total and complete* attention, he missed the exit.	28, 34/p. 97

Part II: Grammar and Usage Review

No matter how confident you are of your command of grammar, you should read through the Grammar and Usage Review to refresh your memory and to become aware of the areas of grammar and style most likely to be tested on the exam. *Both* the multiple-choice and the writing sample sections of the examination will test your knowledge of grammar and sentence structure; the grade on your essay will depend upon your mastery of the mechanics of correct writing as well as your rhetorical skill.

This review has nine sections on the problems of grammar and style that appear most often in the multiple-choice part of the test. After each section, there is a review exercise, and after every three sections, there is a second exercise reviewing the subjects of the three preceding parts. There is also a short section on punctuation and finally a section on sentence combining, a technique you must know to do well on the Improving Paragraphs part of the exam. The grammar review is as concise as it can be made and still cover the questions that the test will ask. It may tell you more about grammar than you *want* to know, but it won't tell you more than you *need* to know for this exam.

1
PARTS OF SPEECH, ADJECTIVES AND ADVERBS, COMPARATIVES AND SUPERLATIVES

PARTS OF SPEECH

The SAT II Writing exam won't ask you to explain a dangling participle or to pick out the adjectives and adverbs in a sentence. But to make the best use of this book, you should know the meaning of several of the important grammatical terms, and you must be able to tell a noun from a verb and an adverb from an adjective.

The test will ask you either to find an error in a sentence or to recognize that a sentence is correct. The most used type of question will ask if the following sentence is correct and, if not, which underlined part has an error.

Freshened by rain that fell during the night, the garden was
    A   B

fragrantly and glistened brightly. No error
   C   D   E

Faced with this question, most students will see that the problem is in the word *fragrantly*. When you ask even those who rightly select choice (C) as the error why they picked choice (C) instead of choice (D), the usual answer is "Choice (C) sounds wrong, and (D) sounds right." Sometimes we have to depend on the *it-sounds-wrong/it-sounds-right* approach. But most of the time, this method is not enough. To perform well on tests of standard written English, you should be able to see what grammatical question the test is really asking. In the example, the real issue is not which sounds better, *was fragrant* or *was fragrantly,* but whether we use an adverb or an adjective with the verb *was.* And so we should begin at the beginning—with a review of the parts of speech on which questions will be based.

- **Noun:** a word used as a person, a place, or a thing.

  Examples: *woman, boy, hope, Boston, car, noun*

- **Pronoun:** a word used as a substitute for a noun.

  Examples: *I, you, he, she, it, me, him, her, we, they, who, whom, which, what, this, that, one, none, someone, somebody, myself, anything, nothing*

- **Verb:** a word used to assert action or state of being.

  Examples: *kill, eat, is, are, remain, think, study, become*

- **Adjective:** a word used to modify a noun or pronoun. To modify is to describe, to qualify, to limit or restrict in meaning. In the phrase *a large, red barn*, both *large* and *red* are adjectives which modify the noun *barn*.

  Examples: *fat, thin, hot, cold, old, new, red*

- **Adverb:** a word used to modify a verb, an adjective, or another adverb. In the phrase *to eat a very large meal very slowly*, the two *very*'s and *slowly* are adverbs. The first *very* modifies an adjective (*large*), the second modifies an adverb (*slowly*), and *slowly* modifies the verb (*eat*).

  Examples: *very, rather, quickly, quite, easily, hopelessly*

ADJECTIVES AND ADVERBS

A common error in the sentences on the exam is the misuse of an adjective or an adverb. Adjectives modify nouns and pronouns; adverbs modify verbs, adjectives, and other adverbs. Errors occur when an adjective is used to do an adverb's job or an adverb to do an adjective's.

Which of the following sentences have adjective or adverb errors?

1. As the debate progressed, the defenders of tax reform grew more and more excited.

2. As the debate progressed, the defenders of tax reform spoke more and more excited.

3. Asleep awkwardly on his side, the man snored loud enough to shake the bedroom.

4. Lying awkward on his side, the sleeper snored loudly enough to shake the bedroom.

Sentence 1 is correct. Sentences 2, 3, and 4 have adjective/adverb errors. In sentence 2, the adjective *excited* modifies the verb *spoke,* describing how they spoke. But we need an adverb to modify a verb, so the correct word here is *excitedly.* The adjective *excited* is correct in the first sentence because it modifies the noun *defenders,* not the verb *grew.* In sentence 3, the adverb *awkwardly* is properly used to modify the adjective *asleep,* but the adjective *loud* should not be used to modify the verb *snored.* Sentence 4 correctly uses the adverb *loudly* but mistakenly uses the adjective *awkward* to modify the verbal adjective *lying.*

Be careful not to confuse *most* and *almost. Most* is an adjective, the superlative of *much* or *many,* as in *most children like ice cream,* but *most* may be used as an adverb to form the superlative of another adjective or adverb, as in *most beautiful* or *most quickly. Almost* is an adverb meaning *nearly.* You can say *most people* or *most men,* but you must say *almost every person* or *almost all men.* A phrase like *most every person* or *most all men* is incorrect because the adjective *most* cannot modify the adjectives *every* or *all.*

COMPARATIVES AND SUPERLATIVES

Adjectives and adverbs have three forms: **positive** (*quick, quickly*), **comparative** (*quicker, more quickly*), and **superlative** (*quickest, most quickly*). Many of the comparatives and superlatives are formed by adding *-er* and *-est* to the adjective stem, although some words (*good, better, best; well, better, best*) change altogether, and some simply add *more* or *most* (*eager, more eager, most eager; quickly, more quickly, most quickly*).

When it is clear that only two are compared, use a comparative, not a superlative. When the comparison involves more than two, use a superlative.

Compared to Smith, Jones is *richer.*

Of all the oil-producing countries, Saudi Arabia is the *richest.*

Of the two finalists, Smith hits *harder.*

Of the eight boxers, Jones hits *harder* than Smith, but Williams hits *hardest* of all.

Don't double comparatives by using phrases like *more richer* or *more faster.* Simply say *richer* or *faster.*

EXERCISE 1
PARTS OF SPEECH, ADJECTIVES AND ADVERBS, COMPARATIVES AND SUPERLATIVES

Choose the correct form in each of the following sentences. Answers are on page 117.

1. (Most, Almost) every person in the stadium was wearing an orange cap.

2. After $2500 worth of cosmetic surgery, he is quite (different, differently) from the man we had known.

3. The ship appeared (sudden, suddenly) out of the fog.

4. Of all the players in the tournament, Smith has the (better, best) volley.

5. Of the two finalists, Jones has the (better, best) serve.

6. The pie was so (bad, badly) baked that he left the piece uneaten.

7. Dickens has a (noticeable, noticeably) more inventive imagination than Gaskell.

8. I am (sad, sadly) about his losing so much money on the lottery.

9. It is impossible to take her claims (serious, seriously).

10. I don't believe him (most, almost) any time he talks about money.

11. If you look very (careful, carefully), the scratches on the car are (clear, clearly) visible.

12. The eland is the (larger, largest) of all the antelopes but not the (slower, slowest).

13. Early in the century, the supply of bison seemed (inexhaustible, inexhaustibly).

14. From a distance, the hill appears to rise (steep, steeply).

15. Sue is the (better, more better) candidate.

16. The team is (quicker, more quicker) this year.

2
CASE

SUBJECT AND OBJECT ERRORS

Nouns and pronouns in English may be used as **subjects** (The *garden* is large. *I* am tired.), as **objects** (David weeded the *garden*. David hit *him.*), and as **possessors** (*David's* garden is large. *His* arm is broken.). Nouns and pronouns, then, have a subjective case, an objective case, and a possessive case.

Since the form of a noun in the subjective case is no different from the form of the same noun in the objective case (The *bat* hit the *ball*. The *ball* hit the *bat.*), errors of case are not a problem with nouns. But several pronouns have different forms as subjects and objects.

Subject	Object
I	me
he	him
she	her
we	us
they	them
who	whom
whoever	whomever

Where are the errors of case (confusions of the subjective and objective form of the pronoun) in the following sentences?

1. I am going to the play with her.

2. Me and her are going to the games.

3. The committee gave prizes to my brother, my sister, and I.

4. For we Americans, July fourth is a special day.

5. Mary invited my cousin, her sister, a friend from New York, and I to the party.

43

Sentence 1 is correct, but there are case errors in sentences 2, 3, 4, and 5. In sentence 2, *me* and *her,* the subjects of the sentence, should be *I* and *she* (or better, *She* and *I*). In sentence 3, *I* should be *me,* the object of the preposition *to,* and in sentence 4, the *we* should be *us,* the object of the preposition *for.* In sentence 5, *I* should be *me,* the object of the verb *invited.* It would be easy to spot the error if the sentences simply said *The committee gave prizes to I* or *Mary invited I,* but when the sentence contains elements that separate the verb or the preposition from the pronoun object, it becomes harder to see the error at once. The question writers know this fact and exploit it. When you see a compound subject or object (that is, two or more subjects or objects joined by *and*), look carefully at the case of pronouns. Imagine how the sentence would read with just the pronoun (*Mary invited I?*).

PRONOUNS IN APPOSITION

An **appositive** is a word or phrase or clause in apposition—that is, placed next to another so that the second explains the first.

Margaret, my sister, and my oldest brother, Hugh, are in New York.

In this sentence, *sister* is in apposition to *Margaret,* and *Hugh* is in apposition to *brother.* A pronoun in apposition is in the same case as the noun or pronoun to which it is in apposition. Thus, in a sentence like *The outfielders, Jack, Joe, and I, are ready to play,* the *I,* which is in apposition to the subject, *outfielders,* is subjective. But in a sentence like *The class elected three representatives, Jack, Joe, and me,* the objective *me* is correct because it is in apposition to *representatives,* which is the object of the verb *elected.*

WHO AND *WHOM*

The demons of case are *who* and *whom.* Fortunately, SAT II sticks to the easier pronouns. There have been no multiple-choice questions on the choice of *who* or *whom* on the exam.

EXERCISE 2
CASE

Choose the correct form in each of the following sentences. The answers are on page 118.

1. The study suggests that (we, us) New Englanders are not practical.

2. Everybody at the table chose steak except Tom and (I, me).

3. It was (I, me) who telephoned the fire department.

4. It is difficult to imagine how such an invention will affect you and (I, me).

5. My uncle, you, and (I, me) should invest together in this project.

6. They will award the trophy to one of the finalists, either Jack or (I, me).

3
AGREEMENT

An agreement error is the faulty combination of a singular and a plural. Agreement errors occur between subjects and verbs and between pronouns and their **antecedents** (the word, phrase, or clause to which a pronoun refers). SAT II Writing tests agreement frequently, and on some tests, as many as one fourth of the questions in the usage or sentence error section will be on agreement.

SUBJECT AND VERB AGREEMENT

Use a singular verb with a singular subject and a plural verb with a plural subject. The key to seeing errors of subject-verb agreement is identifying the subject correctly. Often, the sentences will try to mislead you by separating the subject and verb.

1. The *sound is* beautiful. (singular subject/singular verb)

2. The *number seems* to increase. (singular subject/singular verb)

3. The *sound* of birds singing and crickets chirping all about the sunlit lakes and woods *is* beautiful. (singular subject/singular verb)

4. The *number* of boats pulling water-skiers on the lakes *seems* to increase every summer. (singular subject/singular verb)

In sentences where there are two or more subjects joined by *and,* use a plural verb. Don't confuse compound subjects (two subjects joined by *and*) with prepositional or parenthetical phrases introduced by such words or phrases as *with, as well as, in addition to, along with, in the company of, not to mention,* and the like. A singular subject, followed by a phrase of this sort, still takes a singular verb.

1. The actress and the director *are* in the dressing room.

2. The chairman of Mobil, as well as the president of Texaco and the vice president of Gulf, *is* attending the meeting.

3. The fullback, accompanied by two ends, two guards, and the 340-pound tackle, *is* leaving the field.

4. The conductor, with his 125-piece orchestra, two small brass bands, and the Mormon Tabernacle Choir, *is* ready to begin the concert.

In the first example, there are two subjects (*actress* and *director*) joined by *and,* so the verb is plural. But in the second, third, and fourth sentences, the subject is singular (*chairman, fullback, conductor*), and all the plurals that intervene between the subject and the verb don't change the rule that the verb must be singular to agree with the singular subject.

Two singular subjects joined by *and* (a compound subject) must have a plural verb, but two singular subjects joined by *or, nor, either . . . or,* or *neither . . . nor* take singular verbs.

1. Mary *and* Jill *are* in the play.

2. Mary *or* Jill *is* in the play.

3. *Neither* Mary *nor* Jill *is* in the play.

In sentences with *either . . . or* or *neither . . . nor,* if one subject is singular and one is plural, the verb agrees with the subject nearer the verb.

1. Neither the hunter nor the *rangers are* in sight.

2. Neither the rangers nor the *hunter is* in sight.

3. Either the dog or the *cats are* in the yard.

4. Either the cats or the *dog is* in the yard.

In sentences 1 and 3, the subjects nearer the verb are the plurals rangers and cats, so the verb is plural. In sentences 2 and 4, the singular subject is nearer the verb, so the verb is singular.

The test will frequently include agreement errors in sentences in which the verb precedes the subject, often by using an opening of *There is* or *There are*.

1. There *are* hidden away in a lonely house out on the heath a brother and sister living alone.

2. There *is* in London and New York newspapers a self-satisfaction that is not found in the papers of smaller cities.

Both of these sentences are correct, although it would be easy to miss the agreement error if the first had used *is* and the second *are*. Don't let the singular nouns in the prepositional phrases in the first sentence or the plurals in the second distract you from finding the subjects of the verbs—the compound subject *brother and sister* in the first and the singular *self-satisfaction* in the second. The test writer's technique here is like that in those sentences that pile up plurals between a singular subject at the beginning of the sentence and the verb at the end. But in this case, the verb comes first.

PRONOUN AGREEMENT

Since personal pronouns have distinctive singular and plural forms (*he/they, his/their, him/them*), pronoun agreement errors are as common as noun-verb agreement errors. The number (that is, singular or plural) of a pronoun is determined by its **antecedent** (the word, phrase, or clause to which it refers), and pronouns must agree in number with their antecedents. Most of the rules that apply to the agreement of nouns and verbs also apply to the agreement of pronouns and their antecedents.

1. The *workers* finished *their* job on time.

2. The *group* of workers finished *its* job on time.

3. The *men* earn *their* money.

4. The *man* earns *his* money.

5 The *men* who earn *their* money are tired.

In sentence 1 here, the plural *their* agrees with the plural *workers*. In sentence 2, the singular *its* agrees with the singular subject, the collective noun *group*. In sentences 3 and 4, the antecedents are *men* and *man,* so the pronouns are *their* and *his*. In sentence 5, the antecedent to the pronoun *their* is *who*. To determine whether *who* is singular or plural, we must look at its antecedent. In this sentence, it is the plural *men*.

In the subject-verb agreement questions, so long as you know whether the subject is singular or plural, you should have no trouble. In pronoun agreement questions, you must know what word is the antecedent of the pronoun and whether that word is singular or plural.

LOGICAL AGREEMENT

Read carefully to be sure the relation of the singulars and plurals in a sentence makes sense. If a sentence begins with *three men,* we can reasonably expect that they have three heads, not just one. Sentences like the following may seem too easy to be true, but you shouldn't be surprised to find sentences on the exam testing this kind of agreement error. Each of the following sentences is incorrect.

1. The *three men* put their *head* together to try to find a solution.

2. *Seven women* in my math class are studying to become *a computer programmer.*

3. We bought *roses and lilies* and arranged *the flower* in a vase.

EXERCISE 3
AGREEMENT

Choose the correct form in each of the following sentences. Answers are on page 118.

1. No one (is, are) willing to speak to that organization.

2. Either the general or the sergeant-at-arms (is, are) responsible for greeting the new Greek minister.

3. The salads and the dessert at this restaurant (is, are) delicious.

4. Mr. Lombardi, as well as his wife and three children, (was, were) found before midnight.

5. The newly discovered evidence, together with the confirming testimony of three eyewitnesses, (make, makes) his conviction certain.

6. The many criteria for admission to Yale Law School in New Haven (includes, include) a score of above 600 on the test.

7. Precise and symmetrical, the basalt columns of the Devil's Postpile in the Sierras (looks, look) as if (it, they) had been sculpted in an artist's studio.

8. Neither the teacher nor the student (is, are) in the classroom.

9. Mr. and Mrs. Smith, in addition to their four children, (is, are) vacationing in Orlando.

10. Jack (has, have) reached the final heat.

11. The number of penguins killed by pesticides (increases, increase) each year.

12. Either I or Mary Jane (is, are) going to Detroit.

13. All of the men in the theater, filled with more than six hundred people, (was, were) bored.

14. Neither Sally nor the twins (has, have) finished (her, their) practice teaching.

15. Neither the twins nor Sally (has, have) finished (her, their) practice teaching.

16. Neither she nor I (was, were) dancing, for we felt tired.

17. The president, no less than all the other members of the first family, (enjoy, enjoys) bowling.

18. The number of books about corruption in the government written by participants in the scandal (seem, seems) to grow larger every month.

19. Many of the books about NASA (has, have) been translated into Russian.

20. The information used in determining your federal tax (is, are) to be submitted with your letter of appeal.

REVIEW EXERCISE: SECTIONS 1, 2, AND 3

Some of the following sentences may be correct. Others contain problems covered in sections 1, 2, and 3 of the Grammar and Usage Review. There is not more than one error in any sentence.

If there is an error, it will be underlined and lettered. Find the one underlined part that must be changed to make the sentence correct. Choose (E) if the sentence contains no error. Answers are on page 119.

1. No one <u>but</u> the president, secretary, <u>and me</u> <u>was</u> at the
   $\qquad$ A $\qquad\qquad\qquad\qquad$ B $\quad$ C

   meeting, and we voted <u>unanimously to spend</u> all of the money
   $\qquad\qquad\qquad\qquad\quad$ D

   in the treasury. <u>No error</u>
   $\qquad\qquad\qquad$ E

2. Many young men of twenty-five or thirty <u>has dreamed</u> of
   $\qquad\qquad\qquad\qquad\qquad\qquad\qquad$ A

   retiring at fifty, but few, when they reach <u>that age</u>, find that the
   $\qquad\qquad\qquad\qquad\qquad\qquad\qquad$ B

   sum <u>they had thought</u> <u>could support them</u> is adequate.
   $\qquad$ C $\qquad\qquad$ D

   <u>No error</u>
   E

3. <u>Having lived</u> for two years <u>near both the highway</u> and the
   $\qquad$ A $\qquad\qquad\qquad$ B

   airport, I am used to the noises of cars and planes, <u>and they</u> no
   $\qquad\qquad\qquad\qquad\qquad\qquad\qquad$ C

   longer <u>disturb my sleep.</u> <u>No error</u>
   $\qquad$ D $\qquad\qquad$ E

4. The book's <u>public-relations prose</u>, <u>its long-windedness</u>, and its
   $\qquad\qquad$ A $\qquad\qquad\qquad$ B

   tendency <u>uncritically to list</u> ideas ultimately <u>makes it</u> a wholly
   $\qquad\qquad$ C $\qquad\qquad\qquad\qquad$ D

   useless study that should never have been published. <u>No error</u>
   $\qquad\qquad\qquad\qquad\qquad\qquad\qquad\qquad$ E

5. It is depressing to realize <u>that in</u> a country <u>as rich as this,</u>
   $\qquad\qquad\qquad\qquad$ A $\qquad\qquad$ B

   thousands of people live out <u>their life</u> without <u>ever having</u>
   $\qquad\qquad\qquad\qquad$ C $\qquad\qquad\qquad$ D

   enough to eat. <u>No error</u>
   $\qquad\qquad$ E

6. My family <u>has</u> several serious and responsible members,

A

   including <u>my sister and I</u>, for example, but <u>even we</u> have had

B   C

   <u>next to no</u> influence on public life. <u>No error</u>

D   E

7. The result of all the tests, <u>according to</u> the surgeon, <u>was not</u>

A   B

   <u>likely to alarm</u> either her husband <u>or her</u>. <u>No error</u>

C   D   E

8. <u>There are</u> on both the <u>men's and women's</u> volleyball teams

A   B

   one player <u>who can jump</u> <u>higher than</u> anyone else. <u>No error</u>

C   D   E

9. Though the first question on the test <u>seemed</u> <u>simple</u>, there

A   B

   were <u>simply</u> too many questions <u>for me to finish</u> on time.

C   D

   <u>No error</u>

E

10. There are several runners on the team <u>who are</u> <u>faster</u> in the

A   B

    <u>shorter</u> races than the runners of the opposing team, but in the

C

    field events, they are <u>best</u>. <u>No error</u>

D   E

4
VERBS

When you look up a verb in the dictionary, you'll find an entry like the following:

eat, *v.t.* (ate, eaten, eating)
chop, *v.t.* (chopped, chopped, chopping)
be, *v.i.* (was or were, been, being)
go, *v.i.* (went, gone, going)
run, *v.i., t.* (ran, run, running)

The *v.* indicates that the word is a **verb,** and the *t* or *i* that it is **transitive** (that is, takes an object) or **intransitive** (that is, doesn't take an object). Some verbs, like *run,* can be either intransitive (I run faster than David) or transitive (I run a factory in Kansas City).

The **present infinitive** of the verb is formed by adding the preposition *to* to the form given first (*to eat, to chop, to be, to go, to run*), and most verbs (although *not* the verb *to be*) form their **present tenses** from the infinitive (*I eat, I chop, I go, I run*). The second form of the verb, given in the parentheses, is the **past tense** (*ate, chopped*), and the third is the **past participle** (*eaten, chopped*), the form which is combined with an auxiliary to form the **perfect tenses** (*I have eaten, I have chopped, I will have gone*). The *-ing* form is the present participle.

VERB TENSES

To deal more fully with verb errors, we'll need to review and define some additional terms. Each verb has **number, person, voice,** and **tense.**

Number is simply singular or plural.

The three **persons** of a verb are **first** (*I, we*), **second** (*you*), and **third** (*he, she, it, they*).

Active (I hit the ball) and **passive** (The ball was hit by me) are the **voices** of verbs. If the subject of a verb performs the action of the

55

verb, the verb is active, while if the subject receives the action, the verb is passive.

The **tenses** of a verb are the forms that show the time of its action or state of being. Most of the verb errors that appear on the exam are errors of agreement or errors of tense. The following chart gives the tenses of the verbs *to be* and *to chop*.

Present Tense: Action or State of Being in the Present

	Singular	*Plural*
First Person	I am I chop	we are we chop
Second Person	you are you chop	you are you chop
Third Person	he, she, it is he, she, it chops	they are they chop

Past Tense: Action or State of Being in the Past

	Singular	*Plural*
First Person	I was I chopped	we were we chopped
Second Person	you were you chopped	you were you chopped
Third Person	he, she, it was he, she, it chopped	they were they chopped

Future Tense: Action or State of Being in the Future

	Singular	*Plural*
First Person	I will be I will chop	we will be we will chop
Second Person	you will be you will chop	you will be you will chop
Third Person	he, she, it will be he, she, it will chop	they will be they will chop

Present Perfect Tense:
Action in Past Time in Relation to Present Time

	Singular	*Plural*
First Person	I have been I have chopped	we have been we have chopped
Second Person	you have been you have chopped	you have been you have chopped
Third Person	he, she, it has been he, she, it has chopped	they have been they have chopped

Past Perfect Tense:
Action in Past Time in Relation to Another Past Time

	Singular	*Plural*
First Person	I had been I had chopped	we had been we had chopped
Second Person	you had been you had chopped	you had been you had chopped
Third Person	he, she, it had been he, she, it had chopped	they had been they had chopped

Future Perfect Tense:
Action in a Future Time in Relation to Another Time Even Farther in the Future

	Singular	*Plural*
First Person	I will have been I will have chopped	we will have been we will have chopped
Second Person	you will have been you will have chopped	you will have been you will have chopped
Third Person	he, she, it will have been he, she, it will have chopped	they will have been they will have chopped

There should be no trouble with the present, past, and future tenses, but some examples of the perfect tenses may be helpful. Remember that the **present perfect** tense is used to describe action in *past* time in relation to the present.

An example of a **past tense** is

I chopped wood last week.

An example of a **present perfect tense** is

I have chopped wood every Tuesday for three years.

That is, the wood chopping is an action begun in the past and continuing to the present.

An example of a **past perfect** tense is

I had chopped wood every Tuesday until I bought a chain saw.

That is, the wood chopping was an action in the past that preceded another past action, buying a chain saw. In this sentence, *had chopped* is a past perfect tense, and *bought* is a past tense.

An example of the **future perfect** tense is

By 1999, I will have chopped enough wood to heat six houses.

That is, the wood chopping will continue into the future but will be past in 1999.

Almost all verb tense errors on the exam occur in sentences with two verbs. Always look carefully at the tenses of the verbs in a sentence. Does the time scheme make sense? Is it consistent and logical? Since tense reflects the time of the actions, there can be no single rule about what tenses should be used. Meaning, in this case, the time scheme of the action, will determine tense. Sometimes, the meaning will require a change of tense. For example,

Yesterday, I ate breakfast at seven o'clock, and tomorrow I will eat at nine.

We have both a past (*ate*) and a future (*will eat*) in this sentence, but other words which explain the time scheme (*yesterday, tomorrow*) make it clear that both a past and a future tense are necessary. On the other hand, consider this example.

In the seventeenth century, the performances at public theaters took place in the afternoon, and the actors dress in splendid costumes.

In this sentence, the change from the past (*took*) to the present (*dress*) makes no sense. Both verbs refer to past actions (*in the seventeenth century*); both should be in the past tense (*took, dressed*).

To spot errors in verb tense, you must look carefully at the verbs and the other words in the sentence that establish the time scheme. Adverbs like *then, subsequently, before, yesterday,* and *tomorrow* and prepositional phrases like *in the Dark Ages* and *in the future* work with the verbs to make the time of the actions clear. The following are sentences very much like those used on the examination to test verb tenses. Which of the italicized verbs are correct?

1. The winds blew sand in the bathers' faces, so they gathered up their towels and *will leave* the beach quickly.

2. The new variety of plum was developed by Burbank, who *begun* to work with fruits after the Civil War.

3. In the year 2010, I *am* fifty years old.

4. I *had spoke* with her briefly many times before, but today's conversation was the first in which she *spoke* frankly about her political ambitions.

All but one of the italicized verbs are incorrect. In the first sentence, the shift to the future tense (*will leave*) makes no sense after the two other verbs in the past tense. The verb should be *left*. In the second sentence, the past tense, *began,* or better, the past perfect, *had begun,* is necessary. The *am* of the third sentence should be *will be,* a future tense. In the fourth sentence, *had spoke* incorrectly tries to form the past perfect tense using the past tense (*spoke*) instead of the past participle *spoken*. The second *spoke* is a correct use of the past tense.

Participles, the form of the verb used as an adjective, have only two tenses, present (*going, chopping, eating*) and past (*having gone, having chopped, having eaten*), but tense errors are possible, Be sure that sentences with a participle have a coherent time sequence. A sentence like

> Eating my lunch, I took the car to the gas station.

makes sense if you eat and drive at the same time. If your meaning is *after lunch,* you must write

> Having eaten my lunch, I took the car to the gas station.

LIE/LAY, RISE/RAISE, SIT/SET

So far, SAT II Writing has *not* had questions on these verbs. You can skip this section if you're short of time.

Lie/Lay

Lie is an intransitive verb (that is, it takes no object) meaning *rest* or *recline. Lay* is a transitive verb (it must have an object) meaning *put* or *place.* The confusion between the two verbs probably arose because the past tense of the verb *to lie* (to recline) is the same as the present tense of the verb *to lay* (to place).

Yesterday I *lay* in bed till noon.
(intransitive verb, past tense, no object)

I *lay* the paper on the table.
(transitive verb, present tense, object [*paper*])

Lie and Lay			
	Present Tense	*Past Tense*	*Past Participle*	*Present Participle*

	Present Tense	*Past Tense*	*Past Participle*	*Present Participle*
to rest, to recline (intransitive)	lie	lay	lain	lying
to place, to put (transitive)	lay	laid	laid	laying

1. I like *laying* my head in a pile of sand when I am *lying* on the beach.

2. I *laid* the book on the table and *lay* down on the couch.

3. I have *laid* the book on the table.

4. I have *lain* in bed all morning.

Rise/Raise, Sit/Set

Like *lie, rise* and *sit* are intransitive verbs. Like *lay, raise* and *set* are transitive verbs.

Rise and Raise/Sit and Set			
	Present Tense	*Past Tense*	*Past Participle*	*Present Participle*
to go up, to ascend (intransitive)	rise	rose	risen	rising
to lift (transitive)	raise	raised	raised	raising
to be seated (intransitive)	sit	sat	sat	sitting
to put (transitive)	set	set	set	setting

1. I *raise* the window shade and watch the sun *rise*.

2. I *raised* the shade after the sun had *risen*.

3. The sun *rose* before I had *raised* the shade.

4. *Raising* the shade, I watched the sun *rising*.

EXERCISE 4
VERBS

Choose the correct verb form in the following sentences. Answers are on page 120.

1. Because I (eat, ate) too many potato chips yesterday, I am ill now.

2. When you light a candle at only one end, it (lasts, lasted) longer than one lighted at both ends.

3. I (waited, have waited) for her on the platform, but she never arrived.

4. I (have waited, had waited) for her for two hours when she arrived at noon.

5. He (will go, will have gone) to the city tomorrow.

6. When I (am, was) thinner, I (buy, will buy) a new wardrobe.

7. The thief climbed up the trellis, opened the window, and (steps, stepped) quietly into the room.

8. The letters (lying, laying) on the table have been (lying, laying) there for a week.

9. I (lay, laid) my briefcase on the table and (lay, laid) down on the couch.

10. In this car, the windows (rise, raise) at the press of a button.

11. (Sitting, Setting) the flowers on the table, she noticed the cat (sitting, setting) on the chair nearby.

12. At nine o'clock, a grill (rises, raises) to prevent any entry into the vault.

13. When I reach retirement age in 2005, I (will be, will have been) sixty years old.

14. When I reach retirement age in 2005, I (will work, will have worked) for the post office for thirty years.

15. You (are, were) more careful when you borrow a car.

16. You (make, made) fewer mistakes last week.

5
MISPLACED PARTS, DANGLING MODIFIERS

MISPLACED PARTS

The grammatical errors discussed in parts 1, 2, 3, and 4 are likely to be tested in a question which asks you to identify an error in a single sentence. The first part of this section discusses misplaced parts of the sentence. Since a misplaced part is often awkward but not, strictly speaking, a grammatical error, the questions testing for misplaced parts usually present five versions of the same sentence and ask you to select the sentence that is not only grammatically correct but also clear and exact, free from awkwardness and ambiguity.

A well-written sentence will be clear and concise. Given a choice between two sentences which say all that must be said and are error free, choose the shorter version. This is *not* to say that any shorter sentence is the right answer. Sometimes, a shorter sentence will have a grammatical error, omit part of the original thought, or change the meaning. Here's a sample question.

Fifteen women have formally protested <u>their being overlooked for promotion</u>.

(A) their being overlooked for promotion
(B) themselves being overlooked for promotion
(C) their overlooking for promotion
(D) overlooking themselves for promotion
(E) themselves as overlooked for promotion

Answer (C) is the shortest of the five choices here, but it is the wrong answer. It changes the meaning by leaving out *being* and makes the women the ones who overlooked. The right answer is choice (A). The shorter version, then, is not always the best answer, but the right answer will be as short as it can be without sacrificing grammatical correctness and clarity of content.

The basic rule for dealing with misplaced parts of the sentence is *keep related parts together.* Avoid any unnecessary separation of closely related parts of the sentence. Avoid odd or unnatural word order. Keep modifiers as near as possible to the words they modify.

1. I bought a jacket in a Westwood shop *made of leather.*

   I bought a jacket *made of leather* in a Westwood shop.

2. The soprano had dreamed of singing at the Met *for many years.*

   For many years, the soprano had dreamed of singing at the Met.

3. The committee decided *after the next meeting* to hold a dance.

   The committee decided to hold a dance *after the next meeting.*

4. The ice cream cone I licked *rapidly* melted.

   The ice cream cone I licked melted *rapidly.*

   The ice cream cone I *rapidly* licked melted.

In the first version of sentences 1, 2, and 3, the placement of the italicized phrases makes the meaning of the sentence unclear, but the revisions place the phrases closer to the words they modify. In the first version of sentence 4, the adverb *rapidly* may modify either *licked* or *melted,* but it isn't clear which meaning is intended. The two revised versions are clear, with two different meanings.

The normal word order in an English clause or sentence is subject-verb-object:

The dog bit the boy.

Although there are bound to be times when another word order is necessary, keep in mind that the clearest sentences will move from subject to verb to object and keep the three elements as close as possible.

The following is an example of a typical question testing your ability to revise a sentence with misplaced modifiers.

A bright red dress was found in the children's department by Mrs. Mason that had Barney the dinosaur embroidered on the back.

(A) A bright red dress was found in the children's department by Mrs. Mason
(B) In the children's department, a bright red dress was found by Mrs. Mason
(C) A bright red dress was found by Mrs. Mason in the children's department
(D) Mrs. Mason found a bright red dress in the children's department
(E) In the children's department, Mrs. Mason found a bright red dress

Answers (A), (B), and (C) use the passive voice and place the *that had Barney* clause to modify *Mrs. Mason* or *the children's department*, when it should be next to *dress*. Answer (D) gets rid of the passive but still separates *dress* and its modifier. In (E), the clearest word order—subject, verb, object—also places *dress* next to the clause that modifies it.

DANGLING MODIFIERS

Dangling modifiers are phrases that have nothing to modify. They most frequently occur at the beginning of a sentence and are usually verbals: **participles** (verbal adjectives), **gerunds** (verbal nouns), and **infinitives.**

Participles

A **participle** is a verb used as an adjective. The **present participle** ends in -*ing* (*eating, seeing, writing,* for example), while the **past participle** is that form of the verb used to form the perfect tense (*eaten, seen, written,* for example). Whenever you see a sentence that begins with a participle, check to be sure that the participle logically modifies the subject that immediately follows the comma that sets off the participial phrase. In the following sentences, the first version begins with a dangling participle. The revised versions correct the sentence to eliminate the error.

1. *Waiting* for the bus, the sun came out.

   While we were waiting for the bus, the sun came out.

2. *Fishing* for trout, our canoe overturned.

   While we were fishing for trout, we overturned our canoe.

   Fishing for trout, we overturned our canoe.

3. *Having finished* chapter one, chapter two seemed easy.

   After I had finished chapter one, chapter two seemed easy.

   Having finished chapter one, I found chapter two easy.

4. *Having had* no soup, the salad was welcome.

   Because I had no soup, the salad was welcome.

   Having had no soup, I found the salad welcome.

Sentences 1 and 2 use present participles; sentences 3 and 4 use past participles. The second of the two revisions of these sentences illustrates that a sentence can begin with a participle that does *not* dangle, and the exam will probably contain sentences that begin with a participle used correctly. But you may be sure that it will also contain sentences that begin with dangling participles to test your ability to recognize this error.

Gerunds

Gerunds, verbal nouns, look like participles, but they are used as nouns rather than adjectives. In the sentence

Waiting for the bus is very boring.

waiting is a gerund, used as a *noun* and the subject of the sentence.

But in the sentence

Waiting for the bus, I became bored.

waiting is a participle, used as an *adjective* and modifying the subject, *I.*

The following sentences contain dangling gerunds, corrected in the revision or revisions that follow.

1. By changing the oil regularly, your car will run better.

   By changing the oil regularly, you can make your car run better.

2. By working very hard, better grades will result.

   By working very hard, you will get better grades.

3. After sneezing, my handkerchief was useful.

   After sneezing, I found my handkerchief useful.

   After I sneezed, my handkerchief was useful.

Infinitives

An **infinitive** is the simple, uninflected form of a verb, usually written with the preposition *to*. *To go* is an infinitive, while *goes* or *going* are inflected forms, that is, with additional sounds (*es, ing*) added to the infinitive. Dangling infinitives show up much less frequently on the exam than dangling participles or gerunds, but the principle of the error is the same. As with dangling participles and gerunds, you can correct a sentence with a dangling infinitive by making sure that the subject of the sentence that follows the comma is what the infinitive really modifies. The first version of the following sentences contains a dangling infinitive, corrected in the revision.

1. To play the violin well, constant practicing is necessary.

   To play the violin well, you must practice constantly.

2. To make cookies, sugar and flour are needed.

   To make cookies, you need sugar and flour.

Prepositional Phrases and Elliptical Clauses

An **ellipsis** is the omission of a word or words. An **elliptical clause** or **phrase** is one in which the subject and verb are implied but omitted. For example, in the sentence

> When in New York, I stay at the Plaza.

the implied subject and verb of *When in New York* are *I am,* but they have been omitted. It is acceptable to use an ellipsis like this, but if the implied subject doesn't follow, the phrase will dangle.

1. Though rich and beautiful, her marriage was a failure.

2. While on guard duty, her rifle was lost.

3. When a very young child growing up in Brooklyn, his father sent him to summer camp in New Hampshire.

4. On the ship's observation deck, three gray whales were sighted.

The first three of these sentences begin with dangling elliptical clauses. Adding *she was* in the first and second clause and *he was* in the third, that is, filling in the ellipsis, will correct the sentences. The fourth sentence illustrates that even a prepositional phrase may dangle. An observer, not the three whales, is much more likely to be on this ship's observation deck. Dangling modifiers are, like this one, often not only incorrect but ridiculous too. Whenever you see a sentence that begins with a participle, gerund, elliptical phrase, or infinitive, look very carefully to see whether or not the phrase dangles. And remember that some will be correct.

EXERCISE 5
MISPLACED PARTS, DANGLING MODIFIERS

All of the following sentences contain misplaced parts or dangling modifiers. Rewrite each sentence to eliminate the errors. Answers are on page 122.

1. After making a par despite a very bad drive, the crowd cheered loudly for Nancy Lopez.

2. Having failed to read the book carefully, his remarks in class were either imperceptive or irrelevant.

3. By keeping your eye on the ball and not on your partner, the overhead may become your most consistent shot.

4. Hoping to win a place on the team, her free-skating performance must be first-rate.

5. To do well in this exam, both stamina and concentration are absolutely essential.

6. For months we had anticipated seeing Elton John's performance, and to get the best possible view of the stage, our seats were on the center aisle in the front row.

7. When only eight years old, he sent his son to boarding school in Arizona.

8. Though only five feet four, his quickness of reflex and the uncanny accuracy of his volley have made him the best doubles player on the team.

9. At temperatures below 250 degrees, you should stir the boiling syrup very briskly.

10. By applying the insecticide carefully, damage to the environment can be avoided.

6
PARALLELISM

Errors of **parallelism** will occur when two or more linked ideas are expressed in different grammatical structures. In a sentence like

I am interested in *nuclear physics, to play tennis,* and *going to the theater.*

each of the three elements of the series is in a different grammatical form: a noun, an infinitive, and a gerund phrase. To make the series parallel, one would use any *one* of the forms three times.

I am interested in *nuclear physics, tennis,* and *theater.*
(three nouns)

I am interested in *studying nuclear physics, playing tennis,* and *going to the theater.*
(three gerunds)

I like *to study nuclear physics, to play tennis,* and *to go the theater.*
(three infinitives)

To find errors of parallelism, look first to be sure there are two or more ideas, words, or phrases that are similar; then check to see that the coordinate ideas are expressed by the same part of speech, verb form, or clause or phrase structure. The first version of the following sentences is *not* parallel. The revision or revisions that follow each sentence correct the parallelism errors.

1. I admire *his cheerfulness* and *that he perseveres.*

   I admire *his cheerfulness* and *his perseverance.*

2. *To dance* and *singing* were his favorite pastimes.

   Dancing and *singing* were his favorite pastimes.

   To dance and *to sing* were his favorite pastimes.

3. *Her cleverness* and *that she looks innocent* helped her to escape.

   Her cleverness and *innocent appearance* helped her to escape.

4. *To ship* a package by air freight is more expensive than *if you send* it by parcel post.

   To ship a package by air freight is more expensive than *to send* it by parcel post.

COMMON PARALLELISM ERRORS

The following are common parallelism errors in the SAT II Writing exam. In the examples, the first version is in error; the revision or revisions correct the sentence.

Unnecessary Shifts in Verb Tenses

1. She *bought* her ticket at the box office and *sits* in the first row.

   She *bought* her ticket at the box office and *sat* in the first row.

2. Every day he *runs* five kilometers and *swam* half a mile.

   Every day he *runs* five kilometers and *swims* half a mile.

   Every day he *ran* five kilometers and *swam* half a mile.

Unnecessary Shifts from an Active to a Passive Verb

1. John *plays* tennis well, but ping-pong *is played* even better by him.

   John *plays* tennis well, but he *plays* ping-pong even better.

2. The editor *wrote* his article in thirty minutes, and it *was typed* by him in five.

   The editor *wrote* his article in thirty minutes and *typed* it in five.

Unnecessary Shifts in Person

We divide personal pronouns into three classes: the **first person** (singular, *I;* plural, *we*), the **second person** (*you*), and the **third person** (singular, *he, she, it, one;* plural, *they*). Although it's possible that a sentence will refer to more than one person (*I* went to Florida, and *she* went to Georgia), in sentences where the change of person isn't part of the meaning, the pronouns should be consistent. The first version of each of the following sentences is incorrect, and the revisions correct the sentence.

1. *One* should drive slowly, and *you* should keep your eyes on the road.

   One should drive slowly and keep *one's* eyes on the road.

   You should drive slowly and keep *your* eyes on the road.

2. To win at poker, *a player* must know the odds, and *you* must observe *your* opponents carefully.

   To win at poker, *you* must know the odds and observe *your* opponents carefully.

   To win at poker, *a player* must know the odds and observe *his or her* opponents carefully.

Parallelism Errors in a List or Series

Parallelism errors are likely to occur in a list or series. In the following examples, the second version of the sentences corrects the parallelism errors.

1. The game has three steps: *getting* your pieces to the center, *capturing* your opponent's pieces, and you must *end* with a throw of double six.

   The game has three steps: *getting* your pieces to the center, *capturing* your opponent's pieces, and *ending* with a throw of double six.

2. I talked on, trying to be *charming, gracious,* and *to keep* the conversation going.

I talked on, trying *to be* gracious and charming and *to keep* the conversation going.

The second example begins with a series of two adjectives (*charming, gracious*), but the expected third adjective is an infinitive. The revised version eliminates the series and makes the two infinitives (*to be, to keep*) parallel.

Sentences incorporating a series set up expectations of parallel structures. In a series of three or more, the first two elements will establish a pattern. Assume a series is to include three parts: *mow the grass, weed the garden,* and *empty the trash.* One can say

I want you to mow the lawn, weed the garden, and empty the trash.
or
I want you to mow the lawn, to weed the garden, and to empty the trash.

In the first sentence, the series begins with the infinitive using *to,* and the *to* is understood in the next two parts. The series is *mow, weed, empty.* In the second sentence, the *to* is used with all three verbs. But if the sentence read

I want you to mow the lawn, weed the garden, and to empty the trash.

the parallelism would be lost.

Don't expect every element in parallel structures to be identical all the time. It is proper, for example, to say

I want you to clean the kitchen and the bathroom, go to the store, and cash a check at the bank.

The parallel elements here are *to clean,* (*to*) *go,* and (*to*) *cash,* but other elements within the series are different.

Correlatives

One sure sign of a sentence that must have parallel grammatical constructions is the use of **correlatives.** Correlatives are coordinating conjunctions used in pairs to express similarity or equality in thought. Whenever any of the following correlatives are used, they should be followed by similar grammatical constructions. Memorize this list, and whenever you see these words in a sentence on the exam, look for parallelism as a problem in the question.

both . . . and	first . . . second
not only . . . but also	not merely . . . but
not only . . . but	not so much . . . as
not . . . but	as much . . . as
either . . . or	more . . . than
neither . . . nor	less . . . than

In a sentence with *both . . . and,* look first to see exactly what the grammar is immediately after the *both;* then make sure the same structure follows the *and.* In the following examples, the first version illustrates an error, corrected in the revision or revisions.

1. The opera is *both* a complex work *and* original.

   The opera is *both* complex *and* original.
   (*both,* adjective, *and* adjective)

   The opera is *both* a complex *and* an original work.
   (*both,* article, adjective, *and,* article, adjective)

2. He *not only* is selfish *but also* deceitful.

   He is *not only* selfish *but also* deceitful.
   (*not only,* adjective, *but also,* adjective)

   He *not only* is selfish *but also* is deceitful.
   (*not only,* verb, adjective, *but also,* verb, adjective)

3. The book is *not only* about pigs *but also* flowers.

The book is *not only* about pigs *but also* about flowers.
(*not only,* preposition, noun, *but also,* preposition, noun)

4. The letter is *either* for you *or* your husband.

The letter is for *either* you *or* your husband.
(*either,* pronoun, *or,* pronoun, noun)

The letter is *either* for you *or* for your husband.
(*either,* preposition, pronoun, *or,* preposition, pronoun, noun)

Note that in the fourth sentence the corrected versions are not identical (for *you*/for *your husband*). The parallel must be in structure, but one part may contain additional words. It is correct to write

The letter is either for you or for your handsome, first husband.

since both *either* and *or* are followed by prepositional phrases beginning with *for.*

EXERCISE 6
PARALLELISM

If there is an error in the following sentences, choose the underlined, lettered part in which the error occurs. Some of the sentences will contain no errors. Answers are on page 123.

1. Because I grew up in Switzerland, I read and speak
        A   B   C
   both French and German. No error
       D   E

2. It is not his reckless spending of my money but that he spends
     A   B
   it on other women that has led me to file for divorce. No error
    C   D   E

3. A <u>person's aptitude</u> for foreign languages <u>is</u> important to State
        A   B

   Department examiners, but on this exam, <u>it</u> is your ability to
                                                         C

   read French <u>that will make</u> the difference. <u>No error</u>
                      D   E

4. Law school <u>not only enables</u> one to practice law,
                   A

   <u>but also teaches</u> <u>you</u> to <u>think more clearly.</u> <u>No error</u>
        B   C   D   E

5. I want you <u>not only</u> to <u>paint</u> and sand the screens <u>but also</u>
               A   B   C

   to <u>put</u> them in the cellar. <u>No error</u>
    D   E

6. What <u>one expects</u> <u>to get out of</u> a long term investment
          A   B

   <u>should be</u> considered carefully <u>before</u> you see your broker.
      C   D

   <u>No error</u>
    E

7. <u>Come</u> to the next class meeting <u>prepared</u> to take notes, to
    A   B

   speak <u>briefly,</u> and <u>with some questions to ask.</u> <u>No error</u>
        C   D   E

8. Her grace and charm, <u>her ability to see</u> both sides of a
                            A

   question, and <u>her willingness to</u> accept criticism <u>are</u> qualities
                    B   C

   <u>that I especially admire.</u> <u>No error</u>
    D   E

9. We <u>must look</u> <u>closely</u> <u>both at the data</u> in this year's report and
$\qquad$ A $\qquad$ B $\qquad$ C

the results of last <u>year's</u> analysis. <u>No error</u>
$\qquad\quad$ D $\qquad\qquad$ E

10. The process of natural selection <u>requires that</u> animals be able
$\qquad\qquad\qquad\qquad\qquad\quad$ A

to adapt <u>to changing climates,</u> to discover new foods,
$\qquad\qquad$ B

<u>and defend themselves</u> against <u>their</u> enemies. <u>No error</u>
$\qquad\qquad$ C $\qquad\qquad\quad$ D $\qquad\qquad$ E

11. The new employee <u>soon</u> <u>proved himself</u> <u>to be</u> not only capable
$\qquad\qquad\qquad\quad$ A $\qquad$ B $\qquad$ C

but also <u>a man who could be trusted.</u> <u>No error</u>
$\qquad\qquad$ D $\qquad\qquad\qquad$ E

12. <u>As soon as</u> school <u>ended,</u> he jumped into his car, drove to the
$\qquad$ A $\qquad\qquad$ B

pool, <u>changes</u> his clothes, and <u>swam</u> twenty laps. <u>No error</u>
$\qquad\quad$ C $\qquad\qquad\qquad$ D $\qquad\qquad$ E

13. To complete your application, <u>you</u> must fill out three forms,
$\qquad\qquad\qquad\qquad\qquad$ A

<u>pay</u> the enrollment fee, <u>submit</u> a recent photograph, and
$\quad$ B $\qquad\qquad\qquad$ C

<u>enclose</u> a copy of your high-school transcript. <u>No error</u>
$\quad$ D $\qquad\qquad\qquad\qquad\qquad\qquad$ E

14. I must remember <u>to buy soap and a toothbrush,</u>
$\qquad\qquad\qquad\qquad$ A

<u>to have the car washed,</u>
$\qquad\quad$ B

<u>to order my Christmas cards and gift subscriptions,</u>
$\qquad\qquad\qquad\qquad$ C

<u>and cash a check</u> before the bank closes. <u>No error</u>
$\qquad$ D $\qquad\qquad\qquad\qquad$ E

REVIEW EXERCISE: SECTIONS 4, 5, AND 6

Some of the following sentences may be correct. Others contain problems covered in sections 4, 5, and 6 of the Grammar and Usage Review. There is not more than one error in any sentence.

If there is an error, it will be underlined and lettered. Find the one underlined part that must be changed to make the sentence correct. Choose (E) if the sentence contains no error. Answers are on page 124.

1. <u>Laying aside</u> his guns, the western hero seems <u>to lose</u> his
      A   B

   distinguishing feature, and <u>he became</u> <u>like anyone else.</u>
                                C   D

   <u>No error</u>
    E

2. Attila campaigned <u>to provide</u> plunder <u>for his army,</u>
                           A   B

   <u>which resembles</u> a vast mobile city <u>existing only for</u> conquest
        C   D

   and pillage. <u>No error</u>
              E

3. In calling <u>*Vanity Fair* a "novel without a hero,"</u> Thackeray
                      A

   <u>suggests</u> that none of his characters,
     B

   <u>not even Amelia or Dobbin,</u> is <u>completely</u> admirable. <u>No error</u>
            C   D   E

4. The fog of myth and superstition <u>was dispelled</u> not by
                                          A
   professors <u>but men like</u> Prince Henry the Navigator and his
              B
   captains <u>who went out</u> to explore the globe <u>and to chart</u> the
            C   D
   known world. <u>No error</u>
                   E

5. <u>Raising the window shade slowly,</u> the bright sunshine <u>poured</u>
                   A   B
   into the room and <u>illuminated</u> the broken crystal <u>lying</u> on the
                      C   D
   floor. <u>No error</u>
          E

6. <u>Having narrowly missed colliding with another car</u> while trying
                          A
   to change lanes on the freeway, all three of my passengers told

   <u>me</u> that <u>I was</u> <u>a terrible driver.</u> <u>No error</u>
   B   C   D   E

7. The prince was <u>embarrassed but not injured</u> when a
                            A
   demonstrator broke through the <u>cordon</u> of security guards
                                  B
   <u>and splashes</u> red paint on <u>his</u> white suit. <u>No error</u>
   C   D   E

8. After beginning at the bottom <u>as a stockboy,</u> <u>he</u> <u>rose</u> to the
                                 A   B   C
   presidency of the store <u>in only eight years.</u> <u>No error</u>
                           D   E

9. You must be very careful <u>to read the instructions</u> on the test
                                              A
   booklet, <u>to mark the correct space</u> on your answer sheet, and
                          B
   <u>stop writing</u> as soon as the proctor <u>announces</u> the end of the
        C   D
   exam. <u>No error</u>
              E

7
AMBIGUOUS PRONOUNS

In conversation and in informal writing, we often use pronouns that have no single word as their antecedent. *This* happens all the time, for example, the *this* that begins this sentence. It refers to the general idea of the preceding sentence but not to a specific noun. In the exam, you should regard a pronoun that does not have a specific noun or word used as a noun as its antecedent a defect. This construction is more likely to occur in the kind of question which gives you choice of revisions. The best answer will either get rid of the ambiguous pronoun or supply a specific antecedent. Which is the best version of the following sentence?

1. The sun was shining brightly, *which* pleased me.
2. The sun was shining brightly, and *this* pleased me.
3. The sun was shining brightly, and *that* pleased me.
4. Because the sun was shining brightly, *this* pleased me.
5. There was bright sunshine, and *this* pleased me.

The fifth is the best version because the pronoun *this* has a specific antecedent (*sunshine*). In the first four sentences, none of the pronouns has a specific antecedent. A revision like *That the sun was shining brightly pleased me* would also be correct, since this version simply removes the ambiguous pronoun. The four other answers demonstrate that you cannot correct an ambiguous pronoun by substituting another pronoun. The ambiguity will remain until you revise to supply a specific antecedent or to get rid of the pronoun altogether.

You must also be careful with sentences with a pronoun and a choice of antecedents. In a sentence like *Mark told Luke that he owed him five dollars,* we cannot know for certain who owes money to whom. A sentence with an ambiguity of this sort may appear in a question asking you to select an underlined error.

For many years, the American consumer <u>preferred</u> <u>a cola</u> to a
                                                    A   B

lemon, orange, or grapefruit flavored drink; recent surveys <u>show</u>
                                                            C

a surprising rise in the consumption <u>of it</u>. <u>No error</u>
                                        D   E

The error here is choice (D), the ambiguous pronoun *it,* which may refer to any one of four flavors.

EXERCISE 7
AMBIGUOUS PRONOUNS

All of the following sentences contain ambiguous pronouns. Identify the ambiguous pronoun and revise the sentence to eliminate the error. Answers are on page 125.

1. I came in fifteen minutes late, which made the whole chemistry class incomprehensible to me.

2. I want to go to law school because this is the best way to prepare myself for a career in politics.

3. I wrote checks for my phone bill, the gas bill, and my union dues, and this made my account overdrawn.

4. He ate a salad, a pizza, an order of chili, and a large wedge of apple pie in only seven minutes, and, needless to say, this gave him indigestion.

5. I bought a radio and a record player at the second-hand store, but when I plugged it in, it would not work.

6. Both Dave and Vince were scheduled to work Saturday morning, but because his car wouldn't start, he didn't appear until noon.

7. I am told that I think clearly and write well, and these are important in historical studies.

8. Marine iguanas have armored skin, strong claws, and sharp teeth, and this makes them seem ferocious, though they are harmless vegetarians.

8
OTHER ERRORS OF GRAMMAR

Chances are that more than fifty percent of the grammar errors on the first two parts of the SAT II Writing multiple-choice exam will be errors of case, agreement, verb tense, parallelism, or misplaced parts, and most of these errors will appear more than once. The errors discussed in this section occur regularly, though usually only once or twice in each exam.

SENTENCE FRAGMENTS

A complete sentence must be an independent clause; that is, it must have a subject and a verb and stand by itself as a sentence. Don't assume that a subject and a verb automatically make a complete sentence. *I go,* although it is only two words long, is a complete sentence, while *When he had finished eating his dinner, had pushed back his chair, placed his napkin by his empty wine glass, and risen from the table* is not. It is a dependent clause, a sentence fragment. All of the following are sentence fragments.

1. Hoping to be elected on either the first or second ballot.

2. Because the jurors had very carefully examined the evidence presented in the twenty-two days of testimony.

3. The runners from six South American countries, together with the volleyball teams from Canada, Cuba, and the United States.

To complete the first sentence, we must add a subject and verb either in an independent clause following this dependent clause or by changing *Hoping* to *He hoped, She hoped, Carol hoped,* or something of the kind. The *Because* at the beginning of the second sentence marks it as a dependent clause. The third sentence has no main verb.

DOUBLE NEGATIVES

It's hard to miss the double negative in a sentence like *I don't want no peas*. The errors are much less obvious with other negative adverbs such as *hardly, but, scarcely, seldom, rarely,* and the like. When you see these words in a sentence, be on the lookout for a double negative like the following.

1. I spent ten dollars on gasoline, and now I don't have hardly any money.

   (Correct to: *I have hardly any money*)

2. In the twilight, a batter can't hardly see a fastball.

   (Correct to: *can hardly see*)

3. I don't have but a dollar, and that will not scarcely pay my check.

   (Correct to: *I have but . . . will scarcely pay*)

OMISSION OF NECESSARY WORDS

Good writing is concise. Given a choice on the exam between two grammatically correct sentences whose meaning is the same, you should choose the shorter version. But be sure there are no necessary words missing. When we read carelessly, sentences like these (which are *not*) appear to be complete.

1. People who read rapidly can easily and often have overlooked important details.

2. I am uninterested and bored by shopping.

The first sentence needs two main verbs and tries to do the work with one. The verb *have overlooked* is complete, but we cannot say *can overlooked*. We must write *can easily overlook and often have overlooked*. In the second sentence, we cannot say *uninterested by;* we must say *uninterested in and bored by*.

The exam is likely to test comparisons which make no sense because of a missing word or words. Be certain that the two elements that are compared are equivalent. You cannot say *The man's time in the hundred meters was much faster than the woman* because the two elements being compared are different—*time* versus *woman*. The sentence must read *The man's time in the hundred meters was much faster than that of the woman* or *The man's time in the hundred meters was much faster than the woman's*.

What words must be added to correct the following sentences?

1. He is more interested in getting a good job than a rich wife.

2. The amount of vitamin C in eight ounces of tomato juice is much greater than eight ounces of milk.

3. There are far fewer single parents in Maine, Vermont, and New Hampshire than Massachusetts or Connecticut.

Sentence 1 needs a phrase like *than in getting a rich wife*. Sentence 2 should end with *than that in eight ounces of milk*. Sentence 3 should read *than in Massachusetts or Connecticut*.

Another form of question testing the same error is a sentence with a *like* . . . or *unlike* . . . at the beginning or end.

1. Like Shelley, Byron's poetry is sensuous.

2. Like New York, Chicago's traffic is snarled on Friday afternoons.

3. The market in Boston never closes, like New York.

4. Her bank account is never overdrawn, unlike her husband.

In all of these sentences, the two compared elements are not parallel. The first sentence compares *Byron's poetry* with *Shelley*, not with *Shelley's poetry*, and the second compares *New York* and the *traffic* in Chicago. The third sentence compares the *market* and *New York*. Any of the following revisions will correct the first sentence.

Like Shelley, Byron wrote sensuous poetry.
(*Shelley = Byron*)

Like Shelley's, Byron's poetry is sensuous.
(*Shelley's poetry = Byron's poetry*)

Like that of Shelley, Byron's poetry is sensuous.
(*Shelley's poetry = Byron's poetry*)

Similarly, the fourth sentence, which compares a *bank account* to a *husband,* must be revised. Either of the following is correct.

Her bank account is never overdrawn, unlike her husband's.

Her bank account is never overdrawn, unlike that of her husband.

WHO, WHICH, AND THAT

Given a choice among *who, which,* or *that,* use *who* when the antecedent is a single human being (*the man who; John Smith, who*) or a group thought of as individuals (*the lawmakers who, the players who, the jurors who*). Use *that* or *which* for a group thought of as a group (*the senate that; the team, which; the jury that*).

The questions on SAT II Writing will probably not ask for more than the distinction between the human (*who*) and the nonhuman (*which* or *that*) in cases where there can be no doubt.

The girl, the baby, Mrs. Gilbertson
(*who*)

The bat, the key, the government
(*which* or *that*)

EXERCISE 8
OTHER ERRORS OF GRAMMAR

Answers are on page 126.

Part A

Identify the sentence fragments in the following.

1. Representing the farm belt attitude toward price subsidies, the delegations from Kansas, Nebraska, and Iowa, as well as food processors from Texas, Louisiana, and Georgia.

2. So David wept.

3. The Colt Company, a leader in the industry, and celebrated for introducing the first energy-efficient nine-room house at a cost under sixty thousand dollars.

4. Is he?

5. When glaciers ground extensive tracts of the granite to a highly polished finish.

Part B

All of the following sentences contain errors described in section 8. Identify the error and correct the sentence.

1. The price of meat has gone up steeply in the past six months, according to an unofficial government survey, but there is some consolation for yogurt eaters; yogurt prices haven't risen hardly at all.

2. Making *Coming of Age in Samoa* the required summer reading for those who have enrolled in the anthropology class.

3. There are scarcely no batteries left in the store.

4. Like the Borgias in Florence, Rome had the all-powerful Orsini family.

5. Water plants can be as effective as purification of water by chlorine.

6. Although the stadium seats one hundred thousand people, there are rarely no tickets available.

7. If you use two tablespoons of soy sauce, you will not need scarcely any salt.

8. The train is as fast as and perhaps even faster than passengers by car.

9. Unlike the reviewers in the *Times,* the film turned out to be well photographed and carefully constructed.

10. The musical plays of Sondheim are less popular and less frequently recorded than Cole Porter.

11. Like France, Spanish navigators were eager to claim vast territories in the Americas.

12. Buying the turkey at Jack's Market, he saved more money than Lucky Mart.

9
ERRORS OF DICTION, IDIOM, AND STYLE

DICTION

The cause of a diction error, the choice of the wrong word, is not knowing exactly what each word means. Obviously, the more words you know, the fewer diction errors you will make. But the usage section of the exam is not intended to test the range of your vocabulary, and the words that are misused are rarely obscure or difficult. They are much more likely to be words we all know—or think we know—but confuse with words that look or sound similar.

IDIOM

This Grammar and Usage Review began by saying that you must not choose your answers by the *it-sounds-right/it-sounds-wrong* principles, but unless you have memorized every idiom in the English language—and no one has—there is nothing to rely on in choosing between idioms except the it-sounds-right principle. Should I say *agree with, agree to,* or *agree upon?* Depending upon the sentence, any one of the three may be right.

I *agree with* your opinion.

The plaintiff *agreed to* pay damage of one hundred dollars.

The committees have *agreed upon* a compromise.

Idioms are the usual way in which educated people put words together to express thought. Careful speakers or writers say *different from,* not *different than,* and *other than,* not *other from.* Most of the idiom problems arise from the use of prepositions. Since prepositions are so often insignificant words (*to, from, of, by*), it is easy to miss an obvious idiom error if you read carelessly.

There are no rules for idiom, and as the example of *agree* illustrates, idiom will often depend upon meaning. The exam occasionally uses an idiom uncertainty to distract you from a real error. Which is the better of these two sentences?

1. The issue are how can we make our streets free of crime.

2. The issue are how can we make our streets free from crime.

Is it *free from* or *free of*? Neither sounds wrong, and in fact, either is acceptable. The sentence is really testing agreement; the *are* should be *is*.

The most frequently asked idiom question on the exam asks you to choose between a three-word phrase made up of a noun or adjective followed by a preposition and a gerund (a word ending in *-ing*) or a similar phrase with the same noun or adjective followed by an infinitive (the preposition *to* and the verb): *hope of going or hope to go; ability in running or ability to run; afraid of jumping* or *afraid to jump.* You must, finally, depend upon your ear and the context, but if neither version sounds clearly right or wrong, choose the infinitive as the correct usage. It is the better percentage play.

Apes have demonstrated some *ability for reasoning deductively.*

Apes have demonstrated some *ability to reason deductively.*

STYLE

To this point, we have been concerned with errors of grammar, usage, diction, and idiom. With errors of this sort, you can point to a problematical single word or phrase and identify an error. In the second part of the multiple-choice section, you will be asked to choose among several versions of a sentence, which may not contain a specific error of grammar or usage. One of the answers will be better than the others for reasons of style, that is, because it conveys meaning with superior precision, conciseness, clarity, or grace.

Between an awkward sentence that is grammatically correct and a smoother sentence with a grammatical error, you must always prefer the correct version. But when neither of the two sentences has an error, you must base your decision on style. *Verbosity,* or unnecessary wordiness, is the most tested stylistic weakness. In Improving Sentences questions, you will often be able to eliminate three of the five sentences for grammar or usage errors and have to decide between two grammatically correct sentences, one of which is less verbose.

> After the shipment of bananas had been unloaded, a tarantula's nest was discovered by the foreman in the hold of the ship.

(A) After the shipment of bananas had been unloaded, a tarantula's nest was discovered by the forman

(B) After unloading the shipment of bananas, a tarantula's nest was discovered by the foreman

(C) Having unloaded the shipment of bananas, a tarantula's nest was discovered by the foreman

(D) After the shipment of bananas had been unloaded, the foreman discovered a tarantula's nest

(E) After the shipment of bananas had been unloaded, the foreman discovers a tarantula's nest

Choices (B), (C), and (E) cannot be right—choices (B) and (C) because of the dangling gerund and dangling participle, choice (E) because of the improper verb tenses (a past perfect and a present). Both choices (A) and (D) are grammatical, but because it uses the passive voice, choice (A) is wordier than choice (D). Given a choice like this, prefer the sentence in the active voice. It is impossible to write the same sentence using a passive verb without using at least two more words than the active voice requires.

I hit the ball.
(four words, active)

The ball was hit by me.
(six words, passive)

You should note also the ambiguity in choice (A); you are not sure if the *foreman,* the *nest,* or both are in the *hold* of the ship.

In our eagerness to be expressive, we sometimes waste words by saying the same thing twice.

1. His prose is *clear* and *lucid.*

2. The *annual* celebration *takes place every year.*

3. Her argument was *trivial,* and *it had no importance.*

There are many phrases which take two or more words to say what one word can say equally well. *Due to the fact that* takes five words to say what *because* says in one. A verbose sentence will use a phrase like *his being of a generous nature,* using six words where a phrase like *his generous nature* would say the same thing in three and *his generosity* in two. The following are examples of verbose phrases and formulas with a concise alternative.

Verbose	Concise
due to the fact that	*because*
owing to the fact that	*because*
inasmuch as	*because*
which was when	*when*
for the purpose of + gerund	*to* + verb
for the purpose of eating	*to eat*
in order to + verb	*to* + verb
in order to fly	*to fly*
so they can + verb	*to* + verb
so they can appreciate	*to appreciate*
not + negative adjective	positive adjective
not useless	*useful*
each and every	*every*
he is a man who is	*he is*
. . . is a . . . that	*is*
soccer is a game that is	*soccer is*
the truth is that	often omit altogether
the truth is that I am tired	*I am tired*
the fact is that	often omit altogether
the fact is that you were late	*you were late*
it is	often omit altogether
it is money that talks	*money talks*
there are	often omit altogether
there are some flowers that are poisonous	*some flowers are poisonous*
in a situation where	*where*
in a condition where	*where*

EXERCISE 9
ERRORS OF DICTION, IDIOM, AND STYLE

Answers are on page 127.

Part A

Some of the following sentences contain an error of diction or idiom. Identify the error and correct the sentence.

1. He is suspected to embezzle over two million dollars in less than a year.

2. He has detained a highly priced lawyer to handle his defense.

3. The judge has no expectation to finish jury selection this week.

4. The prosecution lawyer is reluctant in speaking about the case to the press.

5. Her client has despaired to find the money to post the high bail.

6. He is resigned to spending several months in jail.

7. The tabloid magazines are eager in interviewing anyone remotely connected to the case.

8. The judge may prohibit the press to bring cameras into the courtroom.

9. Almost thirty percent of the local news broadcast is devoted to the coverage of this case or news relevant to it.

10. Many people will be glad in seeing the end of this trial.

Part B

All of the following sentences are verbose. Cross out all the unnecessary words without changing the meaning of the sentences.

1. Though trailing thirty-one to ten, the team showed great resilience and an ability to bounce back; when the fourth quarter ended, the score was thirty-one to thirty.

2. She is so compulsive about avoiding noise that she refuses to begin to do her homework until there is total and complete silence in the dorm.

3. When I look back in retrospect on all that has happened, it is clear that I made the right decision.

4. At the present moment in history, there are now over two thousand unregistered handguns in Alpine County alone.

5. Raised in a well-to-do and affluent suburb of New York, she was unable to adjust to the lack of physical comforts in rural Saskatchewan.

6. Unless the president presents a workable and practicable program to conserve and keep energy from being wasted, none of the New England states are likely to support him.

7. The true facts of the case made it clear that he was obviously a victim of a hideous injustice.

8. The subtle distinctions and nice discriminations of her philosophical essays are too fine for any but the most learned and erudite to understand, even with several rereadings.

9. Many dramatists and playwrights, Congreve among them, wrote about the elegance and corruption of the Restoration society.

10. The photography of the mountainous hill regions where the peasants live is beautiful; unfortunately, the film opened when the potential audience to whom it might have appealed had sated its appetite for travelogues.

REVIEW EXERCISE: SECTIONS 7, 8, AND 9

If there is an error of grammar, diction, or verbosity in the following sentences, choose the underlined and lettered part in which the error occurs. Some of the sentences will contain no errors. Answers are on page 128.

1. Gordon's novel, written <u>with an eye to</u> conservative readers,
   A

   has <u>fewer scenes</u> of action and more with moral lessons <u>than</u>
   B C

   <u>any other book or volume</u> published this year. <u>No error</u>
   D E

2. An independent clause <u>can stand alone</u> <u>as a sentence</u>; a
   A B

   dependent clause <u>occupies</u> a subordinate position and cannot
   C

   <u>by itself</u> be a complete sentence. <u>No error</u>
   D E

3. Although his lawyer <u>argued his case</u> concisely, cogently, and
   A

   <u>succinctly</u>, Jones <u>was still</u> found guilty <u>and sentenced</u> to three
   B C D

   years in jail. <u>No error</u>
   E

4. Since the mountains in California are higher <u>than New York</u>, I
                                                         A
and my cousins <u>who like to ski</u> <u>prefer</u> <u>to spend</u> the winter on
                      B   C   D
the West Coast. <u>No error</u>
                      E

5. The courtly lover of Provence worshipped both <u>the Virgin</u> and
                                                       A
an earthly lady and <u>paid his</u> tribute <u>to her</u> in <u>ornate</u> lyric
                          B   C   D
poems. <u>No error</u>
            E

6. Although he <u>took</u> careful notes, <u>studied</u> in the library every
                    A   B
night, and <u>wrote</u> two extra papers, this industry
                 C
<u>did not affect or influence</u> his grade in the class. <u>No error</u>
              D   E

7. <u>Like</u> a large room, the American continent once offered
     A
<u>an exhilarating spatial freedom</u>, impressing western settlers
                  B
<u>first with</u> its sublime beauty and afterward with
       C
<u>its opportunities for exploitation.</u> <u>No error</u>
                  D   E

8. When the Queen entered, the <u>musicians which were</u> on the
                                              A
stage withdrew quietly, but the actors were <u>too surprised</u>
                                                        B
<u>to be able</u> <u>to know what to do.</u> <u>No error</u>
       C   D   E

9. I have <u>no interest</u> <u>to become</u> involved with <u>this foolish debate</u>
          A   B   C

about priorities <u>in</u> Central America. <u>No error</u>
                 D   E

10. We will <u>have to start for home</u> much earlier this week, <u>for</u>
                     A   B

there are <u>not but two or three hours</u> of good driving conditions
                      C

<u>if we leave</u> after two o'clock. <u>No error</u>
     D   E

10
PUNCTUATION

This section will certainly not tell you all you ought to know about punctuation to write well. It will describe the kind of punctuation errors that appear most often on the exam. You aren't likely to find sentences that test the use of the dash or the colon or that ask you whether to put the comma inside or outside a parenthesis. The testing of punctuation on the SAT II Writing exam will appear in the Improving Sentences section, where run-on sentences or sentences with comma splices will occur, usually at least once and perhaps more often.

The punctuation marks you must know are the comma and the semicolon. The comma is used to indicate a slight separation of sentence elements. The semicolon indicates a greater degree of separation, and the period marks the end of a sentence. The punctuation errors that will appear most frequently on the exam are the use of a comma where a semicolon is needed and the use of a semicolon where a comma is needed. In compound sentences, that is, sentences with two independent clauses, a semicolon and a comma are *not* interchangeable.

Punctuate the following sentences with either a comma or a semicolon.

1. I had come to China to buy silk and I was not planning to buy anything else.

   I had come to China to buy silk I was not planning to buy anything else.

2. I got my needles from Frankfurt while my threads came from London.

   I got my needles from Frankfurt my threads came from London.

In both examples, the first version needs a comma before the conjunction (*and, while*). In the second, a semicolon should follow

105

silk and *Frankfurt*. The principle is the same in both. With two independent clauses joined by a conjunction, use a comma. With two independent clauses that are not joined by a conjunction, use a semicolon.

Now punctuate the following sentences with either a comma or a semicolon.

1. I looked for a house for sale on the lake hoping to be able to finish my book there.

2. They bundled themselves into the car waved once and drove away.

3. He was not at all interesting a man who talked endlessly about himself and how much money he had.

4. The editorials in *Ghost Magazine* are infuriating to some readers delightful to others.

All four sentences need commas and only commas: after *lake* in sentence 1, after *car* and *once* in sentence 2, after *interesting* in sentence 3, and after *readers* in sentence 4. The clauses or phrases after the commas cannot stand by themselves as complete sentences. If they were set off by semicolons, they would be sentence fragments.

COMMA

Use a comma

1. **in a series of three or more with a single conjunction.**

   He bought red, green, and blue neckties.

   I must stop at the bank, have the car washed, and leave my shirts at the laundry.

2. **to set off parenthetic expressions.**

The result, I imagine, will be in the paper.

The check, you will be glad to know, is in the mail.

3. **to set off nonrestrictive relative clauses.**

In 1600, when *Hamlet* was first acted, the Globe was London's largest public theater.

Montpelier, Concord, and Augusta, which are all small cities, are the capitals of the northern New England states.

4. **to separate the two parts of a sentence with two independent clauses joined by a conjunction.**

The film is over, and the audience has left the theater.

The mayor is present, but the governor is not here.

5. **to set off introductory words, phrases, or clauses.**

Unfortunately, he left his wallet in the car.

Having looked in the glove compartment, he discovered his wallet was missing.

6. **to set off appositives.**

Mr. Smith, the mayor, called the meeting to order.

The leading batter in the league is John Jones, the first baseman.

Do *not* use a comma to join two independent clauses *not* joined by a conjunction. Use a period or a semicolon.

Her novels are always bestsellers; they are translated into three languages.

The boat crossed the lake in fifteen minutes; the canoe took two hours.

SEMICOLON

Use a semicolon

1. **to separate two independent clauses in a compound sentence when there is no conjunction between them.**

   The hurricane came ashore near Lake Charles; its winds were measured at more than one hundred miles per hour.

   The warnings were broadcast early in the day; thus, there was no loss of life.

2. **to separate a series when one or more of the elements of the series contain commas.**

   He bought a red, a green, and a blue tie; three button-down shirts; and a pair of penny loafers.

   We will stop in Maumee, Ohio; Erie, Pennsylvania; Albany, New York; and Amherst, Massachusetts.

Questions on the following punctuation marks are not likely.

COLON

Use a colon after an independent clause

1. **to introduce a series.**

   The following vegetables should be planted in March: radishes, carrots, leeks, turnips, and cabbage.

   In this sentence, the clause before the colon is independent. In a sentence like *In March, you should plant radishes, carrots, leeks, turnips, and cabbage,* where there is no independent clause before the series, you must *not* use a colon.

2. **to join two independent clauses when the second amplifies or interprets the first.**

A preliminary step is essential to successful whipped cream: you must chill the bowl and the beaters.

3. **to introduce a quotation.**

Every English schoolchild knows the opening line of *Twelfth Night:* "If music be the food of love, play on."

OTHER MARKS OF PUNCTUATION

Dash

Use a *dash* to indicate an abrupt break and to set off parenthetical elements already broken up by commas.

I believe—no, I know—he is guilty.

I—er—you—er—forget it!

The general—overdecorated, overconfident, overweight— spoke to the troops on the benefits of self-sacrifice.

The speech—the harangue, I should say—lasted for three hours.

Apostrophe

Use an *apostrophe* to indicate the omission of a letter or letters in a contraction (*I'm, I've, you'd, don't, who's, we're*).

Form the possessive of singular nouns by adding *'s* (*tiger's, cat's, man's*). Form the possessive of plural nouns by adding just the apostrophe (') if the plural ends in *s* (*tigers', cats', dogs'*). Form the possessive of plural nouns that do not end in *s* by adding *'s* (*mice's, men's, children's*).

EXERCISE 10
PUNCTUATION

Punctuate the following sentences. Answers are on page 129.

1. Anything it seems is worth fighting about when there's money to be made.

2. Beside those tried trusty and true brown paper bags you'll find plastic ones.

3. Some argue that plastic bags are more easily portable especially for those who walk to the store that they don't leak when wet and that they can be used several times.

4. Paper bags stand on their own so to speak in the trunk of a car they can be cut up and used to cover books or to make Halloween masks.

5. Not surprisingly those who live alone in city apartments prefer plastic to paper bags they find them easier to carry.

6. Recently plastic bags have been improved they are now recycled.

REVIEW EXERCISE: SECTIONS 1–10

When you take the exam, you ought to be able to recognize the kind of error that is being tested for. Certain words or sentence structures should warn you at once of the kind of error likely to occur in the sentence. All of the following words or structures should alert you at once to one or two likely errors. What are these errors? Answers are on page 130.

1. a sentence beginning with a participle

2. a sentence beginning with *Both*

3. a sentence containing a series

4. a sentence beginning with *Either*

5. a sentence containing the word *not*

6. a sentence beginning with a prepositional phrase beginning with *Like*

7. a sentence beginning with *There is*

8. a sentence beginning with the word *One*

9. a sentence beginning with an elliptical phrase

10. a sentence containing the word *hardly*

11. a sentence containing a comparison

12. a sentence containing the phrase *as well as*

11
SENTENCE COMBINING

In the improving paragraphs (or revision in context) section of the exam, a third or more of the questions may ask you to revise and combine sentences from a sample of student writing. Although your revision choices will be influenced by the rest of the paragraph, you can practice the technique with two or three sentences that are not part of a paragraph or essay.

The sentences the exam will ask you to work with will probably be grammatically correct, but they will be choppy, or wordy, or dull. There may be a series of very short sentences.

Iris is twenty. She is getting married in June. She is designing a dress. It is white.

Or the sentences may be mindlessly coordinated.

Iris is twenty, and she is getting married in June, and she is designing a dress, and the dress is white.

Your combined and revised version might read like this.

Twenty-year-old Iris is designing a white dress for her June wedding.

The purpose of sentence combining is to clarify the relationship between thoughts and to eliminate wordiness or choppiness. The techniques the exam questions will call for most often are **coordination** and **subordination.** To coordinate is to make equal; to subordinate is to place in a less important position. The parts of speech used to control sentence elements in these ways are the coordinating and subordinating conjunctions. On the exam, you may find a question which asks you to select the best coordinating or subordinating conjunction.

Common Coordinating Conjunctions

and	nor	so
but	or	yet
for		

Common Subordinating Conjunctions

after	how	unless
although	if	until
as	in order that	when
as . . . as	provided that	whenever
as if	since	where
as long as	so . . . as	wherever
as soon as	so that	whereupon
as though	than	while
because	that	why
before	though	

The best way to begin a problem in combining sentences is to determine which thought you wish to emphasize. If the two ideas are equally significant, use the coordinating conjunction that best expresses their relationship. If one idea is more important, subordinate the other. If you haven't already done so in your English class, practice different ways of combining sentences, especially sentences that seem awkward to you. It will help you on the multiple-choice section of the exam and will improve your own writing.

The sentence combining questions appear in two forms. In one, part of the end of one sentence and part of the beginning of the next will be underlined, and you will be given five revisions to choose from. In the second type, the question will ask for the best way to revise and combine two or three complete sentences from the passage. Unlike the exam, the exercise that follows does not give you five answers to choose from; you must write your own revisions.

EXERCISE 11
SENTENCE COMBINING

Suggested answers are on page 131.

Part A

Revise the underlined portions of the following sentences to combine the two into one.

1. In Luxembourg, the absence of inexpensive housing increases the number of the homeless. People with no address cannot qualify for welfare benefits.

2. The result of tighter money is slower economic growth. The result is also a lower rate of inflation.

3. About 100,000 cases of polio still occur annually throughout the world. Many cases occur in Pakistan, Poland, and the former Soviet Union.

4. Recent studies have shown that high-density lipoproteins can protect against atherosclerosis. Atherosclerosis is the buildup of fatty deposits that can produce heart attacks.

5. On Mt. Washington, the year-round temperature is below freezing. It is the wind on Mt. Washington that most interests climatologists.

Part B

Revise and combine the following sentences.

1. Immobilizing animals with anesthesia is not a new practice. Zoos have used this procedure for many years. The practice is common.

2. Some animals require anesthesia because they might endanger the physician administering to them. Large carnivores are usually anesthetized. Lions and tigers are large carnivores.

3. The crowned crane is found in the open grasslands of West Africa. It stands about three feet tall and has a wingspan of five feet.

4. Azerbaijan was the home of Scythian tribes in ancient times. In the eleventh century, the Turks overran Azerbaijan, and it was conquered by the Russians in the nineteenth century.

5. Many successful wind turbines were perfected on Mt. Washington. It was not easy to do so. Often winds blew too hard, destroying the turbines.

6. Symptoms of chronic fatigue syndrome include debilitating tiredness and low-grade fever. The tiredness persists for more than six months. Swollen lymph glands and sleep disorders are also symptoms.

7. Great religious art was created in Mexico in the sixteenth and seventeenth centuries. The rich heritage of Mexican art does not lie in the religious art alone.

8. Music by American pop stars is routinely mixed into the radio formats of salsa and samba stations in Central and South America. In the United States, Latin-influenced music is primarily limited to Spanish-speaking radio stations.

9. In 1823, President Monroe outlined United States foreign policy in the Western Hemisphere. The policy is that the United States would regard as unfriendly any European nation's interference in the affairs of countries in the Western Hemisphere.

10. Earthquakes in California are very different from those elsewhere around the world. In California, the earthquakes are centered a few miles below the earth's surface, and elsewhere they may occur many miles deeper below the earth's surface.

ANSWERS TO THE GRAMMAR AND USAGE REVIEW EXERCISES

EXERCISE 1
PARTS OF SPEECH, ADJECTIVES AND ADVERBS, COMPARATIVES AND SUPERLATIVES

1. *Almost*—an adverb, modifying the adjective *every.*

2. *different*—an adjective. In this sentence, *different* modifies *he,* not *is.*

3. *suddenly*—an adverb, modifying *appeared.*

4. *best*—the superlative. There are more than two players.

5. *better*—the comparative, with only two compared.

6. *badly*—an adverb modifying *baked.*

7. *noticeably*—an adverb, modifying the adverb *more.*

8. *sad*—an adjective, modifying *I* with the verb *to be.*

9. *seriously*—an adverb, modifying the verb *take.*

10. *almost*—an adverb, modifying the adjective *any.*

11. *carefully*—an adverb, modifying the verb *look.*
    clearly—an adverb, modifying the adjective *visible.*

12. *largest*—the superlative. There are many antelopes.
    slowest—the superlative. Again, there are more than two.

13. *inexhaustible*—an adjective, modifying the noun *supply,* not the verb *seemed.*

117

14. *steeply*—an adverb, modifying the verb *rise.*

15. *better*—Use only one comparative adjective.

16. *quicker*—Use only one comparative adjective.

EXERCISE 2
CASE

1. *we*—subject of the clause *we are not.*

2. *me*—object of the preposition *except.*

3. *I*—subjective case, agreeing with the subject *It.*

4. *me*—object of the verb *affect.*

5. *I*—one of the three subjects of the sentence.

6. *me*—objective case, in apposition to *finalists,* the object of the preposition.

EXERCISE 3
AGREEMENT

1. *is*—The subject of *is* is the singular *No one.*

2. *is*—The singular *sergeant-at-arms* is the subject of the verb.

3. *are*—The subject is the compound *salads and dessert.*

4. *was*—The subject is the singular *Mr. Lombardi.*

5. *makes*—The subject is the singular *evidence.*

6. *include*—The subject is the plural *criteria*. The singular is *criterion*.

7. *look, they*—The subject is the plural *columns,* which is also the antecedent of *they.*

8. *is*—The subject is the singular *student.*

9. *are*—The subject is compound, *Mr. and Mrs. Smith.*

10. *has*—The subject is the singular *Jack.*

11. *increases*—The subject of *increases* is the singular *number.*

12. *is*—The subject is the singular *Mary Jane.*

13. *were*—The subject is the plural *All.*

14. *have, their*—The plural *twins* is the subject of *have* and the antecedent of *their.*

15. *has, her*—The singular *Sally* is the subject of *has* and the antecedent of *her.*

16. *was*—The subject is the singular *I.*

17. *enjoys*—The subject is the singular *president.*

18. *seems*—The singular *The number* is the subject.

19. *have*—The subject here is *Many.*

20. *is*—The subject *information* is singular.

REVIEW EXERCISE: SECTIONS 1, 2, AND 3

1. (E) The *me* is the object of the preposition *but;* the subject is the singular *No one,* so *was* is also correct.

2. (A) The subject, *men,* is plural. The correct verb would be the plural *have dreamed.*

3. (E) The agreement in this sentence is correct.

4. (D) The subject is plural, a compound subject with *and.*

5. (C) Since *thousands* is plural, *life* should be *lives.*

6. (B) The phrase *my sister and I* is the object of *including. I* should be *me.*

7. (E) The singular *was* is correct with the singular subject *result. Her* is the object of *alarm.*

8. (A) The plural *There are* does not agree with the singular subject *player.*

9. (E) The adjective *simple* is correct. It modifies *questions.* The adverb *simply* modifies the adverb *too.*

10. (D) With a comparison of two teams, *better,* not *best,* should be used.

EXERCISE 4
VERBS

1. *ate*—The *yesterday* indicates a past action.

2. *lasts*—Since the fact continues to be true, use the present tense.

3. *waited*—The second verb, *arrived,* is in the past tense, so only the past tense makes sense for the first.

4. *had waited*—Here, the other verb in the sentence is the past tense *arrived.* Action in past time in relation to another past time is expressed by the past perfect tense.

5. *will go*—The sentence expresses a simple future (*tomorrow*). The future perfect would be used only if the action were related to another time even farther in the future.

6. *am, will buy*—The sentence makes sense only as projection of the future. When the projected condition is true (*I am thinner*), the future action (*I will buy*) can take place.

7. *stepped*—The first two verbs (*climbed, opened*) are in the past tense. There is no reason to change tenses, so the third verb should also be in the past tense.

8. *lying, lying*—The verb here is the intransitive *lie* (to rest). The participial form of *lie* is *lying*.

9. *laid, lay*—The first verb is the transitive verb *lay* (to place) in the past tense. The second verb is the intransitive verb *lie* (to recline) in the past tense. The first verb has an object (*briefcase*); the second has none.

10. *rise*—The intransitive verb *rise* in the present tense is correct here.

11. *Setting, sitting*—The first verb is the transitive *set* with *flowers* as the object; the second verb, the intransitive *sit,* has no object.

12. *rises*—The intransitive verb *rise* in the present tense is correct here.

13. *will be*—The future tense, not the future perfect, is correct here. There is no time even farther in the future to which this verb is related.

14. *will have worked*—Here, the future perfect is correct because the opening clause defines a time which is even farther in the future. In sentence 13, 2005 is in the future but not farther in the future than the time at which I will be sixty. But in the second sentence, 2005 will come at the end of the period of thirty years' work.

15. *are*—Since *borrow* is a present, the first verb should also be present tense.

16. *made*—The words *last week* make clear the action is in the past, not the present.

EXERCISE 5
MISPLACED PARTS, DANGLING MODIFIERS

There are several ways to rewrite these sentences and eliminate the errors. The following are a few of the possible revisions.

1. As it stands now, the participial phrase at the beginning of the sentence dangles and appears to modify the *crowd* rather than *Nancy Lopez*. One can correct the sentence by beginning *After she made a par . . .* or by leaving the participial phrase unchanged and writing *Nancy Lopez was cheered* after the comma.

2. The sentence also begins with a dangling participle. It can be corrected by beginning with *Because he failed . . .* or by writing *he made remarks in class that were . . .* after the comma.

3. Again, the error is a dangling participle. Revise the sentence to begin with *If you keep . . .* or write something like *you may make the overhead . . .* after the comma.

4. A dangling participle once more. The corrected sentence could begin *If she hopes to win . . .* or could say *she must give a first-rate free-skating performance* after the comma.

5. The error here is a dangling infinitive, which makes it appear that *stamina* and *concentration* are taking the exam. Either add a human agent in the first phrase (*For you to do well*) or begin the second with *you must have. . . .*

6. This is a very difficult sentence because the dangling infinitive is not at the beginning of the sentence but in the middle (*to get the*

best possible view). As it stands, the *seats,* not the ticket holders, are getting the best view. By revising the last clause of the sentence to read *we bought seats on the center aisle . . .* , we eliminate the error.

7. The elliptical phrase here dangles, so the sentence suggests that the father is eight years old. To remove the error, we can remove the ellipsis and write *When his son was only eight years old. . . .* If we wish to keep the opening unchanged, we must write *his son was sent . . .* after the comma.

8. Like sentence 7, this sentence opens with a dangling elliptical phrase. The simplest way to correct the error is to write *Though he is only. . . .*

9. Here the prepositional phrase which begins the sentence seems to modify *you.* Beginning the sentence with the *you* clause and putting the prepositional phrase at the end will correct the error.

10. The opening gerund *applying* dangles. Write *By applying the insecticide carefully, you can avoid damage to the environment.*

EXERCISE 6
PARALLELISM

1. (E) The parallelism here is correct.

2. (B) With the correlatives *not . . . but,* the words after *but* should be parallel to those after *not: not his reckless spending . . . but his spending.*

3. (A) Since the pronoun *your* is used later in the sentence (and cannot be changed, since it is not underlined), the first phrase in the sentence should read *Your aptitude.*

4. (C) Since the pronoun *one* is used earlier in the sentence, *you* should be *one.*

5. (E) The parallelism here is correct.

6. (A) Since the pronoun *you* is used at the end of the sentence, *one* should be *you.*

7. (D) The series of infinitives (*to take, to speak*) should be completed with another infinitive (*to ask some questions*).

8. (E) The series in this sentence maintains parallelism.

9. (C) With the correlatives *both . . . and,* the structure following should be parallel. The correct version is *at both the data.*

10. (C) To maintain the series of infinitives, the sentence should read *and to defend.*

11. (D) With the correlatives *not only . . . but also,* the sentence should read *not only capable but also trustworthy.*

12. (C) The past tense should be used in all the verbs—*ended, jumped, drove, changed,* and *swam.*

13. (E) The parallelism here is correct.

14. (D) The final verb in this series should be an infinitive (*to cash*) to be parallel with the others.

REVIEW EXERCISE: SECTIONS 4, 5, AND 6

1. (C) Since the main verb in the first part of the sentence is in the present tense (*seems*), there is no reason to shift to a past tense.

2. (C) To keep the verb tenses consistent, *resembles* should be *resembled.*

3. (E) The sentence is correct as given.

4. (B) With the correlatives *not . . . but,* the *but* should be followed by the preposition *by* to be parallel.

5. (A) *Raising* is the right verb (not *rising*), but the phrase is a dangling participle. It looks as if the *sunshine* raised the shade.

6. (A) Another dangling participle. The *I* of the sentence, not the passengers, narrowly missed the collision.

7. (C) The other verbs of the sentence (*was, broke*) are in the past tense, so *splashed* is correct here.

8. (E) The beginning phrase modifies *he* and does not dangle.

9. (C) The series should have three infinitives: *to read, to mark,* and *to stop.*

EXERCISE 7
AMBIGUOUS PRONOUNS

All of the following are *possible* answers, but certainly not the only right response.

1. The *which* has no specific antecedent. To avoid the ambiguous pronoun, one might write *My coming in fifteen minutes late made* . . . or *I came in fifteen minutes late and found.* . . . One cannot correct the error by substituting another pronoun for the ambiguous *which.*

2. The ambiguous pronoun is *this.* The sentence can be corrected by simply omitting the phrase *because this is* and adding a comma after *school.*

3. The ambiguous pronoun is *this.* Effectively revised, the sentence would read *By writing checks for . . . I overdrew my account.*

4. The ambiguous pronoun is *this*. It can be eliminated by concluding the sentence with *and, needless to say, had indigestion*.

5. The antecedent of *it* could be either the radio or the record player. The simple solution is to say *when I plugged the radio* (or *the record player*) *in, it would not work.*

6. The antecedent of *his* and *he* is unclear. As in sentence 5, the solution is to use the noun (*Dave* or *Vince*) in place of *he*.

7. The *these* is ambiguous. One solution is to write *these abilities*.

8. The *this* is ambiguous. One could write *this appearance makes them seem ferocious* or *and they appear ferocious, though.* . . .

EXERCISE 8
OTHER ERRORS OF GRAMMAR

Part A

1. A fragment—There is no main verb, only a participle.

2. A complete sentence—*David* (subject) *wept* (verb).

3. A fragment—There is no verb.

4. A complete sentence—*Is* (verb) *he* (subject).

5. A fragment—The clause is dependent.

Part B

1. Double negative—*haven't risen hardly*.

2. Sentence fragment—no main verb.

3. Double negative—*scarcely no*.

4. Illogical comparison—*Borgias* (a family) and *Rome* (a city).

5. Illogical comparison—*water plants* and *purification.*

6. Double negative—*rarely no.*

7. Double negative—*not . . . scarcely.*

8. Illogical comparison—*train* and *passengers.*

9. Illogical comparison—*reviewers* and *film.*

10. Illogical comparison—*plays* and *Cole Porter.*

11. Illogical comparison—*France* and *navigators.*

12. Illogical comparison—*money* and *Mart.*

EXERCISE 9
ERRORS OF DICTION, IDIOM, AND STYLE

Part A

1. The sentence should read *suspected of embezzling.*

2. The word *detained* (confined, delayed) has been mistakenly used for the word *retained* (hired, continued to use).

3. With *expectation,* the preposition *of* and the gerund *finishing* should replace the infinitive.

4. The idiom is *reluctant to speak.*

5. The idiom here is *despaired of finding.*

6. This sentence is correct.

7. Here, the idiom is *eager to interview.*

8. The sentence should read *prohibit . . . from bringing.*

9. This sentence is correct.

10. The idiom here is *glad to see.*

Part B

1. *Resilience* and *ability to bounce back* mean the same thing.

2. One could omit *to do. Total* and *complete* mean the same thing.

3. Since *retrospect* means *a looking back,* the prepositional phrase is unnecessary.

4. The phrase *At the present moment in history* is unnecessary with the use of *now.*

5. *Well-to-do* and *affluent* mean the same thing.

6. *Workable* and *practicable* mean the same thing. You also do not need both *conserve* and *keep . . . from being wasted.*

7. Both *true* and *obviously* are unnecessary words here.

8. Either *subtle distinctions* or *nice discriminations* and either *learned* or *erudite* can be eliminated.

9. A *dramatist* is a *playwright.* One or the other is sufficient.

10. With *mountainous, hill* is unnecessary, and *potential* is equivalent to *to whom it might have appealed.*

REVIEW EXERCISE: SECTIONS 7, 8, AND 9

1. (D) *Book* and *volume* are redundant.

2. (E) The sentence is correct as given.

3. (B) *Succinctly* repeats *concisely.*

4. (A) The sentence should read *than those in New York.*

5. (C) The antecedent of *her* is ambiguous. It could be either *the Virgin* or *an earthly lady.*

6. (D) *Affect* and *influence* are redundant.

7. (E) There is no error in this sentence.

8. (A) Since the musicians are human, the pronoun should be *who.*

9. (B) The sentence should read *no interest in becoming.*

10. (C) The *not* and *but* are both negatives. Eliminate *not.*

EXERCISE 10
PUNCTUATION

1. Add commas after *Anything* and *seems.* The phrase *it seems* is parenthetical.

2. To this series of three adjectives, add commas after *tried* and *trusty.* There should also be a comma after *bags,* at the end of the introductory phrase.

3. The sentence needs a comma after *portable.* The series of clauses should be separated by semicolons after *store* and *wet.*

4. The sentence needs commas before and after *so to speak* and a semicolon after *car.*

5. The parenthetical *Not surprisingly* should be followed by a comma. This is a run-on sentence unless a semicolon or period follows *bags.*

6. A comma should follow the inductory *Recently*. And again, a semicolon (after *improved*) will correct the run-on sentence.

REVIEW EXERCISE: SECTIONS 1–10

1. Dangling participle.

2. Either agreement (the subject will be plural) or parallelism with *both . . . and.*

3. Parallelism.

4. Either agreement (the verb will agree with the word nearer the verb) or parallelism with *either . . . or.*

5. Double negative or parallelism with *not . . . but.*

6. Illogical comparison or parallelism with the prepositional phrase.

7. Agreement, with the subject far from the verb.

8. Agreement (*One* is singular) or change of person, the incorrect use of *you* later in the sentence.

9. Dangling elliptical phrase.

10. Double negative.

11. Illogical comparison or parallelism (be sure like elements are compared) or omission of necessary words such as *other.*

12. Agreement (*as well as* is parenthetical and will not make a singular subject plural).

EXERCISE 11
SENTENCE COMBINING

Part A

1. The choices to answer this question would include coordinating conjunctions like *and* or *so,* but the correct answer is *but* or *yet,* to point a contrast rather than a connection between the two sentences. Their point is the catch-22, that the homeless, who most need welfare benefits, cannot qualify because they are homeless.

2. When combining sentences, look for repetitions of a phrase or words. Usually the repeated words can be eliminated altogether or replaced by a pronoun or a synonym. Here, the second *the result is* and the *also* can be cut and replaced by *as well as* or simply *and.*

3. The repetitious *cases occur* can be eliminated here, and a revised sentence might read . . . *throughout the world, with many in.* . . .

4. The same words end one sentence and begin the next. By cutting *Atherosclerosis is,* you can make the second sentence an appositive by changing the first period to a comma.

5. Here, a conjunction like *but* or *yet* will clarify the relation of the two sentences. The second *on Mt. Washington* should be dropped, leaving . . . *below freezing, but it is the wind that.* . . .

Part B

1. The repetitions here include the two uses of *practice,* plus its synonym *procedure*, and *for many years* and *not new*. A revision like the following eliminates the repetition: *For many years, zoos have used the common practice of immobilizing animals with anesthesia.*

2. The obvious repetition here is *large carnivores*. By combining the second and third sentences and embedding the phrase in the first, the three sentences become one: *Some animals, large carnivores like lions and tigers, for example, require anesthesia because they might endanger the physician administering to them.*

3. Since the three facts are equally important, they can be presented in a series, with all three verbs in the active voice: *The crowned crane lives in the open grasslands of West Africa, stands about three feet tall, and has a wingspan of five feet.* Or, one of the three elements can be subordinated: *Found in the open grasslands of West Africa, the crowned crane stands about three feet tall and has a wingspan of five feet.*

4. The second sentence contains a shift from an active (*overran*) to a passive verb (*was conquered*). By subordinating the first sentence and using only one verb, we can eliminate two of the three verbs as well as the repetition of *century: The home of Scythian tribes in ancient times, Azerbaijan was overrun by the Turks in the eleventh century and by the Russians in the nineteenth.*

5. The combined sentence will probably put more emphasis on the difficulty and eliminate *It was not easy to do so: Perfecting wind turbines on Mt. Washington was difficult because the destructive winds often blew too hard.*

6. A repeated word will often tell you what can be subordinated. Here, the second sentence's description of *tiredness* can be subordinated to *tiredness* in the first: *Symptoms of chronic fatigue syndrome include swollen lymph glands, sleep disorders, low-grade fever, and debilitating tiredness that persists for more than six months.*

7. The word *art* is used three times here, and the relation of the two sentences can be expressed more clearly: *Although the religious works of the sixteenth and seventeenth centuries are great, the rich heritage of Mexican art does not lie in the religious art alone.* Another version might read *However great the religious works of the sixteenth and seventeenth centuries, the rich heritage of Mexico does not lie in religious art alone.*

8. Since the point here is to contrast American and Latin American radio formats, a *but* would call attention to the opposition: *Music by American pop stars is routinely mixed into the radio formats of salsa and samba stations in Central and South America, but in the United States, Latin-influenced music is primarily limited to Spanish-speaking stations.*

9. The repeated *policy* suggests that the phrase *the policy is* is expendable, and there is no need for two *Western Hemisphere's*: *In 1823, President Monroe outlined the policy that the United States would regard as unfriendly any European nation's interference in the affairs of countries in the Western Hemisphere.*

10. The notion of difference can be expressed much more concisely by a *but* or by a word or phrase like *however* or *on the other hand*: *In California, earthquakes are centered a few miles below the earth's surface, but elsewhere they occur many miles deeper.* Or . . . *below the earth's surface; elsewhere, however, they occur. . . .* Or *below the earth's surface; on the other hand, elsewhere they occur. . . .*

Part III:
Introduction to the Essay Exam

THE ESSAY QUESTION

THE INSTRUCTIONS

THE GENERAL INSTRUCTIONS

The SAT II Writing exam begins with a twenty-minute writing sample. The first instructions on the page will look something like this.

PART A	Time—20 Minutes 1 Question	ESSAY

In twenty minutes, write an essay on the topic below. YOU MAY NOT WRITE ON ANOTHER TOPIC. AN ESSAY ON ANOTHER TOPIC WILL NOT BE SCORED.

The essay is intended to give you the chance to show your writing skills. Be sure to express your ideas on the topic clearly and effectively. The quality of your writing is much more important than the quantity, but to deal adequately with this topic, you should probably write more than one paragraph. Be specific.

These general instructions will appear on all SAT II Writing Subject Tests. There are several points to remember here. You must take the shrill, capitalized warning not to write on a different topic seriously. Essays that are considered to be off-topic earn nothing, and you can't afford to give away one third of the possible points. Do *not* take the essay writing time as an opportunity to complain about how overpriced SAT tests are or how badly your English class was taught; your cry will go unheard, and your money will be wasted. Even a weak essay will add some points to your score and raise it more than even the most eloquent off-topic diatribe.

The general instructions on every exam include the sentence suggesting that *you should probably write more than one paragraph.* This remark is a polite way of saying that if you expect to score well, you'd *better* write more than one paragraph. Very short essays usually receive very low scores. The scored samples in the *Official Guide to SAT II* use essays of only one paragraph to illustrate the two lowest grades, while the high scoring papers have at least three paragraphs. A very long paper written with no marked paragraph divisions, that is, an essay of several paragraphs in length and content but without the indentations to separate the paragraphs, would receive a good score, but it would receive an even better grade if the paragraph divisions were clear.

The general instructions will say *Be specific,* and chances are that the topic instructions will repeat this order. Your readers are not, as you may suppose, combing your essay for split infinitives. They are looking for specific details, for concrete evidence of some kind used to support your points. Perhaps the most obvious difference between the content of the good upper-half essay (scored a 4, 5, or 6) and the content of the weak lower-half paper (a 3, 2, or 1) is the inclusion of supporting detail. Before you begin to write, jot down as many good supporting details as you can think of, and use the best ones in your essay.

THE ADDITIONAL INSTRUCTIONS

Additional instructions and the topic itself will follow the general instructions. They will look something like this:

> Think carefully about the following quotation and the assign-ment that follows. Then plan and write your essay according to the instructions.
>
> "Don't take risks; better safe than sorry."
>
> Do you agree with this statement? Write an essay in which you support your opinion with specific examples from history, contem-porary life, readings, or personal observation.

The exam will provide one and only one topic for your essay. It will probably not be the most engaging you have ever written about or the dullest. The topics must be general enough to allow all the students who take the exam to find something to say in their essays. The topic will not be controversial, and it will not require any specialized information.

Your essay must be completed in twenty minutes, and if you finish in less time, you can use the few extra minutes on the multiple-choice questions. If you finish the multiple-choice questions in less than forty minutes, you can't go back and use the additional time on your essay.

The essay topic will usually take the form of a quotation with wide-ranging applications. Chances are it will be a statement with which it is easy to agree or disagree. (On the quotation above, one can argue that if no one takes a risk, nothing new will be discovered; on the other hand, risks are, by definition, risky.) It doesn't matter which side you take so long as you complete the tasks set by the question and write well. It is theoretically possible that a top-scoring essay could argue for the extermination of all English composition teachers (though it is unlikely that a quotation that would invite such a response would appear on the exam). Your score will be determined by the coherence of your essay and the quality of your writing, not by the political correctness or incorrectness of what you say.

WRITING THE ESSAY

There is no single right way to approach writing a timed essay. If you've been practicing for this exam in your English class, and you and your teacher are satisfied with the way you handle the twenty-minute analytical essay, you can skip this chapter and continue to write your essays your way. If you aren't confident about your technique, consider the following straightforward approach.

Before you get to the exam, you should be familiar with the general instructions and the kind of essay you're likely to be assigned.

THE STEPS

Step One

Read the topic and the assignment very carefully. Underline if that is your habit. Reread the assignment. If there are several tasks given, number them and write them down. Let the nature of the assignment determine the structure of your essay.

Step Two

Before you begin to write, take some time to think about what your essay will contain. If, as is likely, the question asks you to take a stand on an issue, decide which side you will take. (Pro? Con? Pro with some reservations? Con with some reservations?)

Next, write down any usable specific details that support your position. List as many as you can think of and decide later which ones you can use. If, as is usual, the directions say to support your position with details from your reading and/or from your personal observations, try to think of examples from both, but if you can't, don't worry about it.

Determine if you can how many paragraphs you will write and what each will be about. Let the question and your evidence help you to determine how you will put your essay together.

Step Three

Carefully write your essay. Keep in mind what the tasks are, what each paragraph is to contain, and what specific details you will use. Take some extra time with the transitions from one paragraph to another.

Step Four

Reread your essay, looking carefully for errors in the spelling, punctuation, and grammar. Make sure the writing is legible.

AN EXAMPLE

Assume you have opened your test booklet and found this topic for your essay:

"All advertising for tobacco products should be banned."

Write an essay in which you agree or disagree with this statement. Support your opinion with information from your reading or personal experience.

Before you begin to write your essay, you determine that the topic has only one task, that is, to make a case for or against advertising for tobacco products. You decide to disagree with the statement. You might jot down notes like these:

issue of freedom of speech, first amendment
economic impact
harm to advertising firms
harm to magazines and billboard companies, to tobacco
    companies, to tobacco farmers
loss of state and federal tobacco tax revenues

At this point, you could decide to give one paragraph to the "moral" argument (the free speech issue) and two paragraphs to the economic consequences of the ban. What order will be best? Why not begin with the practical argument about private economic losses, proceed to the public loss of revenues, and conclude with an appeal to fair play for all, for freedom of speech? But what about the argument for limiting freedom of speech, the fact that some speech should be forbidden, such as shouting *Fire!* in a crowded room? Since this consideration can only weaken your case, you forget about it at once.

Having completed your essay, three paragraphs, about three hundred words long, you reread it carefully, checking the grammar, spelling, and punctuation. Are there any words that could be improved? Have you used the same word too often? Finally, is the essay legible, with the *i*'s dotted and the *t*'s crossed?

As a final check, you ask yourself these questions:

- Does the essay focus on the topic and complete the assigned task?
- Is the essay coherently developed and consistent in argument?
- Does the essay use specific supporting detail?
- Is the writing correct?

If you can answer *yes* to these questions, you can go on, with confidence, to the multiple-choice section of the exam.

EIGHT ESSAY-WRITING AXIOMS

1. Try to be genuinely interested in the topic.

2. Don't worry about the answer you think "they" want you to write.

3. Don't be afraid to be honest.

4. Avoid clichés.

5. Write naturally.

6. Choose your words with some thought and don't use words whose meaning you're unsure about.

7. Don't be afraid to use contractions, figures of speech, even slang, but do so tactfully.

8. Don't be wishy-washy.

ANSWERS TO YOUR QUESTIONS ABOUT
THE ESSAY EXAM

Should I make an outline before I write my essay?

If you can write better essays without an outline, don't change your writing habits. But keep in mind that your reader will be looking for good organization and development in your essay, and an outline, however brief, will probably help you to organize your ideas. The outline itself will not be graded or counted in the scoring. There is room on the page with the essay question and a blank page before or after it on which you can write your outline or notes. You shouldn't use the pages provided for the essay for this purpose. The exam allows two pages of lined paper with twenty-four lines per page for your essay. To be sure your essay will fit, don't skip lines.

Should I write a five-paragraph essay?

If you write a well-organized, well-developed, specific, and interesting essay, no one will notice how many paragraphs it has. If you're most comfortable with the five-paragraph format, continue to use it. Be sure that you write in paragraphs and that you write more than one. The lowest scored student sample essays in the *Official Guide to SAT II* have only one paragraph; the essays with the highest scores have four. Rather than deciding in advance how many paragraphs you will write, let the logic of your essay determine the number.

How long an essay should I write?

You won't be graded on the length of your essay, and you have only twenty minutes. Keep in mind that very short essays will probably not be sufficiently developed. Each essay is scored by two readers using a scale of from 1 to 6. In the sample essays the College Board has released, the scores of 12 (that is, two readers give the essay a score of 6) are essays of four paragraphs and about 300 words. The second highest scores (10) have three or four paragraphs and 275 words. Scores of 8 have two or three paragraphs and about 250 words. In the lower half of the scale, the 6 scores are two-paragraph essays of 185 words, the 4 scores have one or two paragraphs and 140 words, and the 2 scores at the bottom have one paragraph and 100 words.

This is not to say that the longer your essay is, the higher your score will be. If you have nothing to say, say it. Padding out your paper with repetition or verbose phrasing will lower your score. Before you begin to write, plan your essay to cover the topic fully with specific supporting detail.

Are spelling and punctuation important?

The readers will pay no attention to one or two minor spelling or punctuation errors. They understand that your essay is a first draft written in only twenty minutes. But if the mechanical errors in a paper are so glaring that they interfere with your communicating meaning, they will count heavily against you.

How important is correct grammar?

Even the best papers (two scores of 6) may have occasional errors. In papers in the lower half of the grading scale, errors of grammar are common.

How important is good handwriting?

Readers make an effort to avoid being influenced by good or bad handwriting, but there may be an unconscious hostility to a paper that is very hard to read. You must write with a number two pencil, so make your writing as legible as you can.

Is it better to write about literature, history, or current events than about personal experience?

If you're given a choice, write about the subject that fits the question and that you know best. Contrary to popular belief, the readers do not have any literary or political ax to grind. They don't care what you write about so long as you write well, on the topic, and legibly.

Is there a reward for creativity in an essay?

It depends on what you mean by creativity. If you mean writing a poem or a letter or a dialogue or a diary when the question calls for an essay, the answer is an emphatic *no*. If you mean writing an essay that is on the topic and has an individual voice, original ideas, wit, and style, the answer is *yes indeed*.

How important is the use of detail or specific examples?

It's crucial. The question will almost certainly ask you to give an example or examples from contemporary life, personal experience or observation, or your reading in history, literature, or other areas. If the question calls for one example, choose one that's relevant and that you know well and develop it very fully. One of the most obvious differences between a paper in the upper and the lower half of the scoring scale is its use of, or failure to use, a specific example.

What if I don't finish my essay?

The readers are told again and again to reward students for what they do well. If you've left out only a few sentences of conclusion to your essay, it may well not affect your score at all. If you've written three quarters of your essay on the topic, you'll certainly get full credit for all you've written, and it may be close to a complete answer. Don't get depressed if you haven't finished and let your disappointment harm your performance in Part B, the multiple-choice section of the test. Perhaps you didn't finish because what you were writing was so good.

What if I finish early?

If you finish early and are sure you can't improve your essay, you can go on to the multiple-choice section of the exam.

Do you have any suggestions about style?

- Write naturally.
- Avoid clichés. If the topic suggests a familiar proverb or quotation to you, resist the temptation to quote. Fifty thousand other papers will have used it already.

How many readers will grade my essay?

Two readers grade each essay on a scale from 1 to 6. If there is more than a two-point discrepancy between the two grades, a third reader will score the essay. None of the readers is aware of the scores the other reader or readers have given a paper.

Is there any specific course required before I take the SAT II Writing exam?

No. Almost all students who take the exam have had one to three high school English classes, but most have not had a course exclusively concerned with writing.

How should I practice writing essays before the exam?

On pages 149–153 of this book, there are twenty essay topics you can use for practice. Take your practice exams seriously and pay close attention to the time so that you become accustomed to finishing your essay in the twenty minutes allowed. Be sure to write more than one paragraph.

On the actual test, the answer sheet for your essay is two pages, each eight inches long and seven inches wide, with twenty-four lines to the page, that is, like standard notebook filler paper if you begin on the fifth line. At least once, practice using notebook filler paper cut to this size to be sure your essay will fit.

Ask a friend (or better yet, two friends) or any one or two people able to judge writing to read and score your essay using the scoring guide on pages 155-156 of this book.

You can also use the student essays printed here to refine your editorial, or revising, skills. The essays in the lower half of the scale are especially likely to contain a number of mechanical errors or weaknesses of style that aren't specified in the comments on them. If you can find and correct these errors, you will be able to avoid similar mistakes in your own writing.

What scores will I receive and when will I get them?

The scores reported to you and to the colleges you designate will include a composite score (that is, the total score on the two parts of the exam) given on a 200–800 scale, your multiple-choice score, on a

20–80 scale, and your writing sample score, also on a 20–80 scale. You'll also receive notice of your score's placement in the percentile ranking of students who took the test. Scores are reported from five to ten weeks after the test is taken.

You can calculate your approximate scaled writing sample score by using this table.

Essay Raw Score (2 readers)	Approximate Scaled Score
11–12	65–71
9–10	54–60
7–8	42–48
5–6	33–37
3–4	26–30
0–2	20–23

To find your raw composite score, multiply your raw score on the essay by 3 (if your raw score was 10 or above, multiply by 3.02). Add this result to your raw score on the multiple-choice section. The total of these two figures is your raw composite score. You can get an approximation of your scaled composite score by converting your raw composite score to the 200–800 scale by using the following table.

Composite Raw Score	Approximate Composite Scaled Score
86–96+	730–800
76–85	640–720
66–75	560–630
56–65	490–550
46–55	430–480
36–45	370–420
26–35	320–360
16–25	260–310

ESSAY TOPICS

The following pages present general instructions like those you'll find on the writing sample section of the exam and topics that you can use to practice writing the twenty-minute essays.

GENERAL INSTRUCTIONS

In twenty minutes, write an essay on the topic below. YOU MAY NOT WRITE ON ANOTHER TOPIC. AN ESSAY ON ANOTHER TOPIC WILL NOT BE SCORED.

The essay is intended to give you the chance to show your writing skills. Be sure to express your ideas on the topic clearly and effectively. The quality of your writing is much more important than the quantity, but to deal adequately with this topic, you should probably write more than one paragraph. Be specific.

TOPICS

1. Think carefully about the following quotation and the assignment that follows. Then plan and write your essay according to the instructions.

    "Don't take risks; better safe than sorry."

    Do you agree with this statement? Write an essay in which you support your opinion with specific examples from history, contemporary life, readings, or personal observation.

2. Think carefully about the following quotation and the assignment that follows. Then plan and write your essay according to the instructions.

   "The American dream is to get something for nothing."

   Do you agree with this statement? Write an essay in which you support your opinion with specific examples from history, contemporary affairs, literature, or personal observation.

3. In a well-organized composition, describe a situation in which an event that you had especially *not* looked forward to turned out to be the opposite of what you had expected. Include the following in your essay:

   an account of why you had not looked forward to the event
   an account of why the event turned out well

   Be specific.

4. "The majority is often wrong."

   Choose a specific example from your reading, personal experience, or current events as the basis for an essay that agrees or disagrees with this statement.

5. "Our heroes reflect our values."

   Write an essay which supports or refutes this statement. Support your position with one or more specific examples.

6. "Among young adults, nothing is more powerful than peer pressure."

   Do you agree or disagree with this statement. Write an essay in which you state your position and support it using evidence from personal experience or observation.

7. "The greatest dangers to liberty are not evil men, but zealous men who mean well but lack understanding."

   Write an essay in which you agree or disagree with this statement. Explain what you think the statement means and give at least one example in support of your position.

8. "Some fads are not silly."

   Do you agree? Write an essay about a fad that you think is or is not silly. Explain what the fad was like and why you respond to it as you do.

9. "Americans can always be counted on to do the right thing after all other possibilities have been exhausted."

   Write an essay in which you agree or disagree with this statement. Explain what you think the statement means and use one or more specific examples to support your position. Your examples may be taken from history, current events, or your own observations.

10. In a narrow decision, the Supreme Court ruled that flag burning, as a form of symbolic speech, is protected by the guarantee of freedom of speech.

    Do you agree with this decision? Write an essay in which you explain your position.

11. "It is better to know nothing at all about something than to know only a little."

Do you agree or disagree with this quotation? Write an essay in which you present your position supported by evidence from your readings or personal experience. Be specific.

12. "We all have an *unfavorite* holiday."

Write an essay in which you explain why one holiday is your unfavorite. You may write on either the holiday that you like less than the others or on a specific holiday that disappointed you.

13. "Less is more."

Write an essay in which you show how this apparent contradiction can make sense. Use specific evidence from your reading, current events, or personal experience to support your ideas.

14. "People nowadays use the past chiefly as a club with which to beat the present."

Write an essay in which you discuss what you think the author of this quotation means and whether or not you agree. Be specific and support your arguments.

15. "The law protects the rich better than it protects the poor."

Do you agree? Write an essay using specific supporting detail in which you agree with or refute this idea.

16. "Lotteries increase state revenues at the expense of the people who can least afford to throw away five or ten dollars every week."

Write an essay in which you refute or support this quotation.

17. "A major element in every generation's choice of the music it makes popular is the hope of outraging an older generation."

Write a well-supported essay in which you take a position either in favor of or against this contention.

18. "Good movies may help us to escape from our troubles, but great films will help us to face them."

Write an essay in which you explain what you think this quotation means and why you agree or disagree with it. Use at least one specific example to support your case.

19. "We can learn more from our failures than from our successes."

Do you agree? Write an essay in which you describe a personal experience that either supports this idea or calls it into question.

20. "These days, it is hard to tell the difference between a television news broadcast and the half-hour tabloid 'news' shows."

What criticism of television news does this statement make? Do you agree? Support your position as specifically as you can.

SAMPLE STUDENT ESSAYS
AND ANALYSIS

The following pages present three sets of student essays written under SAT II exam conditions. The papers are reproduced exactly as they were written, so they contain some mechanical errors and some bad writing. The high school students wrote the essays in twenty minutes or less, the time limit on the SAT II Writing exam. The scoring guide used to grade the essays is given first, followed by the general instructions. The general instructions and scoring guide are the same on all three essay topics. Each set of essays is preceded by the exam topic, and each essay is scored and followed by an analysis.

SCORING GUIDE

Since the student has only twenty minutes to write the essay, minor errors of grammar or mechanics will not affect the score. The essays scored at 6 will not be errorless—they are, after all, first drafts—but they will be superior to the other essays.

Score of 6

These consistently competent essays are characterized by the following:

- the effective coverage of the tasks required by the exam question
- good organization and development, with relevant supporting details
- command of standard written English with a range of vocabulary and variety of syntax

Score of 5

These competent essays are characterized by the following:

- the coverage of the tasks required by the exam question
- generally good organization and development, with some supporting details

155

- good handling of standard written English with some range of vocabulary and variety of syntax

Score of 4

These adequately competent essays are characterized by the following:
- the coverage of the tasks required by the exam question
- adequate organization and development with some supporting details
- adequate handling of standard written English, but with minimal variety of syntax and some grammatical or diction errors

Score of 3

These marginal papers are characterized by the following:
- failure to cover fully the required tasks
- weak organization and/or development
- failure to use relevant supporting detail
- several errors of grammar, diction, and syntax

Score of 2

These inadequate papers are characterized by the following:
- failure to cover the assignment
- poor organization and development
- lack of supporting detail
- many errors of grammar, diction, and syntax

Score of 1

These incompetent papers are characterized by the following
- failure to cover the assignment
- very poor organization and development
- errors of grammar, diction, and syntax so frequent as to interfere with meaning
- extreme brevity

GENERAL INSTRUCTIONS

In twenty minutes, write an essay on the topic below. YOU MAY NOT WRITE ON ANOTHER TOPIC. AN ESSAY ON ANOTHER TOPIC WILL NOT BE SCORED.

The essay is intended to give you the chance to show your writing skills. Be sure to express your ideas on the topic clearly and effectively. The quality of your writing is much more important than the quantity, but to deal adequately with this topic, you should probably write more than one paragraph. Be specific.

ESSAYS

SET 1

Topic

"Don't take risks; better safe than sorry."

The papers on this topic used personal events, history, and contemporary affairs about equally as supporting examples. For some reason, students wrote longer essays on this topic than on the others.

Essay: Score of 6

Stagefright

The fear of speaking in front of a group of people is sometimes called stagefright. When I was in the sixth grade, my teacher assigned our class roles in a play about colonial times for President's Day. I was chosen to play the leading part, Betsy Ross. At that time, I was terrified of standing in front of my sixth grade classmates. The idea of speaking to parents and other classes in a large auditorium was too scary to imagine. I couldn't do it.

"Miss Allen," I said, "I don't feel too good, I think I have flu, I don't think I'll be able to practice my part." "Then you'll have to play the part without practice," said Miss Allen, seeing through my plan to convince her to let me out of the play. The expression on her face told me she would not be fooled. So rehearsals went on, and the day of the performance drew nearer. The idea of standing on the big auditorium stage peering out at all those faces staring back at me was overwhelming.

On the day before the play, Miss Allen sat me down and said, "I know how hard it is for you to get up and speak to people; that is why I chose you for this part. You have done exceptionally well in rehearsals, and I think you are very special." Supported by these words, I gathered all my courage, and played my part without a hitch.

When it was over, my family was proud of me, and I gave myself a purple heart for bravery. Though I am not what you call a risk-taking person, my sixth grade acting experience showed me what can be lost if you are afraid to try something for the first time. It is a lesson I have never forgotten.

Analysis

It is not until we reach the final paragraph of this essay that its connection to the topic becomes clear, but it is, nevertheless, a good response. The writing is varied, making a good use of dialogue. The paragraphs are well developed, and the organization is clear.

Essay: Score of 5

"Jump!" "I dare you to!" Sound familiar? These are calls to risk. What are the consequences of jumping? What good could it possibly do? Life? Death? A rush of adreneline? By taking risks and trying new things, people can save their lives (in a fire) or kill themselves (on a foolish dare). But by taking risks and trying new things, people have advanced in this world. Safe is good but boring. You may live longer, but you die eventually, and have missed something. To take a risk is to step forward and without moving forward to a new field or area you can't evolve as a person.

I disagree with "Don't take risks; better safe than sorry." The Pilgrims took a risk in leaving England and discovered a new world.

They would have been unable to worship their way in England, so they took a risk and it paid off. This may not always be the case. Many of the Pilgrims died on the voyage or in America, and would have been better safe in England than dead.

NASA took a risk and now they launch people into space every month or so. If they didn't, they would never have reached the moon and learned so much more about space. They could of stayed here and looked from the earth, but to learn more they had to take a risk. They ended up better than safe and much better than sorry. Of course, Challenger blew up, but they took charge again and will soon send men to Mars and beyond.

The most basic example is trying new foods. People would never know what they liked and didn't like if they didn't try new foods. Without the risk of trying new foods, they would eat the same thing all the time and that would lead from safe to sorry because food would get so bland and eating would be monotonous. Without taking risks, one cannot live fully, and without fully living, there is no point to living at all.

Analysis

The first paragraph of this essay is especially good, and though the writing falls off as the paper progresses, it is a competent paper. It cites a number of specific examples to support its points. Though there are several careless errors, on the whole, the paper demonstrates a good handling of standard written English.

Essay: Score of 4

Everyone in todays society and in history has taken some risk of some level. I agree with this statement as it reads. If you don't take a risk, you won't take the chance of being sorry. However, great fame and fortune may reward you for taking risks. Risks must be thought out and planned well, if one is to attempt to risk something. Possibly listing the outcomes of both sides of the results would better give an idea, weather the risk is worth it.

People that take risks must ask themselves "What is the reason for taking this risk?" Often times people might try to become famous, but end up no more famous than the average person. Great inventors, generals, and scientists have taken many risks throughout time. Generals in the army risk loosing lives and battles that people might later read in history books. Others might have forged new countries and help start governments. The different outcomes are dramatically different.

Risks are actions, events, and thoughts that people are not familiar with. If a risk already has the chance of being dangerous and the only reason someone wants to take one is to say they have eluded the danger of it, doesn't make sense. There should be the possibility of personal gain for someone. Often times people get in trouble with the law because they take risks that can only hurt them. When risks involve the law the consequences often outweight the chances on gaining even material property.

Personally, I don't take too many large risks. It can be a sign of what kind of person you are. Wheather you are an optomistic or pessimestic person. Maybe you are in great need of a change. People need to take some risks in life so that they may gain certain things in life, they otherwise would not.

Analysis

This essay is uneven. Its attempts to define risk are not very convincing, and its examples are general rather than specific. The organization and handling of syntax and mechanics, though flawed, are adequate.

Essay: Score of 3

The quotation "Don't take risks; better safe than sorry" is a very controversial statement. I definately have mixed feelings about this quotation.

First of all, I feel that if an individual is going to take a risk, he/she should have confidence and a good plan. I myself am a risky person. For instance; I love to try new things. Not only does it give me experience in what I am doing, but it boosts my confidence level so I am determined to do it again. If I make a mistake, then I know not to make the same mistake in the future.

However, it can also work the other way. If a buisnessman risks a lot of money on one single buisness deal, he may lose all of his money or maybe even his buisness altogether. Risks can be fatal too.

If an individual decides to try something dangerous, that person may be injured or even killed.

So there you have it. Risks can work for you in a negative way or they can work for you in a positive way. You just have to be smart when taking them.

Analysis

Though this essay does cite some examples of risk, its paragraphs are undeveloped, and its command of diction, syntax, and spelling are marginal.

Essay: Score of 2

I agree with this topic, and then again I disagree with this topic. I agree with it because over time I've seen people who didn't take the risk of being peer persured into something like, drug, crime, or any thing else of that nature and made a better life for that person and there family. I disagree with this topic because over time in history people have taken alot of risks some for good and some for bad. For example, some for good like Benjiman Franklin discovering electricity or Dr. Martin Luther King for makeing a way for Afro-Americans to be equal to other nationalities. Some for bad is the person who made the first gun and fire arm, the person who started growing drugs in there spare time.

Analysis

This paper does refer to Franklin and King as examples of men who risked, but it is otherwise marred by weak development and many errors of grammar, diction, and syntax.

Essay: Score of 1

I disagree to some extent with the quotation "Don't take risks; better safe than sorry." I think you have to take risks, it is impossible not to take risks, with everything you do their is a risk involved. So I think "Don't take risks" is a bad statement. But I do think that you are better safe than sorry, and that if something can get you hurt or has a good chance of injuring you, you should play it safe and probably not do it. Better to be safe than to be sorry.

Therefore, this statement to me is half right and half wrong because you have to take chances and risks in life, but it is always better to be safe than sorry also.

Analysis

This essay has no specific examples. It is very short and has too many mechanical errors to score higher than one.

SET 2

Topic

"The American dream is to get something for nothing."

Of the three topics, this one gave the most trouble to the students writing the essays. Many failed to understand the point of the quotation. Many took it literally. Only a few saw it as a legitimate criticism of American values. Most of the essays failed to offer specific examples to support or refute the idea, and as always happens when a writer is uncertain of what to say, the writing was unfocused. More than half of the papers fell into the lower half of the scale.

Essay: Score of 6

"Something for nothing" may not be the only American dream, but it is one of them. How else do you explain the explosion of gambling casinos all over the country? Las Vegas was the only big gambling town twenty years ago. Now even half the states in the Bible belt have legalized betting. They put the casinos on riverboats and call it nostalgia not gambling. Dying cities like Atlantic City, New Jersey, and Loghlin, Nevada come to life solely to provide slot machines and poker tables for a public eager to hit a jackpot.

Many states began with small bingo games on Indian reservations. Now these are gambling halls with slot machines. The states that have no casinos or Indians have state lotteries. When the payoff gets over two million dollars, hysteria rules. If this isn't a dream of something for nothing, then what is?

The legal gambling is just the tip of the iceberg. The money spent on legitimate gambling is just a fraction of what is spent on illegal betting. There are bookies, and office pools, and all sorts of rackets which can lead to fixed sports events. There are mail-order lotteries, and horse and dog races. Americans are generous to people in need, but they are also greedy, and the idea that they dream of something for nothing is an idea that is hard to dispute.

Analysis

This essay was one of very few which found a relevant and coherent way of approaching the quotation. By dealing with the single issue of gambling in America, the student writer is able to organize and develop an argument and to offer a very large number of cogent supporting details. The writing is vivid and varied. The essay is conspicuously superior to the five others on this topic.

Essay: Score of 5

There may be a few people who believe the American dream is something for nothing, but the idea is not practical. America has much more to offer than a blind hope. Because we have so much more than many other countries, we may take basic things for granted. Almost anyone would be glad to get something for nothing, but it's a rare occasion when someone doesn't have to break the law to make that dream come true.

If you wish to become famous, you have to work hard. Edison would never have invented a working light bulb, if it weren't for his effort and hard work. Personally, I have rarely received something for nothing. Anybody who works knows that the harder you work, the more money you will earn. Anyone who goes to school knows that the harder you study, the better your grades will be.

Some people may agree, some will disagree with my view of this idea. Everyone must ask what the American dream means, because it is different for everyone. It depends on your needs and what you believe in. I think the American dream is to be successful, but not by doing little and getting something in return. Only a few people can actually believe in this statement. Everyone who has worked or tried hard to accomplish something realizes that there is some sort of reward or satisfaction that goes along with effort.

Analysis

This essay is one that chose to disagree with the quotation. It does cite specific examples to support its argument; it is competently developed and relatively free from errors of grammar, diction, and syntax.

Essay: Score of 4

I strongly disagree that the American dream is "to get something for nothing." I feel that the strength of America lies in the ability of one person, starting from nothing, using only talent and intelligence to achieve his goals. An example of this is the immigrants who came to America, having little more than the shirt on their back, that worked hard and achieved their dreams.

Behind the hope of getting "something for nothing" is lazyness, while the motivation to success is the hope to use the natural ability you possess to benefit both you and others. If you put a lot of effort into a piece of work, that work will turn out well and benefit you later, even if only through memory. If you ever get something for nothing, that something is worth nothing or is next to useless because it is unearned.

There are examples of this today. Where people want to better themselves, they can; when they see something they want, they can work towards it until it is theirs. No one is owed anything by life; that is just like wanting something for nothing. The real power in America is that while not everyone has a good life, all have the right to try.

Analysis

This is an upper-half paper, but barely. It offers a supporting example in the first paragraph, and its organization, development, and handling of standard written English are adequate.

Essay: Score of 3

It's almost everyones dream to get something for nothing. Weather they admit it or not, it is true. The false part of the statement, "the American dream is something for nothing" is that first of all it is impossible and second of all its the whole world and not just American.

We can't stereotype this statement as only Americans are selfish because no matter what anyone says, the entire world is greedy.

Another thing I disagree with on this statement is that why even bring up the fact that a dream is to get something for nothing. It is impossible, one has a better chance in winning the lottery. If everyone in the world wasn't so money hungry than maybe this statement could come true. One could give just to give and take without feeling guilty.

I know for a fact that, even though it might sound selfish, much of the time I dont want to give something and get nothing in return, even if it's a gift sometimes I would like a thank you or some acknowledgement of appreciation. On the other hand, when I get things for nothing, I feel awkward. I feel guilty and don't really know what to say.

So as concluded, I suspect one could say that that statement is mostly false but there is some truth to it. The dream is to get something for nothing when in reality this dream is impossible.

Analysis

Though this essay has vitality and candor, it is a lower-half paper. The argument is incoherent or illogical. The paragraphs are undeveloped or unrelated to one another, and there are a number of errors of grammar, spelling, and punctuation.

Essay: Score of 2

Throughout history people have always been trying to lead a life where they dont have to work hard and can relax and enjoy life. No where is this more evident than America. Here we lead pretty relaxed lives compared to other countries and yet we complain. Maybe its because we have a democracy where we have a say in goverment and try to make things too easy without any regard to the conseqences. But it is clear that we Americans have become a nation of slackers. Look how many people are on welfare. Look at how much better Japan is doing than us. It seems that the work ethic engrained in our founding forefathers has not been passed on to us.

It is pretty safe to say that in most cases the American dream is to get something for nothing.

Analysis

The relevance of this essay to the topic is not always clear. It is marred by a lack of logical argument and of supporting detail. It has many errors of grammar, syntax, and mechanics.

Essay: Score of 1

I agree with this statement In some cases, there are many people who try and get everything for nothing. Most people when they're shopping always shop the sales or try and find the best deal or lowest price. Yeah so I guess that we are trying to get something for nothing.

I guess this is how our society has turned to everybody wants something the easy way out. Nobody wants to work for it. Americans have become lazy and fat and people would rather sit on the couch and watch television than go outside and work for what they want.

Analysis

Like the essay scored 2, this one uses the topic to denounce American society, and like the other paper, it offers no support. Its mechanics are no worse, but its extreme brevity places it at the bottom of the scale.

SET 3

Topic

Describe a situation in which an event that you had especially not looked forward to turned out to be the opposite of what you had expected.

The students writing on this topic had no difficulty with the task, and because it required the writing of a personal essay, the essays on this topic were, as a rule, much better than those on the other two assignments.

Essay: Score of 6

It was almost June. School would be out in three weeks, and I was tired of homework. While other classes were winding down, our English teacher assigned another novel. At that point, it did not matter to me what book it was; I had already decided to hate it. When I thought the situation could not get worse, I learned the book was about farm animals. The only consolation was the book was short. It was called Animal Farm.

The first two pages confirmed my worst expectations of torture (of course, I would have been disappointed if they hadn't). Knowing that my final grade in English could depend on the paper I would have to write about this book, I knew I had to keep going. It was a last wall to climb before I could reach the green hills of summer. Then something strange happened. I was not falling asleep, even when I read in bed. I was reading beyond each day's assignment, and I usually never read more than I have to. I finished the book two weeks ahead of schedule, and—gasp!—I had really liked it.

I still don't know how Animal Farm managed to take such a hold on me. The animals, of course, were more than human, and I found myself, against my will, hating a pig or feeling sorry for a horse. I even had a sense of recognizing my friends and one teacher on the farm. While my sister's English class spent that June sitting around doing crossword puzzles and playing word games, I found myself stuck in a class reading a book I couldn't stop reading, reading a book twice for the first time in my life.

Analysis

This is a good paper. It has a voice of its own, is on the topic, and is largely free from errors of mechanics, diction, or syntax. It has three well-organized paragraphs, a coherent, chronological development. Unusually, it makes use of both metaphor (*green hills of summer,* a phrase from a popular song) and irony (*stuck* in the last sentence). Devices like these are certainly not required in essays with high scores, but if they are well used, the reader will take notice. The sentences are varied, and the mechanics are good. The essay is not errorless (*The animals . . . were more than human* is unclear), but it is clearly one that fulfills the scoring guide's *consistently competent* description of the highest scoring paper.

If you're thinking, *Oh, yeah. This paper got a high score because it says reading is cool and that's what the teachers grading the exam want to hear,* forget it. Any on-topic essay written this well would be scored 6, regardless of what it said about reading books.

Essay: Score of 5

I remember when I was ten years old, my dad signed himself and me up for the Hometown Fair ten kilometer run. I tried to weesel out of it, but my dad was determined it would be good for both of us. Every morning in September, he would wake me an hour earlier than usual, and we would walk over to the school track, and run for thirty or forty minutes. At first, I hated getting up so early, but I had to admit the running was not that bad.

After a while, I began to really like the run. I got stronger and felt better after the run. Before long I had to drag my dad out of bed in the mornings.

In six weeks, the day of the run was getting near. We were up to running five miles every morning, and some days I'd run further. Finally, it was the night before the run. I was really nervous, I was not sure I wanted to run, and I couldn't go to sleep. When the morning came I told my dad I couldn't run, but he wouldn't let me stay home. When we got to the start, my nerves went away. I completed the race in forty four minutes, thirty one seconds, second in my age group. I made the front page of the town newspaper. Now distance running is my favorite recreation.

Analysis

The writing here is not so varied and assured as it is in the 6 paper, but this is certainly a "competent" essay. The organization is clear, the use of detail is good, and the errors are minor (the misspelling of *weasel,* the diction of *not that bad*). The second paragraph is very short, but the brevity contributes to its effective description of the reversal of the father-son roles.

Essay: Score of 4

When my history teacher announced that we were to do a debate, it was enough to ruin my day. I had never been in a debate before, and the idea did not seem very interesting to me. The only good thing about it was we could choose our own teams, and mine was a group with three of my friends.

Two of them were really smart, and that helped. They decided to work on the debate on all three weekend nights, since the debate was on Tuesday. I complained all weekend about how I'd rather be at the movies or the mall, anywhere but at a library doing debate research. On Monday night I began to worry. What if we lost and had wasted a whole weekend and all that work.

I was the first to speak for our group, and though I was shaking, it was not too bad. We had rebuttals for all their arguments, and really beat them bad, because we were so much better prepared. We all got top marks on the debate. For something I dreaded and complained so much about, the debate turned out to be fun, something I never expected when the teacher assigned it.

Analysis

The repeated word on the scoring guide to describe essays in this range is *adequate*. This essay deals with the assignment, is sufficiently developed, and though it has a few awkward or incorrect phrases (*smart, beat them bad*), it belongs in the upper half of the scale.

Essay: Score of 3

Last year I was not looking forward to going to Canada to play hockey because I was really scared of how good the teams up there would be. I thought that we would lose every game. I also did not like the flying too.

Before our first game I was really nervous. I pictured these huge Canadians who would just skate circles around me. I ended up being wrong. They ended up being not that good, and we won.

I also ended up being wrong on not looking forward to the trip because it also ended up being really fun. We won two games. These teams were really good, and we were great and deserved to win the games that we won. The flight was great too.

I often do this where I don't look forward to something and then it ends up being great. I don't know why I do this, I guess it's just the way I am. Maybe I shouldn't jump to conclusions all the time.

Analysis

This essay is an example of the upper range of the lower half of the scale. It does cover the assigned task, but it does so in undeveloped paragraphs, with little or no supporting detail, and in sentences that have hardly any variety. The vocabulary is limited. Three sentences in a row use the verb *ended up* (one of them twice), and three sentences repeat the carelessly used word *great*. There are also a few punctuation errors.

Essay: Score of 2

The event I did not look forward to was coming to a new school. I liked my old school, and was happy there. I had friends, knew people when I past through the halls, and did ok in my classes and enjoyed the life there. When we moved out of that district, I wanted to stay at my old school.

I feared going to this new school for many reasons. One was not knowing a soul. People, classes, teachers, friends, dress all were different then my old school.

After reaching the new school at the begginning of the second semester sophmore year, I was still unhappy of the move. Then I started junior year and am happier meeting friends, but still miss my old school.

Analysis

The scoring guide characterizes the essay scored at 2 as poorly developed, lacking supporting detail, and having errors of grammar, diction, and syntax. This essay contains all of these weaknesses.

Essay: Score of 1

An event that I was in that turned out the opposite way of what I planned to do was a video game contest. I thought I would go all the way because Ive beaten a lot of good people before so I thought it would be easy but I ended up not making it past round three. I guess the reason it turned out like this is because I didnt think there would be a person as good as me. Now I know there is always going to be some one who is as good as or even better than me.

Analysis

Any essay as short as this one must be well written to have any chance of getting a score in the upper half of the scale. This paper combines extreme brevity with meager development and errors of grammar, punctuation, or diction in every sentence.

Part IV:
Five Full-Length Practice Tests

ANSWER SHEET FOR PRACTICE TEST 2
(Remove This Sheet and Use it to Mark Your Answers)

Identifying Sentence Errors

1 Ⓐ Ⓑ Ⓒ Ⓓ Ⓔ
2 Ⓐ Ⓑ Ⓒ Ⓓ Ⓔ
3 Ⓐ Ⓑ Ⓒ Ⓓ Ⓔ
4 Ⓐ Ⓑ Ⓒ Ⓓ Ⓔ
5 Ⓐ Ⓑ Ⓒ Ⓓ Ⓔ

6 Ⓐ Ⓑ Ⓒ Ⓓ Ⓔ
7 Ⓐ Ⓑ Ⓒ Ⓓ Ⓔ
8 Ⓐ Ⓑ Ⓒ Ⓓ Ⓔ
9 Ⓐ Ⓑ Ⓒ Ⓓ Ⓔ
10 Ⓐ Ⓑ Ⓒ Ⓓ Ⓔ

11 Ⓐ Ⓑ Ⓒ Ⓓ Ⓔ
12 Ⓐ Ⓑ Ⓒ Ⓓ Ⓔ
13 Ⓐ Ⓑ Ⓒ Ⓓ Ⓔ
14 Ⓐ Ⓑ Ⓒ Ⓓ Ⓔ
15 Ⓐ Ⓑ Ⓒ Ⓓ Ⓔ

16 Ⓐ Ⓑ Ⓒ Ⓓ Ⓔ
17 Ⓐ Ⓑ Ⓒ Ⓓ Ⓔ
18 Ⓐ Ⓑ Ⓒ Ⓓ Ⓔ
19 Ⓐ Ⓑ Ⓒ Ⓓ Ⓔ
20 Ⓐ Ⓑ Ⓒ Ⓓ Ⓔ

Improving Sentences

21 Ⓐ Ⓑ Ⓒ Ⓓ Ⓔ
22 Ⓐ Ⓑ Ⓒ Ⓓ Ⓔ
23 Ⓐ Ⓑ Ⓒ Ⓓ Ⓔ
24 Ⓐ Ⓑ Ⓒ Ⓓ Ⓔ
25 Ⓐ Ⓑ Ⓒ Ⓓ Ⓔ

26 Ⓐ Ⓑ Ⓒ Ⓓ Ⓔ
27 Ⓐ Ⓑ Ⓒ Ⓓ Ⓔ
28 Ⓐ Ⓑ Ⓒ Ⓓ Ⓔ
29 Ⓐ Ⓑ Ⓒ Ⓓ Ⓔ
30 Ⓐ Ⓑ Ⓒ Ⓓ Ⓔ

31 Ⓐ Ⓑ Ⓒ Ⓓ Ⓔ
32 Ⓐ Ⓑ Ⓒ Ⓓ Ⓔ
33 Ⓐ Ⓑ Ⓒ Ⓓ Ⓔ
34 Ⓐ Ⓑ Ⓒ Ⓓ Ⓔ
35 Ⓐ Ⓑ Ⓒ Ⓓ Ⓔ

36 Ⓐ Ⓑ Ⓒ Ⓓ Ⓔ
37 Ⓐ Ⓑ Ⓒ Ⓓ Ⓔ
38 Ⓐ Ⓑ Ⓒ Ⓓ Ⓔ

Improving Paragraphs

39 Ⓐ Ⓑ Ⓒ Ⓓ Ⓔ
40 Ⓐ Ⓑ Ⓒ Ⓓ Ⓔ

41 Ⓐ Ⓑ Ⓒ Ⓓ Ⓔ
42 Ⓐ Ⓑ Ⓒ Ⓓ Ⓔ
43 Ⓐ Ⓑ Ⓒ Ⓓ Ⓔ
44 Ⓐ Ⓑ Ⓒ Ⓓ Ⓔ
45 Ⓐ Ⓑ Ⓒ Ⓓ Ⓔ

46 Ⓐ Ⓑ Ⓒ Ⓓ Ⓔ
47 Ⓐ Ⓑ Ⓒ Ⓓ Ⓔ
48 Ⓐ Ⓑ Ⓒ Ⓓ Ⓔ
49 Ⓐ Ⓑ Ⓒ Ⓓ Ⓔ
50 Ⓐ Ⓑ Ⓒ Ⓓ Ⓔ

Identifying Sentence Errors

51 Ⓐ Ⓑ Ⓒ Ⓓ Ⓔ
52 Ⓐ Ⓑ Ⓒ Ⓓ Ⓔ
53 Ⓐ Ⓑ Ⓒ Ⓓ Ⓔ
54 Ⓐ Ⓑ Ⓒ Ⓓ Ⓔ
55 Ⓐ Ⓑ Ⓒ Ⓓ Ⓔ

56 Ⓐ Ⓑ Ⓒ Ⓓ Ⓔ
57 Ⓐ Ⓑ Ⓒ Ⓓ Ⓔ
58 Ⓐ Ⓑ Ⓒ Ⓓ Ⓔ
59 Ⓐ Ⓑ Ⓒ Ⓓ Ⓔ
60 Ⓐ Ⓑ Ⓒ Ⓓ Ⓔ

CUT HERE

ANSWER SHEET FOR PRACTICE TEST 3
(Remove This Sheet and Use it to Mark Your Answers)

Identifying Sentence Errors

1 Ⓐ Ⓑ Ⓒ Ⓓ Ⓔ
2 Ⓐ Ⓑ Ⓒ Ⓓ Ⓔ
3 Ⓐ Ⓑ Ⓒ Ⓓ Ⓔ
4 Ⓐ Ⓑ Ⓒ Ⓓ Ⓔ
5 Ⓐ Ⓑ Ⓒ Ⓓ Ⓔ

6 Ⓐ Ⓑ Ⓒ Ⓓ Ⓔ
7 Ⓐ Ⓑ Ⓒ Ⓓ Ⓔ
8 Ⓐ Ⓑ Ⓒ Ⓓ Ⓔ
9 Ⓐ Ⓑ Ⓒ Ⓓ Ⓔ
10 Ⓐ Ⓑ Ⓒ Ⓓ Ⓔ

11 Ⓐ Ⓑ Ⓒ Ⓓ Ⓔ
12 Ⓐ Ⓑ Ⓒ Ⓓ Ⓔ
13 Ⓐ Ⓑ Ⓒ Ⓓ Ⓔ
14 Ⓐ Ⓑ Ⓒ Ⓓ Ⓔ
15 Ⓐ Ⓑ Ⓒ Ⓓ Ⓔ

16 Ⓐ Ⓑ Ⓒ Ⓓ Ⓔ
17 Ⓐ Ⓑ Ⓒ Ⓓ Ⓔ
18 Ⓐ Ⓑ Ⓒ Ⓓ Ⓔ
19 Ⓐ Ⓑ Ⓒ Ⓓ Ⓔ
20 Ⓐ Ⓑ Ⓒ Ⓓ Ⓔ

Improving Sentences

21 Ⓐ Ⓑ Ⓒ Ⓓ Ⓔ
22 Ⓐ Ⓑ Ⓒ Ⓓ Ⓔ
23 Ⓐ Ⓑ Ⓒ Ⓓ Ⓔ
24 Ⓐ Ⓑ Ⓒ Ⓓ Ⓔ
25 Ⓐ Ⓑ Ⓒ Ⓓ Ⓔ

26 Ⓐ Ⓑ Ⓒ Ⓓ Ⓔ
27 Ⓐ Ⓑ Ⓒ Ⓓ Ⓔ
28 Ⓐ Ⓑ Ⓒ Ⓓ Ⓔ
29 Ⓐ Ⓑ Ⓒ Ⓓ Ⓔ
30 Ⓐ Ⓑ Ⓒ Ⓓ Ⓔ

31 Ⓐ Ⓑ Ⓒ Ⓓ Ⓔ
32 Ⓐ Ⓑ Ⓒ Ⓓ Ⓔ
33 Ⓐ Ⓑ Ⓒ Ⓓ Ⓔ
34 Ⓐ Ⓑ Ⓒ Ⓓ Ⓔ
35 Ⓐ Ⓑ Ⓒ Ⓓ Ⓔ

36 Ⓐ Ⓑ Ⓒ Ⓓ Ⓔ
37 Ⓐ Ⓑ Ⓒ Ⓓ Ⓔ
38 Ⓐ Ⓑ Ⓒ Ⓓ Ⓔ

Improving Paragraphs

39 Ⓐ Ⓑ Ⓒ Ⓓ Ⓔ
40 Ⓐ Ⓑ Ⓒ Ⓓ Ⓔ

41 Ⓐ Ⓑ Ⓒ Ⓓ Ⓔ
42 Ⓐ Ⓑ Ⓒ Ⓓ Ⓔ
43 Ⓐ Ⓑ Ⓒ Ⓓ Ⓔ
44 Ⓐ Ⓑ Ⓒ Ⓓ Ⓔ
45 Ⓐ Ⓑ Ⓒ Ⓓ Ⓔ

46 Ⓐ Ⓑ Ⓒ Ⓓ Ⓔ
47 Ⓐ Ⓑ Ⓒ Ⓓ Ⓔ
48 Ⓐ Ⓑ Ⓒ Ⓓ Ⓔ
49 Ⓐ Ⓑ Ⓒ Ⓓ Ⓔ
50 Ⓐ Ⓑ Ⓒ Ⓓ Ⓔ

Identifying Sentence Errors

51 Ⓐ Ⓑ Ⓒ Ⓓ Ⓔ
52 Ⓐ Ⓑ Ⓒ Ⓓ Ⓔ
53 Ⓐ Ⓑ Ⓒ Ⓓ Ⓔ
54 Ⓐ Ⓑ Ⓒ Ⓓ Ⓔ
55 Ⓐ Ⓑ Ⓒ Ⓓ Ⓔ

56 Ⓐ Ⓑ Ⓒ Ⓓ Ⓔ
57 Ⓐ Ⓑ Ⓒ Ⓓ Ⓔ
58 Ⓐ Ⓑ Ⓒ Ⓓ Ⓔ
59 Ⓐ Ⓑ Ⓒ Ⓓ Ⓔ
60 Ⓐ Ⓑ Ⓒ Ⓓ Ⓔ

CUT HERE

ANSWER SHEET FOR PRACTICE TEST 4
(Remove This Sheet and Use it to Mark Your Answers)

Identifying Sentence Errors

1 Ⓐ Ⓑ Ⓒ Ⓓ Ⓔ
2 Ⓐ Ⓑ Ⓒ Ⓓ Ⓔ
3 Ⓐ Ⓑ Ⓒ Ⓓ Ⓔ
4 Ⓐ Ⓑ Ⓒ Ⓓ Ⓔ
5 Ⓐ Ⓑ Ⓒ Ⓓ Ⓔ

6 Ⓐ Ⓑ Ⓒ Ⓓ Ⓔ
7 Ⓐ Ⓑ Ⓒ Ⓓ Ⓔ
8 Ⓐ Ⓑ Ⓒ Ⓓ Ⓔ
9 Ⓐ Ⓑ Ⓒ Ⓓ Ⓔ
10 Ⓐ Ⓑ Ⓒ Ⓓ Ⓔ

11 Ⓐ Ⓑ Ⓒ Ⓓ Ⓔ
12 Ⓐ Ⓑ Ⓒ Ⓓ Ⓔ
13 Ⓐ Ⓑ Ⓒ Ⓓ Ⓔ
14 Ⓐ Ⓑ Ⓒ Ⓓ Ⓔ
15 Ⓐ Ⓑ Ⓒ Ⓓ Ⓔ

16 Ⓐ Ⓑ Ⓒ Ⓓ Ⓔ
17 Ⓐ Ⓑ Ⓒ Ⓓ Ⓔ
18 Ⓐ Ⓑ Ⓒ Ⓓ Ⓔ
19 Ⓐ Ⓑ Ⓒ Ⓓ Ⓔ
20 Ⓐ Ⓑ Ⓒ Ⓓ Ⓔ

Improving Sentences

21 Ⓐ Ⓑ Ⓒ Ⓓ Ⓔ
22 Ⓐ Ⓑ Ⓒ Ⓓ Ⓔ
23 Ⓐ Ⓑ Ⓒ Ⓓ Ⓔ
24 Ⓐ Ⓑ Ⓒ Ⓓ Ⓔ
25 Ⓐ Ⓑ Ⓒ Ⓓ Ⓔ

26 Ⓐ Ⓑ Ⓒ Ⓓ Ⓔ
27 Ⓐ Ⓑ Ⓒ Ⓓ Ⓔ
28 Ⓐ Ⓑ Ⓒ Ⓓ Ⓔ
29 Ⓐ Ⓑ Ⓒ Ⓓ Ⓔ
30 Ⓐ Ⓑ Ⓒ Ⓓ Ⓔ

31 Ⓐ Ⓑ Ⓒ Ⓓ Ⓔ
32 Ⓐ Ⓑ Ⓒ Ⓓ Ⓔ
33 Ⓐ Ⓑ Ⓒ Ⓓ Ⓔ
34 Ⓐ Ⓑ Ⓒ Ⓓ Ⓔ
35 Ⓐ Ⓑ Ⓒ Ⓓ Ⓔ

36 Ⓐ Ⓑ Ⓒ Ⓓ Ⓔ
37 Ⓐ Ⓑ Ⓒ Ⓓ Ⓔ
38 Ⓐ Ⓑ Ⓒ Ⓓ Ⓔ

Improving Paragraphs

39 Ⓐ Ⓑ Ⓒ Ⓓ Ⓔ
40 Ⓐ Ⓑ Ⓒ Ⓓ Ⓔ

41 Ⓐ Ⓑ Ⓒ Ⓓ Ⓔ
42 Ⓐ Ⓑ Ⓒ Ⓓ Ⓔ
43 Ⓐ Ⓑ Ⓒ Ⓓ Ⓔ
44 Ⓐ Ⓑ Ⓒ Ⓓ Ⓔ
45 Ⓐ Ⓑ Ⓒ Ⓓ Ⓔ

46 Ⓐ Ⓑ Ⓒ Ⓓ Ⓔ
47 Ⓐ Ⓑ Ⓒ Ⓓ Ⓔ
48 Ⓐ Ⓑ Ⓒ Ⓓ Ⓔ
49 Ⓐ Ⓑ Ⓒ Ⓓ Ⓔ
50 Ⓐ Ⓑ Ⓒ Ⓓ Ⓔ

Identifying Sentence Errors

51 Ⓐ Ⓑ Ⓒ Ⓓ Ⓔ
52 Ⓐ Ⓑ Ⓒ Ⓓ Ⓔ
53 Ⓐ Ⓑ Ⓒ Ⓓ Ⓔ
54 Ⓐ Ⓑ Ⓒ Ⓓ Ⓔ
55 Ⓐ Ⓑ Ⓒ Ⓓ Ⓔ

56 Ⓐ Ⓑ Ⓒ Ⓓ Ⓔ
57 Ⓐ Ⓑ Ⓒ Ⓓ Ⓔ
58 Ⓐ Ⓑ Ⓒ Ⓓ Ⓔ
59 Ⓐ Ⓑ Ⓒ Ⓓ Ⓔ
60 Ⓐ Ⓑ Ⓒ Ⓓ Ⓔ

CUT HERE

ANSWER SHEET FOR PRACTICE TEST 5
(Remove This Sheet and Use it to Mark Your Answers)

Identifying Sentence Errors

1 Ⓐ Ⓑ Ⓒ Ⓓ Ⓔ
2 Ⓐ Ⓑ Ⓒ Ⓓ Ⓔ
3 Ⓐ Ⓑ Ⓒ Ⓓ Ⓔ
4 Ⓐ Ⓑ Ⓒ Ⓓ Ⓔ
5 Ⓐ Ⓑ Ⓒ Ⓓ Ⓔ

6 Ⓐ Ⓑ Ⓒ Ⓓ Ⓔ
7 Ⓐ Ⓑ Ⓒ Ⓓ Ⓔ
8 Ⓐ Ⓑ Ⓒ Ⓓ Ⓔ
9 Ⓐ Ⓑ Ⓒ Ⓓ Ⓔ
10 Ⓐ Ⓑ Ⓒ Ⓓ Ⓔ

11 Ⓐ Ⓑ Ⓒ Ⓓ Ⓔ
12 Ⓐ Ⓑ Ⓒ Ⓓ Ⓔ
13 Ⓐ Ⓑ Ⓒ Ⓓ Ⓔ
14 Ⓐ Ⓑ Ⓒ Ⓓ Ⓔ
15 Ⓐ Ⓑ Ⓒ Ⓓ Ⓔ

16 Ⓐ Ⓑ Ⓒ Ⓓ Ⓔ
17 Ⓐ Ⓑ Ⓒ Ⓓ Ⓔ
18 Ⓐ Ⓑ Ⓒ Ⓓ Ⓔ
19 Ⓐ Ⓑ Ⓒ Ⓓ Ⓔ
20 Ⓐ Ⓑ Ⓒ Ⓓ Ⓔ

Improving Sentences

21 Ⓐ Ⓑ Ⓒ Ⓓ Ⓔ
22 Ⓐ Ⓑ Ⓒ Ⓓ Ⓔ
23 Ⓐ Ⓑ Ⓒ Ⓓ Ⓔ
24 Ⓐ Ⓑ Ⓒ Ⓓ Ⓔ
25 Ⓐ Ⓑ Ⓒ Ⓓ Ⓔ

26 Ⓐ Ⓑ Ⓒ Ⓓ Ⓔ
27 Ⓐ Ⓑ Ⓒ Ⓓ Ⓔ
28 Ⓐ Ⓑ Ⓒ Ⓓ Ⓔ
29 Ⓐ Ⓑ Ⓒ Ⓓ Ⓔ
30 Ⓐ Ⓑ Ⓒ Ⓓ Ⓔ

31 Ⓐ Ⓑ Ⓒ Ⓓ Ⓔ
32 Ⓐ Ⓑ Ⓒ Ⓓ Ⓔ
33 Ⓐ Ⓑ Ⓒ Ⓓ Ⓔ
34 Ⓐ Ⓑ Ⓒ Ⓓ Ⓔ
35 Ⓐ Ⓑ Ⓒ Ⓓ Ⓔ

36 Ⓐ Ⓑ Ⓒ Ⓓ Ⓔ
37 Ⓐ Ⓑ Ⓒ Ⓓ Ⓔ
38 Ⓐ Ⓑ Ⓒ Ⓓ Ⓔ

Improving Paragraphs

39 Ⓐ Ⓑ Ⓒ Ⓓ Ⓔ
40 Ⓐ Ⓑ Ⓒ Ⓓ Ⓔ

41 Ⓐ Ⓑ Ⓒ Ⓓ Ⓔ
42 Ⓐ Ⓑ Ⓒ Ⓓ Ⓔ
43 Ⓐ Ⓑ Ⓒ Ⓓ Ⓔ
44 Ⓐ Ⓑ Ⓒ Ⓓ Ⓔ
45 Ⓐ Ⓑ Ⓒ Ⓓ Ⓔ

46 Ⓐ Ⓑ Ⓒ Ⓓ Ⓔ
47 Ⓐ Ⓑ Ⓒ Ⓓ Ⓔ
48 Ⓐ Ⓑ Ⓒ Ⓓ Ⓔ
49 Ⓐ Ⓑ Ⓒ Ⓓ Ⓔ
50 Ⓐ Ⓑ Ⓒ Ⓓ Ⓔ

Identifying Sentence Errors

51 Ⓐ Ⓑ Ⓒ Ⓓ Ⓔ
52 Ⓐ Ⓑ Ⓒ Ⓓ Ⓔ
53 Ⓐ Ⓑ Ⓒ Ⓓ Ⓔ
54 Ⓐ Ⓑ Ⓒ Ⓓ Ⓔ
55 Ⓐ Ⓑ Ⓒ Ⓓ Ⓔ

56 Ⓐ Ⓑ Ⓒ Ⓓ Ⓔ
57 Ⓐ Ⓑ Ⓒ Ⓓ Ⓔ
58 Ⓐ Ⓑ Ⓒ Ⓓ Ⓔ
59 Ⓐ Ⓑ Ⓒ Ⓓ Ⓔ
60 Ⓐ Ⓑ Ⓒ Ⓓ Ⓔ

CUT HERE

PRACTICE TEST 1

| PART A | Time—20 Minutes
1 Question | ESSAY |

In twenty minutes, write an essay on the topic below. YOU MAY NOT WRITE ON ANOTHER TOPIC. AN ESSAY ON ANOTHER TOPIC WILL NOT BE SCORED.

The essay is intended to give you the chance to show your writing skills. Be sure to express your ideas on the topic clearly and effectively. The quality of your writing is much more important than the quantity, but to deal adequately with this topic you should probably write more than one paragraph. Be specific.

Think carefully about the following quotation and the assignment that follows. Then plan and write your essay according to the instructions.

"The health of the economy is more important than the health of the environment."

Do you agree with this statement? Write an essay in which you support your opinion with specific examples from history, contemporary life, readings, or personal observation.

WHEN THE TWENTY MINUTES HAVE PASSED, YOU MUST STOP WRITING AND GO ON TO THE MULTIPLE-CHOICE SECTION OF THE TEST. IF YOU FINISH YOUR ESSAY BEFORE THE TWENTY MINUTES HAVE PASSED, YOU MAY GO ON TO THE NEXT SECTION OF THE EXAM.

Directions: The following sentences may contain one error of grammar, usage, diction, or idiom. No sentence will contain more than one error, and some have no error. If there is an error, it will be underlined and have a letter beneath it. Sections of the sentence that are not underlined cannot be changed. In selecting your answer, observe the requirements of standard written English.

If there is an error, choose the one underlined part that must be changed to correct the sentence. If there is no error, choose (E).

EXAMPLE:

The film <u>tell the story</u> of a cavalry captain and <u>his wife</u>
      A   B

who <u>try to</u> <u>rebuild their lives</u> after the Civil War. <u>No error</u>
   C   D   E

Correct answer: A

1. When the weather is humid, <u>as it is now</u>, the heat <u>seems to be</u>
                            A   B

greater than <u>it</u> does <u>at times of lower</u> humidity. <u>No error</u>
       C   D   E

2. Raul Julia won a Tony award in *The Threepenny Opera*, and

he <u>re-creates</u> <u>his role</u> when <u>the play</u> became an
     A   B   C

<u>award-winning film</u>. <u>No error</u>
     D   E

3. The short stories of J. California Cooper <u>addresses</u> the black
                                             A
   experience <u>with colloquial talk,</u> <u>dialect, dots, dashes,</u> and
              B   C
   <u>even musical notes.</u> <u>No error</u>
              D   E

4. The manufacturer of a new pertussis vaccine <u>has requested</u>
                                                A
   federal approval because the new shot <u>is better,</u> <u>not because</u>
                                          B   C
   the old one <u>is unsafe.</u> <u>No error</u>
               D   E

5. Many psychologists <u>claim that</u> slips of the tongue do not mask
                      A
   <u>no deeply concealed wishes</u> but are <u>simply</u> signs
              B   C
   <u>of momentary confusion.</u> <u>No error</u>
              D   E

6. <u>Among scientists,</u> <u>there are widespread</u> interest in the
   A   B
   <u>ability of primates</u> to <u>understand and use</u> language. <u>No error</u>
   C   D   E

7. <u>Most</u> archeological expeditions in Central America <u>focus on</u>
   A   B
   the <u>massive stone cities</u> built and inhabited by
       C
   <u>the most wealthiest of the Mayan aristocracy.</u> <u>No error</u>
       D   E

8. Researchers <u>have extended</u> the life span of laboratory-grown
               A
   cells, <u>a feat</u> <u>that</u> may shed light on the <u>process to age.</u> <u>No error</u>
          B   C   D   E

9. The Africanized bees <u>who</u> have <u>been moving northward</u> from
A   B
South America <u>may become</u> less dangerous <u>as they interbreed</u>
C   D
with native populations. <u>No error</u>
E

10. The Dragon Boat Festival <u>is celebrated</u> <u>especially</u>
A   B
<u>enthusiastically</u> in Hunan with colorful races and <u>the eating of</u>
C   D
a traditional dumpling. <u>No error</u>
E

11. The <u>organically grown</u> vegetables sold at this market
A
<u>cost much more</u> than <u>the market</u> selling vegetables
B   C
<u>grown with pesticides.</u> <u>No error</u>
D   E

12. <u>Setting at her typewriter</u> <u>almost every day</u> for fifty-five years,
A   B
Agatha Christie <u>completed</u> eighty-six volumes <u>of prose.</u>
C   D
<u>No error</u>
E

13. The exact causes of glaucoma <u>are unknown,</u> but <u>it</u> occurs when
A   B
<u>abnormally high</u> pressure from fluid in the eye <u>damages</u> the
C   D
optic nerve. <u>No error</u>
E

14. Physicists <u>have synthesized</u> a new third form of solid carbon,
                      A
    <u>known previously</u> <u>to exist</u> <u>for only two forms</u>, graphite and
          B   C   D
    diamond. <u>No error</u>
                  E

15. Thirty years ago, automotive experts <u>expected</u> the
                                              A
    <u>acceptance of</u> the rotary engine <u>to come</u> <u>as easily than</u> any
          B   C   D
    other innovation. <u>No error</u>
                           E

16. The subjects of the <u>Chinese puppet theatre</u> <u>are drawn</u> from
                               A   B
    the same stock of folk tales that professional storytellers

    <u>use to create</u> their <u>story.</u> <u>No error</u>
          C   D   E

17. The great blue heron <u>has survived</u> because it is
                              A
    <u>difficult to stalk,</u> is <u>not particular tasty,</u> <u>and lacks</u> elegant
          B   C   D
    plumage. <u>No error</u>
                  E

18. The scientist <u>operates under</u> the unspoken assumption
                       A
    <u>that there is</u> order <u>underlying</u> the phenomena
          B   C
    <u>they are studying.</u> <u>No error</u>
          D   E

19. Based in Oscar Hijuelos's prize-winning novel, *The Mambo*
     A
Kings has a screenplay by Cynthia Cidres and stars Armand
     B   C   D
Assante. No error
      E

20. Though immunization shots for diphtheria can cause
                     A
acute allergic reactions, medical experts insist that their
      B   C
benefits outweigh the risks. No error
       D   E

Directions: The following questions test correctness and effective expression. In selecting the answer, pay attention to grammar, diction, sentence structure, and punctuation.

In the following questions, part or all of each sentence is underlined. The (A) answer repeats the underlined portion of the original sentence, while the next four offer alternatives. Choose the answer that best expresses the meaning of the original sentence and at the same time is grammatically correct and stylistically superior. The correct choice should be clear, unambiguous, and concise.

EXAMPLE:

The forecaster predicted rain and the sky was clear.

(A) rain and the sky was clear
(B) rain but the sky was clear
(C) rain the sky was clear
(D) rain, but the sky was clear
(E) rain being as the sky was clear

Correct answer: D

21. Using Christian, West African, and Taino traditions, ancient images are re-created in rare rain-forest woods by George Crespo.

(A) ancient images are re-created in rare rain-forest woods by George Crespo
(B) rare rain-forest woods re-create ancient images by George Crespo
(C) George Crespo re-creates ancient images in rare rain-forest woods
(D) George Crespo is the creator of ancient images in rain-forest woods
(E) George Crespo re-creating ancient images of rare rain-forest woods

22. Each year, about fifty thousand books are published in Great Britain, that is as many as in the four-times-larger United States.

   (A) published in Great Britain, that is as many as in
   (B) published in Great Britain; that is as many as in
   (C) published in Great Britain; as many as in
   (D) published in Great Britain; which is as many as in
   (E) published in Great Britain as many as in

23. By her eye-witness reporting, Mary Ward helped to bring America into the war, and Britain's first child-care centers were founded with her help.

   (A) Britain's first child-care centers were founded with her help
   (B) with her help the first British child-care centers were founded
   (C) also helping to found the first child-care centers in Britain
   (D) also Britain's first child-care centers
   (E) she helped to found Britain's first child-care centers

24. David Lynch has directed films and television programs, collaborated on a symphonic work, exhibited his paintings, and written rock lyrics.

   (A) collaborated on a symphonic work, exhibited his paintings, and
   (B) has collaborated on a symphonic work, exhibited his paintings, and
   (C) has collaborated on a symphonic work, and he has exhibited his paintings and
   (D) collaborated on a symphonic work, has exhibited his paintings, and has
   (E) has collaborated on a symphonic work, has exhibited his paintings, and has

25. By the early eleventh century, Muslim scientists knowing the rich medical literature of ancient Greece, as well as arithmetic and algebra.

    (A) knowing the rich medical literature of ancient Greece, as well as
    (B) knew the rich medical literature of ancient Greece, as well as
    (C) know the rich medical literature of ancient Greece, as well as
    (D) having learned the rich medical literature of ancient Greece, as well as
    (E) having been given knowledge of the rich medical literature of ancient Greece, as well as

26. Artist Christina Fernandez originally chose painting as her primary medium, as she now works chiefly in still photography and video.

    (A) as she now works chiefly
    (B) seeing as she now works chiefly
    (C) working chiefly now
    (D) but she now works chiefly
    (E) because she now chiefly works

27. Ending the hope that a single genetic flaw might cause Alzheimer's disease, they say the disorder apparently has multiple causes, as do heart disease and cancer.

    (A) they say the disorder apparently has multiple causes
    (B) they say the disorder has multiple apparent causes
    (C) they say that it apparently has multiple causes
    (D) researchers report the disease has many causes apparent
    (E) researchers report the disorder apparently has multiple causes

28. In 1858, John Speke looked over the waters of <u>Lake Victoria he insisted that it was</u> the source of the Nile.

(A) Lake Victoria he insisted that it was
(B) Lake Victoria and he insisted it to be
(C) Lake Victoria and he insisted that they were
(D) Lake Victoria; insisting that they were
(E) Lake Victoria; he insisted that it was

29. Inhaling hot, steamy air to treat a cold will not make it <u>better, while possibly making it worse.</u>

(A) better, while possibly making it worse
(B) better and may even make it worse
(C) better, making it worse, possibly
(D) better, even worsening it, perhaps
(E) better, and it may even get worse than it is

30. <u>The Prado museum in Madrid has the largest collection of great Spanish paintings in the whole world.</u>

(A) The Prado museum in Madrid has the largest collection of great Spanish paintings in the whole world.
(B) The Prado museum in Madrid has the world's largest collection of great Spanish paintings.
(C) It is the Prado museum in Madrid that has the largest collection of the world's great Spanish paintings.
(D) The greatest collection of Spanish paintings in the world is held by the Prado museum in Madrid.
(E) In Madrid, it is the Prado museum that holds the world's largest collection of great Spanish paintings.

31. The whooping crane population has increased from only fifteen to about two hundred, <u>which is one of conservation's most encouraging stories</u>.

   (A) which is one of conservation's most encouraging stories
   (B) which is one of the most encouraging stories in conservation
   (C) and this is one of conservation's most encouraging stories
   (D) and this growth is one of conservation's most encouraging stories
   (E) and that appears to be encouraging to conservationists.

32. <u>The caribou herds, for centuries, have supported the Gwich'in Indians</u> which migrate to feed in their summer range beside the Beaufort Sea.

   (A) The caribou herds, for centuries, have supported the Gwich'in Indians
   (B) For centuries, the caribou herds have supported the Gwich'in Indians
   (C) For centuries, the Gwich'in Indians have been supported by the caribou herds
   (D) The Gwich'in Indians have been supported by the caribou herds for centuries
   (E) The caribou herds which have for centuries supported the Gwich'in Indians

33. George Eliot did not begin to write fiction until she was nearly <u>forty, this</u> late start accounts for the maturity of even her earliest works.

   (A) forty, this
   (B) forty this
   (C) forty, and this
   (D) forty, a
   (E) forty, such a

34. The strike cannot be settled until the growers agree to improve
health-care benefits <u>and improving the workers' housing</u>.

    (A) and improving the workers' housing
    (B) and improving worker housing as well
    (C) and to improve the workers' housing
    (D) and the workers' housing
    (E) and also to the improvement of the housing of the workers

35. Using highly seasoned onions, green peppers, and celery in
almost all of their recipes, <u>Creole cooking had</u> achieved a
popularity throughout the country.

    (A) Creole cooking had
    (B) Creole cooking has
    (C) Creole cooking have
    (D) Creole cooks has
    (E) Creole cooks have

36. Exercising without proper warm-ups can be as harmful to the
body <u>as if you didn't exercise at all</u>.

    (A) as if you didn't exercise at all
    (B) as no exercise at all
    (C) than not exercising at all
    (D) than no exercise
    (E) as your not getting any exercise at all

Directions: The following passages are early drafts of student essays. Some parts of them need to be revised.

Read the selections carefully and answer the questions that follow. There will be questions about sentence structure, diction, and usage in individual sentences or parts of sentences. Other questions will deal with the whole essay or paragraphs and ask you to decide about organization, development, and appropriate language. Choose the answer that follows the requirements of standard written English and most effectively expresses the intended meanings.

Questions 37–43 are based on the following passage.

(1) The desire of excess money has been a part of almost everyone's life. (2) Money buys self-confidence. (3) It also buys comfort and convenience. (4) Regardless of whether wealth is obtained ethically or unethically, money is sought as a source of self-confidence and convenience or comfort.

(5) Economic status plays a role in self-confidence. (6) In most countries, money determines a person's status. (7) This determines the level of self-confidence. (8) People with little money and low status have little self-confidence. (9) Money can buy vacations, luxury cars, and shopping sprees. (10) In some countries the poor are made to feel worthless and not worthy of marriage to wealthy people.

(11) A comfortable life can be bought by money. (12) Everyone takes risks and chances to obtain a more convenient and more comfortable life. (13) Some will even risk their lives to obtain a more comfortable life. (14) Money can buy large, luxurious homes, with pools and tennis courts. (15) Money can buy services that do all the chores. (16) If one has enough money, you can enjoy all the comforts and conveniences of life.

37. Which of the following is probably the best version of the underlined portion of sentence 1 below?

The desire <u>of excess money</u> has been a part of almost everyone's life.

(A) (As it is now)
(B) desire for excess money
(C) desire to possess excess money
(D) desire of excessive money
(E) excessive desire for money

38. Which of the following is the best way to revise and combine sentences 2, 3, and 4 (reproduced below)?

Money buys self-confidence. It also buys comfort and convenience. Regardless of whether wealth is obtained ethically or unethically, money is sought as a source of self-confidence and convenience or comfort.

(A) Money buys self-confidence, and also comfort and convenience, because regardless of whether wealth is earned ethically or unethically, it is sought as a source of these.

(B) Money is sought as a source of self-confidence, convenience, and comfort, as it buys these regardless of how unethically it has been obtained.

(C) Regardless of its ethical background, money is sought as a source of self-confidence, comfort, and convenience.

(D) Regardless of how wealth is obtained, money buys self-confidence, comfort, and convenience.

(E) Money is sought as a source of self-confidence, convenience, and comfort, regardless of how ethically or unethically it was obtained.

39. Which of the following is the best revision and combination of sentences 5, 6, and 7 (reproduced below)?

Economic status plays a role in self-confidence. In most countries, money determines a person's status. This determines the level of self-confidence.

(A) In most countries, money determines status, and thus the level of self-confidence.
(B) In most countries, economic status plays a role in self-confidence, and this is determined by money.
(C) In self-confidence, economic status in most countries determines the level.
(D) Status is determined by money, and self-confidence is determined by status in most countries.
(E) In most countries, status and self-confidence are determined by economic status and money.

40. Which of the following sentences in the second paragraph more logically belongs in the third paragraph?

(A) sentence 6
(B) sentence 7
(C) sentence 8
(D) sentence 9
(E) sentence 10

41. Which of the following revisions would most improve the writing in sentences 11, 12, and 13 (reproduced below)?

A comfortable life can be bought by money. Everyone takes risks and chances to obtain a more convenient and more comfortable life. Some will even risk their lives to obtain a more comfortable life.

(A) Change the verb forms from passive to active voice.
(B) Combine the sentences to eliminate the repetition of "comfortable life."
(C) Eliminate the words "risks" and "even."
(D) Add the phrase "in order" before "to obtain" in 12 and 13.
(E) Make the verbs less assertive by such phrases as "might be bought" (11), "might take" (12), and "might even risk" (13).

42. Which of the following best describes the organization of this passage?

   (A) The first two paragraphs present opposing ideas that are reconciled in the third paragraph.
   (B) Each of the three paragraphs describes a different benefit that money confers.
   (C) The first two paragraphs describe advantages of wealth; the third paragraph describes disadvantages.
   (D) The first paragraph cites two ideas that are developed in the second and third paragraphs.
   (E) The first and third paragraphs are subjective, but the second paragraph is objective.

43. Which of the following is the best version of the last sentence of the passage (reproduced below)?

   If one has enough money, you can enjoy all the comforts and conveniences of life.

   (A) (As it is now)
   (B) If one has sufficient money, you can enjoy all the comforts and conveniences of life.
   (C) If you have enough money, you can enjoy all the comforts and conveniences of life.
   (D) You can enjoy all the comforts and conveniences of life if one has enough money.
   (E) Having enough money, all the comforts and conveniences of life can be enjoyed.

Questions 44–49 are based on the following passage.

(1) Should we keep an electoral system in which a candidate with the most votes can lose an election? (2) The Electoral College comes most into question when presidential elections are very close. (3) The election of 1960 between Nixon and Kennedy was a close election. (4) A few votes changed might have changed the outcome.

(5) The electoral system works as the Founding Fathers intended as a buffer against the popular vote. (6) Sixteen presidents have been elected without a majority of the popular vote. (7) However, three of these actually had fewer votes than another candidate.

(8) The root of the problem is the unit system that count all of a state's electoral votes as one bloc. (9) A candidate who won a state by ten votes might get as many electoral votes as another who won a state of the same size by five hundred thousand. (10) After the close election of 1960, the House voted overwhelmingly in favor of the direct popular election of the President. (11) A Senate filibuster killed the bill. (12) Recent polls show that the public strongly favors the direct popular presidential election, but so far Congress has taken no steps to change the system we have now.

44. Which of the following is the best way to combine sentences 2 and 3 (reproduced below)?

    The Electoral College comes most into question when presidential elections are very close. The election of 1960 between Nixon and Kennedy was a close election.

    (A) The Electoral College comes most into question when presidential elections are very close, like the close election of 1960 between Nixon and Kennedy.

    (B) The Electoral College comes most into question when presidential elections are very close like that of 1960 between Nixon and Kennedy.

    (C) The Electoral College is questioned most at times of close presidential elections like the close election of 1960 between Nixon and Kennedy.

    (D) The Electoral College is most questioned when presidential elections, such as the 1960 election between Nixon and Kennedy, are close.

    (E) When presidential elections are close, like the close 1960 Nixon-Kennedy election, the Electoral College is questioned most.

45. The function of sentence 3 in the first paragraph is to

(A) contradict a commonly held idea
(B) interject a personal opinion
(C) introduce a new idea
(D) provide an example
(E) appeal to the reader's political sympathies

46. In the first paragraph, sentence 4 should probably be revised because it

I. repeats information already clear in sentence 3
II. unnecessarily repeats the word "changed"
III. contains a grammatical error

(A) I only
(B) I and II only
(C) I and III only
(D) II and III only
(E) I, II, and III

47. Which of the following would be the best replacement for *"However"* at the beginning of sentence 7 (reproduced below)?

However, three of these actually had fewer votes than another candidate.

(A) But
(B) Nevertheless
(C) Yet
(D) Still
(E) And

48. Which of the following versions of the underlined portion of sentence 8 (reproduced below) is best?

    The root of the problem is the unit system that count all of a state's *electoral votes as one bloc.*

    (A) is the unit system that count all of the states' electoral votes as a bloc
    (B) is a unit system to count all of the state's electoral votes as a bloc
    (C) is a unit system which will count all of the states' electoral votes as a bloc
    (D) is the unit system that counts all of the state's electoral votes as a bloc
    (E) is a unit system that count as a bloc all of a state's electoral votes

49. All of the following strategies are used in the passage EXCEPT

    (A) selecting specific examples
    (B) referring to several different historical periods
    (C) pointing out a logical inconsistency
    (D) identifying the supporters of an opposing view
    (E) disproving an argument of the opposition

Directions: The following sentences may contain one error of grammar, usage, diction, or idiom. No sentence will contain more than one error, and some have no error. If there is an error, it will be underlined and have a letter beneath it. Sections of the sentence that are not underlined cannot be changed. In selecting your answer, observe the requirements of standard written English.

If there is an error, choose the one underlined part that must be changed to correct the sentence. If there is no error, choose (E).

EXAMPLE:

The film tell the story of a cavalry captain and his wife
      A   B

who try to rebuild their lives after the Civil War. No error
    C   D   E

Correct answer: A

50. By prohibiting discounting by chain stores and supermarkets,
        A   B

British book publishers left smaller private bookstores become
                      C

competitive with the larger distributors. No error
              D   E

51. In the popular imagination, Richard III is the
            A

deformed and evil king who had his two young nephews
        B   C   D

murdered in the Tower of London. No error
                     E

52. The best examples of plays that can be produced with a
          A   B

minimum of expense for settings must be Thornton Wilder's
             C   D

Our Town. No error
       E

53. The results of the survey <u>refute</u> a <u>prevailing</u> popular belief:
                                      A   B
    that <u>it is harder</u> for women <u>winning</u> elections than for men.
                    C   D
    <u>No error</u>
     E

54. When <u>we were</u> in elementary school, <u>there was</u> a competition
           A   B
    <u>between my sister and I</u> that now <u>seems</u> ridiculous. <u>No error</u>
                 C   D   E

55. <u>As early as 500</u> A.D., the Mayans <u>make</u> <u>their homes</u> safe for
      A   B   C
    children <u>by storing</u> knives in the thatched roof. <u>No error</u>
             D   E

56. Neither the pianist nor the violinist <u>know</u> the music
                                  A
    well <u>enough to play</u> <u>so difficult</u> a composition <u>accurately</u>.
          B   C   D
    <u>No error</u>
     E

57. People <u>who drink</u> four or more cups of coffee <u>a day</u> greatly
           A   B
    increase <u>their risk</u> of a heart attack, researchers in Oakland
             C
    <u>advise</u> in a new study. <u>No error</u>
     D   E

58. The identification of a murder victim <u>by genetic fingerprints</u>
                                      A
    <u>has brung</u> <u>to light</u> a crime <u>undetected for eight years</u>. <u>No error</u>
      B   C   D   E

59. In the 1840's, Dickens wrote the Christmas books "The
           A   B

    Chimes" and "The Cricket on the Hearth," but it did not
                                          C

    attain the popularity of *A Christmas Carol*. No error
                      D   E

60. Observers hoped that the terrible civil war in nearby Rwanda
                             A

    will warn the warring factions of the grim consequences of
        B   C   D

    intertribal strife. No error
                   E

ANSWER KEY FOR PRACTICE TEST 1

Identifying Sentence Errors

1. E	6. B	11. C	16. D
2. A	7. D	12. A	17. C
3. A	8. D	13. E	18. D
4. E	9. A	14. D	19. A
5. B	10. E	15. D	20. E

Improving Sentences

21. C	25. B	29. B	33. C
22. B	26. D	30. B	34. D
23. E	27. E	31. D	35. E
24. A	28. E	32. C	36. B

Improving Paragraphs

37. E	42. D	46. B
38. D	43. C	47. E
39. A	44. B	48. D
40. D	45. D	49. E
41. B		

Identifying Sentence Errors

50. C	54. C	58. B
51. E	55. B	59. C
52. A	56. A	60. B
53. D	57. E	

PRACTICE TEST 1 SCORING WORKSHEET

You can use the following worksheet to determine your scores. You will need two readers to score your essay. If they are not available, be objective and double the score you decide on yourself.

Part A: Essay

_____ + _____ = _____

first reader's score   second reader's score   essay raw score

Approximate essay scaled score (use the table on page 147) = _____

Part B: Multiple-Choice

_____ – _____ = _____

correct answers   wrong answers × .25   multiple-choice raw
                                          score

Approximate multiple-choice scaled score (use the table on page 30) = _____

Composite Score

_____ + _____ = _____

essay raw score times 3   multiple-choice   composite
(or 3.02 for scores of 10–12)   raw score   raw score

Approximate composite scaled score (use the table on page 147) = _____

ANSWERS AND EXPLANATIONS FOR PRACTICE TEST 1

PART B

1. (E) There are no errors in this sentence. Remember that there are likely to be four or five sentences without errors in each set of twenty questions. Here, the *as* (not *like*) is correct; the pronoun *it* refers to *heat*.

2. (A) The verb *re-creates* should be *re-created,* a past tense. The past tense is necessary to be consistent with the verb *became.*

3. (A) The subject *stories* is a plural. To agree, the verb should be the plural *address.*

4. (E) There are no errors in this sentence. Don't assume that two sentences with no errors will not occur near one another.

5. (B) The error here is the double negative: *do not mask . . . no.*

6. (B) This is another agreement error, the plural *there are* and the singular *interest.*

7. (D) Use either *most wealthy* or *wealthiest* but not both to express the superlative.

8. (D) The problem is in the phrase *process to age,* a use of the infinitive when the correct idiom is *of aging.*

9. (A) This is a pronoun error. The relative pronouns *who, whom,* and *whoever* are used to refer to humans, while relative pronouns like *that, which,* or *what* refer to the nonhuman, such as bees.

10. (E) There are no errors in this sentence.

211

11. (C) The sentence compares the cost of vegetables with the cost of a market. To make sense, it should read something like *cost much more than those grown with pesticides* or *cost much more than vegetables grown with pesticides.* In sentences with comparisons, look carefully at exactly what two things are compared; be sure the comparison is a logical one.

12. (A) This is an error of diction, or choice of word. The writer has confused *to sit* (an intransitive verb) and *to set* (a verb that takes an object).

13. (E) There are no errors in this sentence. The *it* refers to *glaucoma,* and *pressure* is the subject of the verb *damages.*

14. (D) The error is the use of the preposition *for;* the correct phrase is *in only two forms.*

15. (D) The correct idiom is *as easily as that of.* The *than* would be used in a phrase like *more easily than.*

16. (D) The singular *story* should be the plural *stories.* It is the object of the plural *storytellers . . . create.*

17. (C) The error is the use of the adjective where an adverb is needed; to modify the adjective *tasty,* the adjective *particular* should be replaced by the adverb *particularly.*

18. (D) This is also an agreement error. The subject is the singular *scientist.* The plural *they are studying* at the end of the sentence does not agree. The sentence can be corrected by changing the phrase *they are studying* to something like *being studied.*

19. (A) The correct preposition idiom here is *Based on* or *Based upon.*

20. (E) There is no error in this sentence.

21. (C) When, like this one, a sentence begins with a participle, be on the alert for a dangling participle. Here, it is the artist, Crespo, not the carvings, who uses the three traditions. Choices (C), (D), and (E) avoid the dangling modifier, but (E) has no main verb, and (D) is wordier than (C) and changes *re-creates* to *creates.*

22. (B) The error in the original sentence is the comma splice— joining the two independent clauses (or complete sentences) with just a comma. Correct the error by using a period, a comma with a conjunction, or, as here, a semicolon. Though (C) and (D) use semicolons, they no longer have independent second clauses, while (E), which has made the second clause dependent, omits the comma.

23. (E) The first half of the sentence uses a verb in the active voice, but the second half uses the passive. Choice (B) does not change this error; it just moves the same verb to a different part of the sentence. (D) makes no sense, since it follows *into the war,* and (C) is no better, since it makes the child-care centers a consequence of her eye-witness reporting. Though (E) might have left out *she helped,* it is in the active voice and the only good choice.

24. (A) The issues here are parallelism and verbosity. The auxiliary verb *has* need not be repeated or should be repeated three times to keep all four parts of the series parallel. (E) is not wrong, but since (A) is also correct and shorter, (A) is the better choice.

25. (B) As it stands, this is a sentence fragment, with a participle (*knowing*) but no main verb. (B) and (C) supply a missing verb, but with the phrase *By the early eleventh century,* the past tense (B) makes more sense. (D) and (E) are just participles in a different tense.

26. (D) The two parts of the original sentence lack proper coordination. The two parts present a difference, which only the conjunction *but* makes clear. What the sentence is saying is *x* was true in the past *but* is so no longer.

27. (E) The vague *they* is the problem here. They who? (D) and (E) replace the inexact pronoun with a specific noun. There is no important difference between *many* and *multiple,* but (E) uses *apparently* correctly.

28. (E) The sentence is a fused, or run-on, sentence, joining two independent clauses with no punctuation or conjunctions. (B) and (C) add conjunctions but fail to add the needed commas. (D) adds a semicolon but makes the second clause dependent. Only (E) avoids a punctuation error.

29. (B) Choice (B) replaces the subordinated participial phrase with two verbs coordinated by *and.* (E) is correct, with an independent clause following the comma, but it is more wordy than (B).

30. (B) Although the original version is not ungrammatical, (B) is less wordy, replacing *in the whole world* with the more economical *the world's.* (C) and (E) add the unnecessary *it is,* while (D) uses the passive voice, always more wordy than the active.

31. (D) If it is possible, a pronoun should have a specific antecedent. In this sentence, choice (D) provides a noun as subject of the clause to replace the pronouns *which, this,* and *that.* Changing the pronoun from *which* to *this* or *that* does nothing to correct the ambiguity of the pronoun.

32. (C) Keep related words and phrases as close together as possible. The trouble with this sentence is a misplaced modifier; the clause about migrating to a summer range modifies the caribou, not the Indians. The best version will place *caribou herds* as close to the *which* as possible. Although (D) uses the passive voice, it is the only version that avoids the misplaced modifier. (E) has no main verb.

33. (C) Like the second question in this group, this is a comma splice. It can be corrected by changing the comma to a semicolon or by adding a conjunction like *and* in (C).

34. (D) The phrases *to improve health care* and *improving . . . housing* are repetitive and not parallel. (C) corrects the parallelism error but not the repetition. (E) is wordy. (D) is brief and grammatical.

35. (E) The participle *using* should modify a plural noun, since the phrase also refers to *their recipes*. Since *cooks* is plural, the plural verb *have* is the correct choice.

36. (B) The idiom to use with the construction *as-adjective-. . .* is *as-adjective-as*. (B) is better than (A) because it is shorter and does not change from a third person to a second person subject (*Exercising* to *you*).

37. (E) The phrase as it is written is unidiomatic and unclear. Does the writer mean an excessive desire for or a desire for an excessive amount of money? Of the choices, only (E) is possible. It eliminates the diction error (*excess money*) and uses the idiomatically correct preposition, *for*.

38. (D) A concise revision will eliminate the repetition of the verb (*buys*) and the subject (*money*). Getting rid of the passive *is sought* and the awkward phrase *obtained ethically or unethically* will also improve the passage. (A) combines the redundant verbs and subject but adds the ambiguous pronoun *these*. (B) has a passive construction and alters the meaning. The problem in (C) is the phrase *its ethical background,* as well as the passive voice. (E) is better than (A), (B), or (C), but the diction weakness remains in the phrase *ethically or unethically*. (D) is the best version of a badly written passage.

39. (A) In (B), the antecedent of *this* is unclear. Is it *confidence* or *status*? In (C), the opening prepositional phrase (*In self-confidence*) garbles the intended meaning of the sentence. (D) and (E) are not wrong, but both repeat words (*status*). (A) avoids the passive and the repetitions.

40. (D) The third paragraph is about what money can buy, and like sentence 9, sentences 14 and 15 begin with the phrase *Money can buy*.

41. (B) Choices (D) and (E) would simply make the sentences even more wordy. The change in (A) would affect only one verb. The word *risks* could go, but *even* has a specific purpose. The best choice is (B), eliminating the repetition of *comfortable life*, which is repeated three times.

42. (D) Only (D) accurately describes this passage.

43. (C) This sentence must be revised to make the pronoun subjects of both clauses the same. Either *you . . . you* or *one . . . one* will correct the error. (E) has a different error, the dangling participle *Having*.

44. (B) When combining sentences, try to avoid using the same word more than once. Here, only (B) avoids the repetition of *election*.

45. (D) The second sentence refers to close elections; the third sentence gives an example.

46. (B) There is no grammatical error in the sentence, but it does repeat information already made clear and could do without the first *changed*.

47. (E) The sentence does not contradict the sentence that precedes it as the use of *However* suggests. It gives an additional example of candidates who have lost elections with more popular votes. The only conjunction choice that denotes *also* here is *And*.

48. (D) The problem here is not the difference between *that* and *which,* but the agreement of the plural verb *count* and the singular subject *system.* Only (D) has the correct singular *counts.*

49. (E) The passage does not present any opposition argument to disprove. It does select specific examples (sentence 3), refer to different periods (sentences 3, 6, and 10), point out a logical inconsistency (sentences 7, 9), and identify supporters of an opposing view (sentences 5, 11).

50. (C) Like 12, this is a diction error, confusing *left* and *let.*

51. (E) There are no errors in this sentence.

52. (A) The sentence concludes with a reference to a single play. To make sense of the sentence, the singular (*example*) should replace the plural.

53. (D) The error here is just the reverse of the error in question 8. There, the correct idiom is a gerund (a verbal noun ending in *ing*), not an infinitive (a verb introduced by *to*). Here, the infinitive *to win* should replace the gerund *winning.*

54. (C) The personal pronoun is the object of the preposition *between,* so the phrase should be *between my sister and me.* It is easy to see case errors like this when the pronoun immediately follows the preposition (*to me, like him, without her*), but it is harder when another object intercedes (*to David and me, like Martha and him. with Iris and her*).

55. (B) The opening phrase in this sentence refers to the distant past. This information should determine the tense of the main verb: the past tense *made,* not the present tense *make.*

56. (A) With *neither . . . nor* and two singular subjects like these, the verb should be singular. The correct verb here is *knows.*

57. (E) There are no errors in this sentence.

58. (B) The correct form of the past participle of the verb *to bring* is *brought.*

59. (C) There are two possible antecedents to the singular *it, "The Chimes"* and *"The Cricket on the Hearth."*

60. (B) The verb form here should be *would warn,* not the future *will.*

PRACTICE TEST 2

| PART A | Time—20 Minutes 1 Question | ESSAY |

In twenty minutes, write an essay on the topic below. YOU MAY NOT WRITE ON ANOTHER TOPIC. AN ESSAY ON ANOTHER TOPIC WILL NOT BE SCORED.

The essay is intended to give you the chance to show your writing skills. Be sure to express your ideas on the topic clearly and effectively. The quality of your writing is much more important than the quantity, but to deal adequately with this topic you should probably write more than one paragraph. Be specific.

Think carefully about the following quotation and the assignment that follows. Then plan and write your essay according to the instructions.

"The two genres of American film that are usually branded as mindless entertainment—the Western and the horror film—can be vehicles for serious moral statements."

Choose either the Western or the horror film and write a well-supported essay in which you support or refute this statement.

WHEN THE TWENTY MINUTES HAVE PASSED, YOU MUST STOP WRITING AND GO ON TO THE MULTIPLE-CHOICE SECTION OF THE TEST. IF YOU FINISH YOUR ESSAY BEFORE THE TWENTY MINUTES HAVE PASSED, YOU MAY GO ON TO THE NEXT SECTION OF THE EXAM.

Directions: The following sentences may contain one error of grammar, usage, diction, or idiom. No sentence will contain more than one error, and some have no error. If there is an error, it will be underlined and have a letter beneath it. Sections of the sentence that are not underlined cannot be changed. In selecting your answer, observe the requirements of standard written English.

If there is an error, choose the one underlined part that must be changed to correct the sentence. If there is no error, choose (E).

EXAMPLE:

The film tell the story of a cavalry captain and his wife
       A   B

who try to rebuild their lives after the Civil War. No error
    C   D   E

Correct answer: A

1. The owners hired my husband and I to manage the inn
                  A   B

because we had more experience than the other applicants.
       C   D

No error
 E

2. Pistachios imported from Asia cost more than the orchards of
            A   B   C

California, but they are larger and have more flavor. No error
        D   E

3. <u>There are</u> in the House and Senate general agreement
    A

<u>about the farm bill</u>, but <u>they are</u> far <u>from agreeing about</u> the
    B   C   D

budget. <u>No error</u>
        E

4. Early tomorrow morning, <u>weather permitting</u>, he <u>departed on</u>
                         A   B

an <u>around-the-state run</u> to <u>raise money</u> for the disabled.
        C   D

<u>No error</u>
  E

5. When they <u>had completed</u> the layout of the <u>paper's front page</u>,
         A   B

the editors <u>considered the problems</u> of the <u>sports page</u>.
             C   D

<u>No error</u>
  E

6. The volleyball players <u>which arrived</u> for the team picture
                 A

<u>in the uniforms</u> that they <u>had worn to practice</u> were
    B   C

<u>irritable and tired.</u> <u>No error</u>
    D   E

7. The soil conditions <u>beneath structures</u> may cause <u>more worse</u>
            A   B

damage <u>in an earthquake</u> than the temblor <u>itself</u>. <u>No error</u>
        C   D   E

8. The debate <u>appeared to be stalemated</u>, since <u>there was no</u>
   A   B
   possibility of the conservatives' <u>conceding with</u> their
   C
   opponents' <u>argument.</u> <u>No error</u>
   D   E

9. The region is <u>so dry</u> that <u>there are</u> <u>hardly any</u> animals and
   A   B   C
   <u>scarcely no</u> plant life in the dunes. <u>No error</u>
   D   E

10. Either <u>the U.S. bombing</u> or the subsequent Iraqui attempt
    A
    <u>to quell</u> the Shiite uprising <u>are responsible for</u> the
    B   C
    <u>damage to the shrines.</u> <u>No error</u>
    D   E

11. Japanese defense policy <u>was changed completely</u> when the
    A
    Socialist Party <u>scrapped</u> <u>its age-old</u> insistence <u>to dismantle</u> the
    B   C   D
    armed forces. <u>No error</u>
    E

12. The election of a <u>separatist-dominated</u> Parliament
    A
    <u>has alarmed</u> those <u>who will believe</u> Quebec <u>must not secede</u>
    B   C   D
    from Canada. <u>No error</u>
    E

13. The engineers <u>have designed</u> an offshore drilling platform
                    A
    <u>strong enough</u> <u>to withstand not only</u> Atlantic storms
         B   C
    <u>but also the occasional iceberg.</u> <u>No error</u>
                  D   E

14. In Britain, <u>a nationwide</u> business <u>in buying and selling</u> special
                      A   B
    license plates <u>have developed</u>, and <u>prices rise</u> each year.
                        C   D
    <u>No error</u>
         E

15. If <u>we plan carefully</u> and waste no time <u>on irrelevant topics</u>, you
              A   B
    should <u>be able</u> to <u>finish the essay</u> in twenty minutes. <u>No error</u>
              C   D   E

16. Desperately <u>trying to lead</u> the cat away from the nest, the bird
                    A   B
    <u>had flew</u> within inches of <u>its</u> claws. <u>No error</u>
         C   D   E

17. The citizens of Berlin <u>bid</u> a <u>fondly good-bye</u> to the American
                              A   B
    troops <u>who had occupied</u> much of the city <u>since the war ended.</u>
                  C   D
    <u>No error</u>
         E

18. When the new ambassador <u>first arrived</u> <u>in the capital,</u> though
                                  A   B
    <u>late in May,</u> <u>they found</u> that the larger lakes were still frozen.
         C   D
    <u>No error</u>
         E

19. Encouraged by the success of its weekly Spanish-language
        A   B

    programs, MTV will launch a twenty-four hour Spanish-
                       C   D

    language cable network. No error
                              E

20. Disguised as farmers from the nearby countryside, the archers
         A   B

    snuck into the city unobserved on market day. No error
      C   D   E

Directions: The following questions test correctness and effective expression. In selecting the answer, pay attention to grammar, diction, sentence structure, and punctuation.

In the following questions, part or all of each sentence is underlined. The (A) answer repeats the underlined portion of the original sentence, while the next four offer alternatives. Choose the answer that best expresses the meaning of the original sentence and at the same time is grammatically correct and stylistically superior. The correct choice should be clear, unambiguous, and concise.

EXAMPLE:

The forecaster predicted rain and the sky was clear.

(A) rain and the sky was clear
(B) rain but the sky was clear
(C) rain the sky was clear
(D) rain, but the sky was clear
(E) rain being as the sky was clear

Correct answer: D

21. Some players have no trouble seeing the weaknesses in other people's game and they are quite unable to see faults of their own.

   (A) in other people's game and they
   (B) in other games and they
   (C) in other players' games, and they
   (D) in other people's game, but they
   (E) in other games, but they

22. The Socialist Party is now powerful enough to worry the governing Christian Democrats, <u>and they may win</u> fifty seats in the next election.

   (A) and they may win
   (B) and they might win
   (C) and the Socialists may win
   (D) and the party may win
   (E) winning

23. The Medical Board is supposed to protect consumers from <u>incompetent, grossly negligent, unlicensed, and unethical practitioners.</u>

   (A) incompetent, grossly negligent, unlicensed, and unethical practitioners
   (B) incompetent, grossly negligent practitioners who are unlicensed or unethical
   (C) the incompetent and grossly negligent who practice without ethics or a license
   (D) incompetent practitioners, gross and negligent, unlicensed and unethical
   (E) those practitioners who are incompetent, grossly negligent, unlicensed, and unethical

24. The wall is a continually evolving work of <u>art, it is a</u> forum for messages against violence, war, and cruelty.

   (A) art, it is a
   (B) art; it is a
   (C) art, in that it is a
   (D) art it is a
   (E) art a

25. Before 1984, Australia had a strong tradition of private <u>medical care, but even conservatives now accepting</u> the national health care plan.

    (A) medical care, but even conservatives now accepting
    (B) medical care; but even conservatives now accepting
    (C) medical care, but now with even conservatives accepting
    (D) medical care, conservatives now accepting
    (E) medical care, but now even conservatives accept

26. In the play, <u>great care is given to present the workers' oppression, and the author is uninterested</u> in the psychology of his characters.

    (A) great care is given to present the workers' oppression, and the author is uninterested
    (B) great care is given to present the workers' oppression, but the author is uninterested
    (C) great care is given to the presentation of the workers' oppression, but the author is uninterested
    (D) the author takes great care to present the workers' oppression but is uninterested
    (E) the author is very careful to present the workers' oppression, and he is uninterested

27. Twenty-five thousand troops went to Somalia, and <u>they failed to disarm the warring clans and failed</u> to create a secure environment.

    (A) Twenty-five thousand troops went to Somalia, and they failed to disarm the warring clans and failed
    (B) Twenty-five thousand troops went to Somalia, but they failed to disarm the warring clans and so they failed
    (C) Twenty-five thousand troops went to Somalia, but they failed to disarm the warring clans and
    (D) Twenty-five thousand troops went to Somalia, failing to disarm the warring clans and failing
    (E) There were twenty-five thousand troops who went to Somalia, and they failed to disarm the warring clans, also failing

28. Scott saw that novels had ceased to paint idealized figures of
    romance, reviewing Jane Austen's *Emma,* and would hence-
    forth copy real life.

    (A) Scott saw that novels had ceased to paint idealized figures
        of romance, reviewing Jane Austen's *Emma,* and would
        henceforth copy real life.
    (B) Scott saw that novels had ceased to paint idealized figures
        of romance and would henceforth copy real life, reviewing
        Jane Austen's *Emma.*
    (C) Scott saw that by copying real life novels had ceased to
        paint idealized figures of romance, reviewing Jane Aus-
        ten's *Emma.*
    (D) Reviewing Jane Austen's *Emma,* Scott saw that novels had
        ceased to paint idealized figures of romance and would
        henceforth copy real life.
    (E) Reviewing Jane Austen's *Emma,* that the novel had ceased
        to paint idealized figures of romance and would hence-
        forth copy real life was seen by Scott.

29. The California condor is just one of many highly endangered
    birds others include several species of sparrow.

    (A) birds others
    (B) birds; others
    (C) birds, others
    (D) birds and other endangered birds
    (E) birds and there are others that

30. Many small seed companies were privately owned, but they have been taken over by chemical giants and they depend on large pesticide sales.

   (A) Many small seed companies were privately owned, but they have been taken over by chemical giants and they depend on large pesticide sales.
   (B) Many small seed companies were privately owned, have been taken over by chemical giants, and they depend on large pesticide sales.
   (C) Many small seed companies are privately owned, and they have been taken over by chemical giants that depend on large pesticide sales.
   (D) Many small privately owned seed companies depending on large sales of pesticides have been taken over by chemical giants.
   (E) Chemical giants that depend on large pesticide sales have taken over many small privately owned seed companies.

31. Drawing on resources that include unpublished letters and manuscripts, Anne Atkinson has written a thorough and original biography of Emily Dickinson.

   (A) Drawing on resources that include unpublished letters and manuscripts
   (B) Drawn on resources that include unpublished letters and manuscripts
   (C) She has drawn on resources that include unpublished letters and manuscripts, and so
   (D) Unpublished letters and manuscripts are the resources used, and
   (E) Drawing on unpublished letters and manuscripts as her resources

32. The rites of how an adolescent female is initiated becoming a member of adult society have never been photographed.

    (A) of how an adolescent female is initiated becoming
    (B) initiating an adolescent female so that she becomes
    (C) of the adolescent female's initiation becoming
    (D) which initiate an adolescent female and she becomes
    (E) by which the adolescent female is initiated and becomes

33. Bankrite Company sells a New York tax-free mutual fund, and you can also buy them at Winston Brokerage.

    (A) and you can also buy them at Winston Brokerage
    (B) and Winston Brokerage also sells them
    (C) and they also can be bought at Winston Brokerage
    (D) as does Winston Brokerage
    (E) and they are also available at Winston Brokerage

34. The banking system is stronger now than it has been in many years, which may encourage bankers to reduce their reserves.

    (A) years, which may encourage bankers
    (B) years, and this may encourage bankers
    (C) years, a condition that may encourage bankers
    (D) years, and because of this, bankers may be encouraged
    (E) years; this may encourage bankers

35. This summer, Las Vegas will see a record number of visitors, and a very high percentage of them will be children.

    (A) and a very high percentage of them will be children
    (B) being children in a very high percentage
    (C) and children will be among them in a very high percentage
    (D) among whom a very high percentage of them will be children
    (E) and among them will be children in a very high percentage

36. <u>Nature has provided so that nearly every plant-eating insect has</u> <u>a natural enemy, but</u> most insecticides kill both.

   (A) Nature has provided so that nearly every plant-eating insect has a natural enemy, but
   (B) Nature has seen to it that nearly every plant-eating insect has a natural enemy, and
   (C) Nature provides that nearly every plant-eating insect has a natural enemy, but
   (D) Nearly every plant-eating insect has a natural enemy, but
   (E) Natural enemies of nearly every plant-eating insect have been provided by nature, but

37. By mid-October, black oaks, dogwood, and big-leaf <u>maples</u> <u>which form splashes</u> of yellow, red, and orange.

   (A) maples which form splashes
   (B) maples form splashes
   (C) maples which are forming splashes
   (D) maples forming splashes
   (E) maples that form splashes

38. Throughout the entire work, <u>Huxley is constantly repeating</u> that we have become the slaves of machines.

   (A) Throughout the entire work, Huxley is constantly repeating
   (B) Throughout the entire work, Huxley states repeatedly
   (C) Constantly throughout the entire work, Huxley states
   (D) Throughout, Huxley repeatedly states
   (E) Huxley states

Directions: The following passages are early drafts of student essays. Some parts of them need to be revised.

Read the selections carefully and answer the questions that follow. There will be questions about sentence structure, diction, and usage in individual sentences or parts of sentences. Other questions will deal with the whole essay or paragraphs and ask you to decide about organization, development, and appropriate language. Choose the answer that follows the requirements of standard written English and most effectively expresses the intended meanings.

Questions 39–44 are based on the following passage.

(1) Separation is to pass from one stage of life as we prepare for another stage of life. (2) It is a process that occurs in life all throughout one's development. (3) The process of separation is a large part of the rebellious stage of adolescence. (4) The adolescent struggles with establishing his own identity and to separate from his parents by rejecting parental rules and expectations. (5) The rejection and struggles are parts of this separation process. (6) Unusual clothing, hair-styles and color are frequently the first signs to appear indicating a separation process is taking place. (7) They are an outward display declaring their independence and separation.

(8) A mature adult experiences separation in many areas of life. (9) For example, separation from a job, career, marriage, community, and also by death from a parent or loved one are inescapable events. (10) A separation from a job may be devastating if it is unplanned or a decision made by another. (11) Even a planned job or career change brings on a certain amount of anxiety, especially if the change requires a relocation. (12) Many adults become depressed and have difficulty dealing with separation. (13) A career change is not well planned if it occurs at the same time as other separations like divorce or the death of a parent.

(14) The death of a parent, spouse or loved one brings us to a more terrifying separation anxiety. (15) The healing process is longer and anxiety is high. (16) It awakens our rational and irrational emotions. (17) I can clearly remember being angry when my father died. (18) I

was angry at him for leaving, yet I know he did not choose his time of death. (19) It was a totally irrational feeling, yet it was very real. (20) Fortunately, as we develop our courage to handle separation also grows. (21) Separation never becomes mundane; it always remains a challenge.

39. Which of the following is the best revision of the underlined portion of sentences 1 and 2 (reproduced below)?

    Separation is to pass from one stage of life as we prepare for another stage of life. It is a process that occurs in life all throughout one's development.

    (A) is to pass from one stage of life as we prepare for another stage, and it is a process that occurs in life throughout one's development
    (B) is passing from one stage of life in a process that occurs all throughout one's development
    (C) is to pass from one stage in the process of life's development as we prepare for another stage
    (D) occurs when we pass from one stage in preparation for another stage of life's development
    (E) is a life-long process of passing from one stage of development to another

40. Which of the following is the best version of the underlined portion of sentence 4 (reproduced below)?

    The adolescent struggles with establishing his own identity and to separate from his parents by rejecting parental rules and expectations.

    (A) (As it is now)
    (B) with establishing their own identity and separating themselves from parents by rejecting parental
    (C) with establishing identity and separating themselves from parents by rejecting parental
    (D) to establish his own identity and to separate from his parents by rejecting their
    (E) to establish their own identity and to separate from their parents by rejecting parental

41. Unlike the first paragraph, the second paragraph deals with separations

    (A) that are literal rather than figurative
    (B) that can occur only to adults
    (C) that may involve unhappiness
    (D) that mark a passage from one stage of life to another
    (E) that are exclusively male

42. Which of the following sentences could be deleted with the least disturbance to the sense of the passage?

    (A) sentence 8
    (B) sentence 9
    (C) sentence 10
    (D) sentence 12
    (E) sentence 13

43. Which of the following changes would make sentence 20 clearer?

    (A) Combine sentence 20 with sentence 19.
    (B) Combine sentence 20 with sentence 21.
    (C) Delete the comma after "Fortunately."
    (D) Add a comma after "develop."
    (E) Change "to handle" to "in handling."

44. In the passage, the writer uses all of the following EXCEPT

    (A) generalization
    (B) definition of a term
    (C) extended simile
    (D) reference to personal experience
    (E) self-analysis

Questions 45–50 are based on the following passage.

(1) Almost every week I am guilty of procrastination. (2) The dictionary definition of "procrastination" is "habitually putting off doing something that should be done." (3) For me, the act of procrastinating is a series of excuses for avoiding assigned tasks. (4) I can't say exactly why I go through the agony of waiting till the very last moment of all to begin my chore. (5) But though I always ask "Why do you wait so long?" I keep putting things off to the last minute.

(6) The reasons for procrastinating vary and I am not always sure which category of reasons the enterprise falls into. (7) The easiest reason of all to recognize is that of simply trying to avoid an unpleasant chore. (8) It is not surprising that I would want to put off doing something that would cause emotional distress. (9) Another reason for procrastinating is facing a task that seems insurmountable. (10) "It's too much," I tell myself. (11) Sometimes it is the unfamiliarity that causes this behavior. (12) After all the fear of the unknown requires taking a risk. (13) Taking a risk requires the possibility of failure—could that be the real reason for procrastinating?

(14) Whatever the reasons, the result is the same: a sleepless night filled with guilt and anxiety. (15) Guilt and its by-product anxiety become the major components of the effects of procrastination. (16) I know that I can avoid all the psychological imbalances associated with procrastination. (17) Logically, I can take out my planning calendar and schedule my time to accommodate any task, any chores, or any assignment. (18) And once again procrastination overpowers logic and the last minute rush begins.

45. Which of the following is the best version of sentence 6 (reproduced below)?

   The reasons for procrastinating vary and I am not always sure which category of reasons the enterprise falls into.

   (A) (As it is now)
   (B) The reasons for procrastination vary, and into which category of reasons the enterprise falls is not always sure.
   (C) The reasons for procrastinating are varied and which category fits the enterprise is uncertain.
   (D) The reasons vary, and I am not always sure why I procrastinate.
   (E) The categories of reasons for procrastination vary, and which one fits an enterprise is not always sure.

46. Sentence 7 (reproduced below) could be made more concise by deleting all of the following words EXCEPT

   The easiest reason of all to recognize is that of simply trying to avoid an unpleasant chore.

   (A) reason
   (B) of all
   (C) that of
   (D) simply
   (E) to avoid

47. Which of the following best describes the writer's intention in the second paragraph?

   (A) to suggest reasons to explain behavior
   (B) to summarize evidence of irrational behavior
   (C) to give specific details
   (D) to point a moral conclusion
   (E) to evaluate evidence of irrational behavior

48. Which of the following sentences could be eliminated from the third paragraph without seriously affecting its meaning or coherence?

    (A) sentence 14
    (B) sentence 15
    (C) sentence 16
    (D) sentence 17
    (E) sentence 18

49. Which of the following is the best choice of word to begin the final sentence (18, reproduced below)?

    And once again procrastination overpowers logic and the last minute rush begins.

    (A) (As it is now)
    (B) So
    (C) But
    (D) Perhaps
    (E) Thus

50. Which of the following best describes this passage?

    (A) an analytical essay
    (B) a personal essay
    (C) a logical argument
    (D) a biographical sketch
    (E) a fable

Directions: The following sentences may contain one error of grammar, usage, diction, or idiom. No sentence will contain more than one error, and some have no error. If there is an error, it will be underlined and have a letter beneath it. Sections of the sentence that are not underlined cannot be changed. In selecting your answer, observe the requirements of standard written English.

If there is an error, choose the one underlined part that must be changed to correct the sentence. If there is no error, choose (E).

EXAMPLE:

The film <u>tell the story</u> of a cavalry captain and <u>his wife</u>
        A   B

who <u>try to</u> <u>rebuild their lives</u> after the Civil War. <u>No error</u>
     C   D   E

Correct answer: A

51. The Federal Communications Commission <u>adopted</u> an
                                              A

    installment plan <u>for broadcasting license payments,</u> <u>allowing</u>
                             B   C

    minorities and women <u>to increase their ownership.</u> <u>No error</u>
                                D   E

52. <u>Like</u> the <u>more famous</u> French opera *Carmen, The Wildcat* <u>is a</u>
    A   B   C

    Spanish opera <u>in a tragic love triangle.</u> <u>No error</u>
                      D   E

53. Johnson is the <u>more valuable player</u> on the football team
                         A

    because he is <u>more agile,</u> <u>more durable,</u> and <u>more thoughtful</u>
                  B   C   D

    than anyone else. <u>No error</u>
               E

54. Now living in New York City, novelist James Carr has written
          A   B
    that he is reluctant in admitting his dislike of urban life.
          C   D
    No error
    E

55. In 1912, Roosevelt became dissatisfied with Taft, and,
                             A
    as a candidate of a third party, runs in opposition to Taft and
          B   C   D
    Wilson. No error
            E

56. One archeologist believes that copper and tin were brought
                     A   B
    west for the express purpose of manufacturing bronze tools.
             C   D
    No error
    E

57. Known most widely for his failure to persuade the Senate
          A   B
    to join the League of Nations,
    C
    Wilson's first term was characterized by success. No error
                         D   E

58. There are, though not yet isolated, some disease-carrying
                 A   B
    organism in the water supply that may have caused the
    C   D
    outbreak. No error
             E

59. Using the cover of a dense fog, the frogmen have stole under
         A   B

    the ship and have planted the explosives. No error
                  C   D   E

60. The philosophers of the 1980s did not restore Albert Camus'
                        A   B

    reputation, and at least they read his works with care. No error
             C   D   E

ANSWER KEY FOR PRACTICE TEST 2

Identifying Sentence Errors

1. A	6. A	11. D	16. C
2. C	7. B	12. C	17. B
3. A	8. C	13. E	18. D
4. B	9. D	14. C	19. E
5. E	10. C	15. A	20. C

Improving Sentences

21. D	26. D	31. A	36. D
22. C	27. C	32. E	37. B
23. A	28. D	33. D	38. D
24. B	29. B	34. C	
25. E	30. E	35. A	

Improving Paragraphs

39. E	43. D	47. A
40. D	44. C	48. B
41. A	45. D	49. C
42. D	46. E	50. B

Identifying Sentence Errors

51. E	56. E
52. D	57. D
53. A	58. C
54. D	59. B
55. C	60. C

PRACTICE TEST 2 SCORING WORKSHEET

You can use the following worksheet to determine your scores. You will need two readers to score your essay. If they are not available, be objective and double the score you decide on yourself.

Part A: Essay

_____ + _____ = _____
first reader's score   second reader's score   essay raw score

Approximate essay scaled score (use the table on page 147) = _____

Part B: Multiple-Choice

_____ – _____ = _____
correct answers   wrong answers × .25   multiple-choice raw
                                          score

Approximate multiple-choice scaled score (use the table on page 30) = _____

Composite Score

_____ + _____ = _____
  essay raw score times 3   multiple-choice   composite
(or 3.02 for scores of 10–12)   raw score   raw score

Approximate composite scaled score (use the table on page 147) = _____

ANSWERS AND EXPLANATIONS FOR PRACTICE TEST 2

PART B

1. (A) There is an error in the case of the pronoun *I*. It is the object of the verb *hired* and should be *me*. *The owners hired I* would be easy to spot as an error. Don't let words between related parts of a sentence distract you.

2. (C) As it stands, two unlike objects are compared. The sentence says *pistachios* cost more than *orchards;* what it intended to say was *imported* pistachios cost more than *California* pistachios.

3. (A) The verb *are* (a plural) does not agree with the singular *agreement*. Again, the error would be easy to see if the two words were together. The plural *they* is correct, as it refers to *House* and *Senate*.

4. (B) The verb tense is wrong here. The use of *tomorrow* tells us the action is to take place in the future, but *departed* is a past tense. It should be *will depart*.

5. (E) The sentence has no errors. The verb tense sequence using the past perfect *had completed* followed by the past *considered* is correct.

6. (A) The pronoun *who* should replace the pronoun *which*. To refer to persons, use *who;* to refer to things or animals, use *which*.

7. (B) The comparative here repeats itself, since *worse* already means *more bad*. You could say something like *more harmful* or *worse* but not *more worse*.

8. (C) The choice of preposition here is not idiomatic. We say *concede to,* not *with*.

9. (D) The error is a double negative. The *hardly any* avoids the error, but *scarcely no* has two negatives. A sentence testing this error will probably use either *hardly* or *scarcely* as one of the negatives. A *not* and a *no* (*I don't have no money*) is too easy.

10. (C) This is an agreement error, common in constructions using *either/or*. Here, the subject of the plural verb *are* is the singular *attempt* or the singular *bombing*. It can't be both, since the point of the sentence is that one or the other is responsible.

11. (D) An often-tested idiom error is the interchange of an infinitive (*to dismantle*) and a prepositional phrase (*on dismantling*). Here, the noun *insistence* requires the prepositional phrase. If, however, the sentence had read *refusal* instead of *insistence,* the infinitive would be correct.

12. (C) The use of the future tense of the verb (*will believe*) makes no sense in this context. The present tense, *believe,* should have been used.

13. (E) The sentence uses the correlatives *not only . . . but also,* which often introduce errors of parallelism, but here there are no errors.

14. (C) This is another agreement error; the singular subject *business* requires the singular verb *has developed.*

15. (A) The subject of the second half of the sentence is *you,* and since it is not underlined, it can't be changed. To keep the pronouns consistent, the *we* at the beginning must also be *you.*

16. (C) The verb form *had flew* is the error here. Either the past tense *flew* or the past perfect *had flown* would be correct.

17. (B) There is an adverb-adjective confusion here. The adjective *fond* should be used to modify the noun *good-bye.*

18. (D) The sentence begins with a singular *ambassador* but changes to the unspecified plural *they* in the main clause. They who?

19. (E) The sentence is correct. The singular *its* refers to the singular *MTV,* and the verb tense is reasonable.

20. (C) Though English speakers use the verb *snuck* as widely as they use the standard past tense *sneaked, snuck* is still not standard written English. Fifty years from now, *snuck* may be the preferred form.

21. (D) The correct version should include either *people's* or *players'* to keep from changing the meaning. Since the word *players* has already been used in the sentence, *people's* is the better choice. The second part of the sentence specifically contrasts the two behaviors, so *but* is a better choice of conjunction than *and.* The sentence contains two independent clauses, which should be separated by a conjunction and a comma.

22. (C) The problem in this sentence is the ambiguous *they.* To which of the two parties does it refer? (C) uses more words but makes clear which party may win the election. Both (D) and (E) are also ambiguous.

23. (A) The original version is correct. It consists of a series of four adjectives, with one adverbial modifier (*grossly*). It is also the most concise of the five versions of the sentence. There is no need to break up the series of adjectives, and the other versions add unnecessary words. Choice (D), by changing *grossly* to *gross,* changes the meaning of the sentence.

24. (B) The error in the original sentence is a comma splice, the use of a comma to join two complete sentences. (D), omitting the comma, is even worse. The use of the semicolon in (B) corrects the sentence. Remember that the semicolon is usually the equivalent of a period, not a comma. (E) needs a comma to be correct; (C) is wordy and awkward, though the punctuation is not wrong.

25. (E) Up to the second comma, this is a complete sentence, but the second half has a subject but no main verb. Choices (A), (B), (C), and (D) have only the participle *accepting* (a verbal adjective, not a verb). (E) has a main verb, *accept,* and is the only version that isn't a sentence fragment.

26. (D) The conjunction *but* is a better choice than *and* because the two parts of the sentence present a contrast. In (A), (B), and (C), the sentence needlessly shifts from the passive (*is given*) to the active voice.

27. (C) Again, the *but* is a better conjunction choice than the *and.* Although (B) is not grammatically wrong, it is wordier than (C), the most concise of the five choices. The shift from the active verbs to the participles in (D) and (E) disrupts the parallel structure.

28. (D) The problem here is a misplaced modifier. The participial phrase *reviewing Jane Austen's Emma,* modifies *Scott* and should appear as close to the noun it modifies as possible. The solution is (D), which puts the phrase at the beginning of the sentence, immediately followed by the word it modifies.

29. (B) There are two complete sentences here but no conjunction or punctuation to join them. The run-on sentence can be corrected by putting a period or a semicolon at the end of the first sentence (after *birds*). Choices (D) and (E) are needlessly wordy and lack a needed comma before *and.*

30. (E) The original version has an ambiguous pronoun (does the second *they* refer to the seed companies or the chemical companies?), is wordy (*they* is used twice), and shifts from active to passive voice. (B) has the ambiguous pronoun and the active-passive shift. (C) is wordy and has the active-passive shift. (D) corrects these problems but distorts the meaning. (E) solves all the problems.

31. (A) Although the sentence begins with a participle, *Drawing* doesn't dangle but modifies *Anne Atkinson,* which immediately follows. The original version is the best of the five, avoiding the verbosity of (C), the passive voice of (D), the awkward tense change of (B), and the slight change of meaning in (E).

32. (E) Choice (C) is attractively concise but is so shortened that it doesn't quite make sense. The two verbs here, *initiate* and *become,* are equally important and can be made parallel as in (E); (A) and (B) subordinate one or the other.

33. (D) The plurals *they* and *them* do not agree with the singular *fund.* The original version needlessly shifts from a third person subject (*Bankrite Company*) to a second person (*you*). (C) shifts from an active to a passive verb. (D) eliminates the need for the *they.*

34. (C) Strict grammarians favor a pronoun's having a single word as its antecedent. In this sentence, the pronouns *which* and *this* refer to the idea that the banking system is stronger but not to a single word. (A), (B), (D), and (E) are alike in this reference. Given the choice, (C) is preferable, since its pronoun, *that,* does refer to a single word, *condition.*

35. (A) The original version is the best choice here. (B) is the only one that's shorter, but it's too short to make sense. The other choices aren't bad, but they are wordier than (A). So long as you can be sure the meaning is the same and the grammar is right, choose the version with the fewest words.

36. (D) The issue here is whether the omission of a phrase like *nature has provided* or its equivalent changes the meaning of the sentence. Clearly (D) is the most concise, and *but* is preferable to *and.* Since the clause also uses the adjective *natural,* isn't the *nature has provided* clause redundant?

37. (B) As it stands, this is a sentence fragment; it has no main verb, since *form* is in a dependent clause. The same problem exists in (C) and (E), while (D) is a participle, not a verb. In (B), *form* is the main verb of a sentence with *oaks, dogwood,* and *maples* the subjects.

38. (D) This is another verbose sentence. If you say *throughout,* there is no need to say *the entire work* also, since *throughout* means *all the way through.* Choice (E) pares too much from the sentence, losing the sense of both *throughout* (where) and *constantly* (how often).

39. (E) Both sentences are very wordy: *stage of life* is used twice, *life* is used three times, and *all throughout* is redundant. The revisions in (B) and (E) get rid of the repetitions of *stage,* but (B) keeps the wordy *that occurs all.* Much the best choice is (E).

40. (D) There are two problems here, the lack of parallelism in *with establishing* and *to separate* and the pronoun agreement with the singular *adolescent.* (B), (C), and (E) make the phrases parallel but use a plural pronoun (*their* and *themselves*). (D) has the singular *his* and parallel infinitives *to establish* and *to separate.*

41. (A) One trouble with this essay is its vague use of the word *separation.* In the second paragraph, the essay deals with the literal separation caused by events like divorce or death. But the first paragraph is not concerned with a physical separation. The adolescent may be psychologically distanced from his parents, but the separation is metaphorical. Choices (B), (C), and (D) are not "unlike the first paragraph," and (E) is untrue.

42. (D) The twelfth sentence is not really needed here. It repeats what is implicit in sentence 11. The rest of the paragraph is about kinds of separation rather than their effect.

43. (D) Without the comma, we may read *our courage* as the object of the verb *develop: as we develop . . . courage.* In this sentence, *develop* is intransitive, that is, does not take an object.

44. (C) The passage doesn't use an extended (or, for that matter, any) simile.

45. (D) A good revision of this sentence will eliminate the repetition of *reasons* as well as the vague and pompous *category of reasons* and *enterprise*. (D) keeps the meaning intact and does so with the greatest clarity and fewest words.

46. (E) The sentence could do without (A), (B), (C), and (D), and the word *trying* as well. The slimmed-down sentence will read: *The easiest to recognize is to avoid an unpleasant chore.*

47. (A) The paragraph offers three plausible reasons to explain why the writer procrastinates.

48. (B) The paragraph still reads smoothly without sentence 15, which does little more than repeat the content of sentence 14: that procrastination produces guilt and anxiety.

49. (C) The best choice here is *But. But* points a contrast, while *and, so,* and *thus* suggest a logical next step. The writer's point here is that understanding the problem does not lead to a solution.

50. (B) The passage is a personal essay. As a personal essay, it uses autobiographical information.

51. (E) There are no errors in this sentence. Be sure you have a reason for deciding that an underlined word or phrase is an error.

52. (D) The choice of preposition here is not idiomatic. It is an *opera about a tragic love triangle.*

53. (A) The context calls for a superlative (*most valuable*) rather than the comparative (*more valuable*), since he is compared to more than one other player *on the football team.*

54. (D) This is another example of the use of the preposition and gerund (*in admitting*) where the idiom, here with *reluctant,* calls for the use of the infinitive (*to admit*). In question 11 on this exam, the gerund, not the infinitive, is correct.

55. (C) The verb *became* is in the past tense, so to keep the sequence of tenses logical, *run* (a present tense) should be *ran* (a past tense).

56. (E) This sentence has no error. The verb agrees with the subject, the plural *were brought* agrees with *copper and tin,* and the idiom is correct.

57. (D) The participial phrase which opens this sentence will dangle if *Wilson* is not the subject of the sentence. But the subject here is *term,* and it was the president, not the term, who was *known.*

58. (C) The plural verb (*are*) that begins the sentence does not agree with the singular subject *organism.* Because the subject is widely separated from the verb, it is easy to miss the agreement error.

59. (B) The error is in the verb form. The verb here is in the perfect tense, and the past participle of the verb *to steal* is *stolen.*

60. (C) The choice of *and* as the conjunction here is the weakness. The sentence begins with a negative and ends with a positive statement. The clearer phrasing is *not x but y.*

PRACTICE TEST 3

PART A	Time—20 Minutes 1 Question	ESSAY

In twenty minutes, write an essay on the topic below. YOU MAY NOT WRITE ON ANOTHER TOPIC. AN ESSAY ON ANOTHER TOPIC WILL NOT BE SCORED.

The essay is intended to give you the chance to show your writing skills. Be sure to express your ideas on the topic clearly and effectively. The quality of your writing is much more important than the quantity, but to deal adequately with this topic you should probably write more than one paragraph. Be specific.

Think carefully about the following quotation and the assignment that follows. Then plan and write your essay according to the instructions.

"Television programs shown in public school classrooms should not be permitted to include commercial messages. To expose a captive audience to a sales pitch is too high a price to pay for even the best educational films."

Do you agree with this argument? Write a specific and well-organized essay in which you explain why you do or do not believe television programs with commercials should be played in public school classrooms.

WHEN THE TWENTY MINUTES HAVE PASSED, YOU MUST STOP WRITING AND GO ON TO THE MULTIPLE-CHOICE SECTION OF THE TEST. IF YOU FINISH YOUR ESSAY BEFORE THE TWENTY MINUTES HAVE PASSED, YOU MAY GO ON TO THE NEXT SECTION OF THE EXAM.

Directions: The following sentences may contain one error of grammar, usage, diction, or idiom. No sentence will contain more than one error, and some have no error. If there is an error, it will be underlined and have a letter beneath it. Sections of the sentence that are not underlined cannot be changed. In selecting your answer, observe the requirements of standard written English.

If there is an error, choose the one underlined part that must be changed to correct the sentence. If there is no error, choose (E).

EXAMPLE:

The film <u>tell the story</u> of a cavalry captain and <u>his wife</u>
       A   B

who <u>try to</u> <u>rebuild their lives</u> after the Civil War. <u>No error</u>
    C   D   E

Correct answer: A

1. <u>By paying</u> very close attention to the shape of the gem and
    A

    <u>looking carefully</u> at the setting, you <u>can clearly see</u> that the
       B   C

    ring <u>will not be</u> an antique. <u>No error</u>
         D   E

2. If the election results are <u>as Harris predicts</u>, the new senator
                          A

    will be the man <u>which</u> the people <u>believed</u> made the
                  B   C

    <u>better showing</u> in the televised debate. <u>No error</u>
       D   E

3. Not one of the sixty-five students <u>majoring in economics</u>
                                              A
<u>were prepared for</u> the teacher's <u>asking about</u> Marx on the
        B   C   D
examination. <u>No error</u>
                  E

4. If the <u>best-selling book</u> always won the award, the publishers
             A
<u>who pay for the publicity</u> would withdraw <u>their support</u>, and
            B   C
there wouldn't be <u>no award at all</u>. <u>No error</u>
                        D   E

5. It <u>must be she</u> he had in mind when he spoke of a
          A
well-trained athlete <u>who has won</u> a place
        B   C
<u>on the Olympic squad</u>. <u>No error</u>
          D   E

6. The reasons for <u>his looking so young</u> are <u>his low-fat diet</u>,
                        A   B
<u>his daily exercise</u>, and his regularity
        C
<u>to follow his doctor's recommendations</u>. <u>No error</u>
                  D   E

7. I <u>sincerely believe that</u> a person <u>intelligent enough</u> to be in
        A   B
business <u>by themselves</u> should have the ability
            C
<u>to recognize a dangerous investment</u>. <u>No error</u>
                  D   E

8. The jury must first <u>decide whether or not</u> the defendant <u>was in</u>
                              A   B
   New York and then how he <u>can have had</u> the strength <u>to carry</u>
                                  C   D
   a 200-pound body. <u>No error</u>
                         E

9. <u>The art of American morticians</u> paints death <u>to look like life,</u>
                     A   B
   <u>sealed it</u> away in watertight caskets, and <u>spirits it away to</u>
        C   D
   graveyards camouflaged as gardens. <u>No error</u>
                                          E

10. <u>Many of the compounds</u> that can <u>be produced from</u> the leaves
                  A   B
    of this plant <u>are dangerous,</u> but the plant <u>themselves</u> cannot be
                       C   D
    called toxic. <u>No error</u>
                      E

11. Most of the survivors <u>now recovering</u> neither heard <u>and saw</u>
                                A   B
    anything unusual <u>just before</u> the plane <u>crashed.</u> <u>No error</u>
                          C   D   E

12. *The Young Visitors* is an <u>unusually powerful novel</u> about a
                                        A
    group of <u>cruel and idle young boys</u> who <u>destruct</u> an old man's
                      B   C
    home for no other reason <u>than that it is beautiful.</u> <u>No error</u>
                                  D   E

13. The state legislature <u>has recommended</u> a bill <u>that allows</u> a
                               A   B

married couple <u>not to declare</u> the income of either the
                        C

husband or the wife, depending upon

<u>which income is more lower.</u> <u>No error</u>
                  D   E

14. <u>It seems increasingly obvious</u> that men's clothes are designed
                 A

not to please the men who will wear <u>them,</u> but <u>to impress</u> the
                                    B   C

people who <u>will see them.</u> <u>No error</u>
                D   E

15. <u>Unlike Monet,</u> Graham's oil paintings have <u>few bright colors,</u>
       A   B

<u>are small,</u> <u>and depict</u> only urban scenes. <u>No error</u>
   C   D   E

16. <u>When my broken arm was in a cast,</u> neither the nurse nor I
                  A

<u>were able</u> to <u>shave my face</u> without one <u>or two cuts.</u> <u>No error</u>
   B   C   D   E

17. <u>If I had my way,</u> the driver would be <u>charged for</u> criminal
        A   B

negligence and drunk driving <u>and spend</u> at least <u>a year in jail.</u>
                                 C   D

<u>No error</u>
  E

18. There are at most colleges <u>the requirement that</u> students <u>take</u>
                                    A   B

standardized tests <u>to be used</u> by admissions committees
                   C

<u>to evaluate applicants for entrance.</u> <u>No error</u>
         D   E

19. If westerners <u>acknowledge that</u> the eastern United States
                        A
    <u>has wilderness areas</u>, <u>one probably thinks</u> of the Blue Ridge
            B   C
    Mountains or <u>perhaps Maine</u>. <u>No error</u>
                        D   E

20. Paul Leonard, a philosopher at Princeton, <u>has argued</u> that
                                                    A
    experiments <u>using animals</u> <u>are unethical</u>, since the animals
                        B   C
    <u>cannot consent to the risk</u>. <u>No error</u>
                D   E

Directions: The following questions test correctness and effective expression. In selecting the answer, pay attention to grammar, diction, sentence structure, and punctuation.

In the following questions, part or all of each sentence is underlined. The (A) answer repeats the underlined portion of the original sentence, while the next four offer alternatives. Choose the answer that best expresses the meaning of the original sentence and at the same time is grammatically correct and stylistically superior. The correct choice should be clear, unambiguous, and concise.

EXAMPLE:

The forecaster predicted rain and the sky was clear.

(A) rain and the sky was clear
(B) rain but the sky was clear
(C) rain the sky was clear
(D) rain, but the sky was clear
(E) rain being as the sky was clear

Correct answer: D

21. As they crossed the Atlantic, cheeses were probably made in the galley by the colonists on the *Mayflower*.

(A) cheeses were probably made in the galley by the colonists on the *Mayflower*
(B) probably cheeses were made in the galley by the colonists of the *Mayflower*
(C) cheese was made, probably in the galley, by the colonists on the *Mayflower*
(D) the colonists of the *Mayflower* probably made cheeses in the galley
(E) in the galley of the *Mayflower,* the colonists probably made cheese

22. The series of articles is about the sicknesses of a violent society and also about how these ills can be remedied.

   (A) and also about how these ills can be remedied
   (B) and as well about the ways of remedying these ills
   (C) and remedies for these ills
   (D) and its remedy
   (E) and about remedying these ills

23. This year's alumni and alumnae differ from last year's they support the funding campaign for the new library.

   (A) last year's they support
   (B) last year's; they support
   (C) last year's, they support
   (D) last year's supporting
   (E) last year's in the support they give to

24. In addition to those of gasoline and sugar, the higher grain prices which lead to more expensive meat and poultry.

   (A) the higher grain prices which lead to more expensive meat and poultry
   (B) the higher prices of meat and poultry caused by more expensive grain
   (C) the higher prices in grain, meat, and poultry
   (D) higher grain prices leading to more expensive meat and poultry
   (E) the higher grain prices will lead to more expensive meat and poultry

25. The workers remain in the fields until they are exhausted; and this, in time, will seriously injure their health.

   (A) exhausted; and this
   (B) exhausted; it
   (C) exhausted, which
   (D) exhausted, a practice that
   (E) exhausted, and it

26. When you see, instead of read, a play, it sometimes reveals new strengths or weaknesses.

   (A) it sometimes reveals new strengths or weaknesses
   (B) new strengths or weaknesses are sometimes revealed to you
   (C) you sometimes see new strengths or weaknesses
   (D) sometimes new strengths or weaknesses are revealed
   (E) new strengths or weaknesses can be seen sometimes

27. Carrying the warm water across the yard to melt the ice on the bird bath, the sparrows were gathered in groups a few feet away.

   (A) bird bath, the sparrows were gathered in groups
   (B) bird bath, the sparrows gathered in groups
   (C) bird bath, the groups of sparrows gathered
   (D) bird bath, the groups of sparrows were gathering
   (E) bird bath, I saw groups of sparrows gathered

28. The operas of Mozart are very frequently performed in Austria; Verdi operas are the favorites in Italy.

   (A) Austria; Verdi operas
   (B) Austria Verdi operas
   (C) Austria, although Verdi operas
   (D) Austria; while Verdi operas
   (E) Austria the operas of Verdi

29. The book argues that *Othello* is the better play because of its construction, which is more careful than that of *King Lear*.

   (A) because of its construction, which is more careful than that of *King Lear*
   (B) because its construction, which is more careful than *King Lear*'s
   (C) because of its construction, more careful than *King Lear*'s construction
   (D) because it is more carefully constructed than *King Lear*
   (E) because its construction is more careful than *King Lear*

30. A valuable device taking advantage of the remarkable sensitivity of cesium has just been <u>constructed, and scientists have known of this capability for many years.</u>

   (A) constructed, and scientists have known of this capability for many years
   (B) constructed, which scientists have known about for many years
   (C) constructed, although scientists have known of this capability for many years
   (D) constructed, and this capability has been known to scientists for many years
   (E) constructed, a capability about which scientists have known for many years

31. The doctor visits her patients in intensive care once every three hours, <u>which can be decreased</u> as danger lessens.

   (A) which can be decreased
   (B) a schedule that can be altered
   (C) which can be altered
   (D) to be decreased
   (E) and can be altered

32. <u>Enjoying the look of a movie musical—its sets, costumes, and dances—is</u> as important as enjoying its songs.

   (A) Enjoying the look of a movie musical—its sets, costumes, and dances—is
   (B) The look of a movie musical—its sets, costumes, and dances—is
   (C) The look of a movie musical—its sets, costumes, and dances—are
   (D) In a movie musical, the sets, costumes, and dances are
   (E) The sets, costumes, and dances of a movie musical are

33. Like the mountains that are found in Switzerland, the mountains of Colorado and Wyoming keep their snows for ten months.

   (A) Like the mountains that are found in Switzerland
   (B) Like the mountains located in Switzerland
   (C) Like the mountains found in Switzerland
   (D) Like those in Switzerland
   (E) Like mountains which are Swiss

34. In the *Trenton News,* they report that there are as many as ten thousand homeless people in Washington, D.C.

   (A) In the *Trenton News,* they report that
   (B) In the *Trenton News,* it is reported that
   (C) In the *Trenton News,* they issued the report that
   (D) The *Trenton News* reports that
   (E) The *Trenton News* makes the report that

35. Paris Mayor Jacques Chirac after a multimillion-dollar face-lift dedicated the refurbished Champs Elysées.

   (A) Paris Mayor Jacques Chirac after a multimillion-dollar face-lift dedicated the refurbished Champs Elysées.
   (B) After a multimillion-dollar face-lift, Jacques Chirac, mayor of Paris, dedicated the refurbished Champs Elysées.
   (C) A multimillion-dollar face-lift completed, Paris Mayor Jacques Chirac dedicated the refurbished Champs Elysées.
   (D) After Jacques Chirac, Paris mayor, completed a multimillion-dollar face-lift, he dedicated the refurbished Champs Elysées.
   (E) Paris Mayor Jacques Chirac dedicated the refurbished Champs Elysées after its multimillion-dollar face-lift.

36. Completing the film on time was as satisfying to the director of *Beneath the Sea* <u>as mastering</u> the underwater camera techniques.

   (A) as mastering
   (B) as his being able to master
   (C) as it was when mastering
   (D) than the mastery of
   (E) as the fact that he mastered

37. Lured by the Florida sun, <u>Canadian motorists by the thousands descend annually into St. Petersburg each year.</u>

   (A) Canadian motorists by the thousands descend annually into St. Petersburg each year
   (B) St. Petersburg receives thousands of Canadian motorists each year
   (C) St. Petersburg annually receives thousands of Canadian motorists
   (D) Canadian motorists by the thousands descend on St. Petersburg each year
   (E) thousands of Canadian motorists descend into St. Petersburg each year

38. At the kitchen, he stopped to wipe the mud from his boots, ran a comb through his hair, <u>and knocks loudly at the door.</u>

   (A) and knocks loudly at the door
   (B) and knocks loud at the door
   (C) and knocked loudly at the door
   (D) and then knocks loudly on the door
   (E) knocking at the door loudly

Directions: The following passages are early drafts of student essays. Some parts of them need to be revised.

Read the selections carefully and answer the questions that follow. There will be questions about sentence structure, diction, and usage in individual sentences or parts of sentences. Other questions will deal with the whole essay or paragraphs and ask you to decide about organization, development, and appropriate language. Choose the answer that follows the requirements of standard written English and most effectively expresses the intended meanings.

Questions 39–44 are based on the following passage.

The Majority Is Often Wrong

(1) I agree with the statement the majority is often wrong. (2) The idea that the majority is always right has been disproved by every bad or dishonest politician who has been elected to any political office by the votes of the majority. (3) It is disproved by every jury decision where it turns out later that the prisoner they found guilty was really innocent. (4) It is frequently disproved in high school. (5) It is disproved in Germany when they elected Hitler.

(6) In my school when I was a sophomore there was an election of the student body president. (7) Two boys (who I'll call Jack and Dave) and one girl (Jane) were running for president. (8) Dave was a bad student, and he was popular and a good basketball player. (9) Jack was active in a lot of clubs and in music, and Jane was by far the best student of the three. (10) Dave won by a landslide, but never even finished his sophomore year when he was in a drunk driving accident. (11) This shows how wrong the majority can be.

(12) These examples show how the majority is often wrong is true. (13) The old saying, the majority is always right, is wrong.

39. Which of the following is the best version of sentence 5 (reproduced below)?

It is disproved in Germany when they elected Hitler.

(A) (As it is now)
(B) It is disproved by Germany where they elected Hitler.
(C) It is disproved when the Germans elected Hitler.
(D) Hitler disproves it in Germany.
(E) It was disproved when the Germans elected Hitler.

40. The first paragraph would be most improved by the removal of which of the following sentences?

(A) sentence 1
(B) sentence 2
(C) sentence 3
(D) sentence 4
(E) sentence 5

41. Which of the following does the first paragraph make use of?

(A) emphatic repetition of a phrase
(B) rhetorical question
(C) definition of a term
(D) specific example of a personal experience
(E) elaboration of an example

42. Which of the following is the best version of sentence 6 (reproduced below)?

In my school when I was a sophomore there was an election of the student body president.

(A) (As it is now)
(B) When I was a sophomore, my school held an election for student body president.
(C) In my school, they held an election for student body president when I was a sophomore.
(D) A student body president election was held by my school when I was a sophomore.
(E) When I was a sophomore, they held a student body president election at my school.

43. Which of the following is the best way to combine sentences 11, 12, and 13 (reproduced below)?

This shows how wrong the majority can be. These examples show how the majority is often wrong is true. The old saying, the majority is always right, is wrong.

(A) Thus, it is shown that the majority is often wrong, and the belief that the majority is always right is wrong.

(B) This example and the others go to show how often the majority is wrong and how seldom it is right.

(C) These examples show that the old saying, the majority is always right, is wrong.

(D) This shows how wrong the majority can be, and that the majority is not always right, but wrong sometimes.

(E) Therefore, the majority is wrong and the old saying the majority is always right is also wrong.

44. The advantages of combining sentences 11, 12, and 13 are

   I. It can eliminate an undeveloped paragraph.
  II. It eliminates the repetitions of *"majority."*
 III. It corrects a grammatical error in sentence 13.

(A) II only
(B) I and II only
(C) I and III only
(D) II and III only
(E) I, II, and III

Questions 45–50 are based on the following passage.

Are Americans Getting Lazier?

(1) Too many people today are trying to get what they want by using the least effort the fastest way. (2) Technology has helped this. (3) Calculators now give you the solution to complex equations in seconds, even watches have calculators on them. (4) People drive their cars to the corner to drop off mail because they are too lazy to walk even if it is healthy and possibly faster to just walk.

(5) Americans used to want a house in the suburbs, a family, a job, and something to look forward to when the kids were grown up. (6) Now they want quick money without taking risks, get rich overnight, and live the life of luxury. (7) They no longer plan ahead. (8) They think about today. (9) They don't think about tomorrow at all. (10) People are lazier than ever.

(11) They turn to television and radio for the news. (12) They don't read newspapers. (13) They depend more and more on automation doing things for you. (14) With more things voice automated, Americans will no longer need their remote controls. (15) Without some change, our future may be a nightmare of sloth.

45. Which of the following is the best combined version of sentences 1 and 2 (reproduced below)?

    Too many people today are trying to get what they want by using the least effort the fastest way. Technology has helped this.

    (A) Too many people today are trying to get what they want by using the least effort the fastest way, and technology is helping them.
    (B) With the help of technology, there are too many people today who are trying to get what they want by using the least effort the fastest way.
    (C) Technology is helping too many people who are trying to get what they want by using the least effort in the fastest way.
    (D) Helped by technology, too many people today are trying to get what they want in the fastest way using the least effort.
    (E) Trying to get what they want using the least effort the fastest way, technology today has helped too many people.

46. Which of the following is the best version of sentence 2 (reproduced below)?

Technology has helped this.

(A) (As it is now)
(B) This has been helped by technology.
(C) Technology has helped this effort.
(D) Technology helping this to happen.
(E) But technology has helped this.

47. Which of the following is the best version of sentence 6 (reproduced below)?

Now they want quick money without taking risks, get rich overnight, and live the life of luxury.

(A) (As it is now)
(B) They now want quick money without taking risks, riches overnight, and to live the life of luxury.
(C) Now they want to earn money quickly without risk, to get rich overnight, and to live a life of luxury.
(D) They want quick money now, without taking risks, and they want riches overnight and to live a life of luxury.
(E) What they want now is quick money, no risks, riches overnight, and to live a life of luxury.

48. To eliminate the series of very short sentences in the second paragraph, which of the following is the best way to combine sentences 7, 8, and 9 (reproduced below)?

They no longer plan ahead. They think about today. They don't think about tomorrow at all.

(A) They no longer plan ahead or think about tomorrow; they think about today.
(B) It is today, not tomorrow that they think about; they never plan ahead.
(C) They plan ahead no longer, thinking only of today and not thinking about tomorrow at all.
(D) No longer planning ahead, they think about today, and not at all about tomorrow.
(E) They no longer plan ahead but think only of today.

49. In which of the following pairs of sentences does the writer make the same usage error?

    (A) sentences 3 and 13
    (B) sentences 4 and 7
    (C) sentences 7 and 8
    (D) sentences 9 and 11
    (E) sentences 14 and 15

50. Which of the following describes an organizational weakness in this passage?

    (A) The first paragraph does not develop a single idea.
    (B) The examples in the first paragraph are inappropriate.
    (C) The second paragraph is largely about a different subject from that of the first and third.
    (D) The last sentence of the second paragraph is unrelated to what follows in the third paragraph.
    (E) There is no logical connection between the content of the first paragraph and that of the third.

Directions: The following sentences may contain one error of grammar, usage, diction, or idiom. No sentence will contain more than one error, and some have no error. If there is an error, it will be underlined and have a letter beneath it. Sections of the sentence that are not underlined cannot be changed. In selecting your answer, observe the requirements of standard written English.

If there is an error, choose the one underlined part that must be changed to correct the sentence. If there is no error, choose (E).

EXAMPLE:

The film <u>tell the story</u> of a cavalry captain and <u>his wife</u>
       A   B

who <u>try</u> to <u>rebuild their lives</u> after the Civil War. <u>No error</u>
    C   D   E

Correct answer: A

---

51. <u>Though in only her first year of research</u>, Dr. Jackson
                  A

<u>has discovered</u> a formula <u>that may affected</u> the study of
    B   C

mathematics <u>for years to come.</u> <u>No error</u>
              D   E

52. Last month, by <u>buying</u> economy-size <u>packages of</u> pasta, muffin
           A   B

mix, and detergent, Mrs. Snow <u>saves as much as</u> ten dollars
                             C

<u>per week.</u> <u>No error</u>
  D   E

53. <u>In hoping to find</u> a safe anchorage, ships in the Pacific
      A

<u>could spend</u> two weeks <u>without ever seeing</u> land or
    B   C

<u>another ship.</u> <u>No error</u>
   D   E

54. Heart patients <u>like Drusilla and I</u> prefer meals <u>that are</u> low
                          A   B
in <u>calories</u> and cost <u>to keep down</u> the weight and bills.
        C   D
<u>No error</u>
    E

55. In the <u>newspaper and television advertisements</u> are the
                              A
<u>claim that prunes</u> are <u>not only low</u> in fat <u>but also high</u> in fiber.
        B   C   D
<u>No error</u>
    E

56. The Baseball Writers' Association <u>elected</u> Willie Mays and
                                          A
Willie McCovey <u>to the Hall of Fame</u> because <u>he had been</u> the
                      B   C
<u>league's leading batter.</u> <u>No error</u>
              D   E

57. A public-opinion survey, <u>commisioned as part</u> of a federal
                                      A
anti-noise program, <u>concludes that</u> some of the residents
                          B
<u>are seriously disturbed</u> by <u>aircraft noise.</u> <u>No error</u>
              C   D   E

58. It was Cardinal Richelieu <u>who decided</u> to found the French
                                      A
Academy <u>when he learned</u> that already an <u>eminent group</u> of
              B   C
grammarians <u>will meet in secret</u> to discuss language and
                      D
literature. <u>No error</u>
                  E

59. <u>More than thirty countries from around the world</u> have
　　　　　　　　　　　A

submitted <u>entries for</u> the Best Foreign Language Film Award,
　　　　　　　B

<u>who will be presented</u> at a ceremony <u>in six weeks.</u> <u>No error</u>
　　　　C　　　　　　　　　　　　　　　D　　　　　E

60. <u>Like President Carter's,</u> President Reagan's cabinet
　　　　　　　A

<u>was chosen from</u> former allies <u>in state politics,</u> national party
　　　　B　　　　　　　　　　　　C

leaders, personal friends,

<u>and seasoned professional politicians.</u> <u>No error</u>
　　　　　　　　D　　　　　　　　　　　E

ANSWER KEY FOR PRACTICE TEST 3

Identifying Sentence Errors

1. D	6. D	11. B	16. B
2. B	7. C	12. C	17. B
3. B	8. E	13. D	18. A
4. D	9. C	14. E	19. C
5. E	10. D	15. A	20. E

Improving Sentences

21. D	26. C	31. B	36. A
22. C	27. E	32. A	37. D
23. B	28. A	33. D	38. C
24. E	29. D	34. D	
25. D	30. C	35. E	

Improving Paragraphs

39. E	43. C	47. C
40. D	44. B	48. E
41. A	45. D	49. A
42. B	46. C	50. C

Identifying Sentence Errors

51. C	56. C
52. C	57. E
53. A	58. D
54. A	59. C
55. B	60. E

PRACTICE TEST 3 SCORING WORKSHEET

You can use the following worksheet to determine your scores. You will need two readers to score your essay. If they are not available, be objective and double the score you decide on yourself.

Part A: Essay

_____ + _____ = _____

first reader's score   second reader's score   essay raw score

Approximate essay scaled score (use the table on page 147) = _____

Part B: Multiple-Choice

_____ – _____ = _____

correct answers   wrong answers × .25   multiple-choice raw
score

Approximate multiple-choice scaled score (use the table on page 30) = _____

Composite Score

_____ + _____ = _____

  essay raw score times 3   multiple-choice   composite
(or 3.02 for scores of 10–12)   raw score   raw score

Approximate composite scaled score (use the table on page 147) = _____

ANSWERS AND EXPLANATIONS FOR PRACTICE TEST 3

PART B

1. (D) The sentence begins with two gerunds and a main verb all in the present tense. To keep the sequence of verb tenses consistent, the last verb must be the present *is,* not the future *will . . . be.*

2. (B) The choice of pronoun is in error here. Since the pronoun refers to a man, *who* rather than *which* is the right word.

3. (B) This is the subject-verb agreement error, disguised by the separation of the singular subject *one* and the interrupting plurals in *of the sixty-five students majoring in economics.* The right verb is the singular *was.*

4. (D) Since *wouldn't* contains a negative, the *no* makes a double negative. The corrected sentence can read *would be no* or *wouldn't be any.*

5. (E) You should think twice about the case of the pronouns here, but remember that *who* and *whom* are not likely to appear on the test. The *who* here is right. The *she* is also right. The verb *to be* does not take an object. Don't forget that each test will contain several sentences with no error.

6. (D) The sentence confuses an idiom, using an infinitive (*to follow*) where the conventional usage calls for the prepositional phrase (*regularity in following*).

7. (C) This is a pronoun agreement error. The sentence begins with the singular noun *a person,* but instead of saying *by himself* or *by herself,* switches to the plural *themselves.*

8. (E) The sentence is correct. Though the verb tenses vary, they present a logical time scheme.

9. (C) Here, the verb tenses are not coherent. Two of the verbs (*paints* and *spirits*) are in the present tense, but *sealed* for no reason is a past tense.

10. (D) This is another pronoun agreement error, easy to miss even though the singular noun (*plant*) and the erring plural pronoun (*themselves*) are together.

11. (B) The idiom is *neither . . . nor,* not the *neither . . . and* we have here.

12. (C) The use of *destruct* as the main verb is an error of diction. A better choice would be *destroy.*

13. (D) The comparison which ends this sentence is needlessly doubled. Since *lower* means *more low,* the *more* should be deleted.

14. (E) This sentence appears to be testing parallelism, but the parallel construction *not to please* with *but to impress* is right. The future tenses of the verbs are also correct.

15. (A) The comparison here is not logical. *Monet* (a painter) is compared to *paintings.* The correct sentence should read *Unlike Monet's.*

16. (B) With the *neither . . . nor* construction here, the subject is a singular (either *nurse* or *I*). The verb should be *was.*

17. (B) In this context, the correct idiom meaning *accused of* is *charged with* rather than *charged for.*

18. (A) With the plural *There are,* the noun must also be plural to agree; *the requirement* should be *requirements.*

19. (C) The antecedent of the pronoun *one* is the plural *westerners.* The pronoun should be *they.*

20. (E) The sentence is grammatical.

21. (D) The subject of the dependent clause that begins this sentence is the pronoun *they.* What should follow is a noun to explain who the *they* are. It isn't *cheeses* or *cheese* as in (A), (B), and (C). (D) correctly puts *the colonists* first in the main clause and also gets rid of the passive verbs of (A), (B), and (C). (D) is preferable to (E) because it avoids the separation of the modifying phrase and what it modifies.

22. (C) The original sentence isn't grammatically wrong, but it is wordy. It repeats the preposition *about* and uses the passive voice. (B) is even wordier, though it does get rid of the passive. (D) uses the fewest words, but it is ungrammatical. The pronoun should refer to the plural *sicknesses;* it appears to refer to the singular *society.* (E) repeats the *about* needlessly; all other things being equal, *remedies* is probably better than *remedying,* since it is a noun like *sicknesses* rather than a gerund.

23. (B) There are two complete sentences here with no punctuation or conjunction to join them. The easiest way to correct the run-on sentence is with the semicolon. (E) isn't wrong, but it is wordier.

24. (E) The original sentence has a subject but no main verb, since *lead* is in a dependent clause. (C) has no verb or verbals. (B) and (D) have participles, that is, adjectives, not verbs. Only (E) is a complete sentence with its main verb (*will lead*) in the future tense.

25. (D) This sentence uses a pronoun (*this*) without a specific antecedent; *this* refers to the general idea of the whole first clause. To use a different pronoun, as (B), (C), and (E) do, without supplying the missing specific antecedent, does not correct the sentence. Only (D) solves the problem. The specific antecedent for the pronoun *that* is the noun *practice.*

26. (C) The original sentence begins with a second person subject (*you*) but switches to the third person (*it*). Only (C) keeps *you* as the subject of the main clause and also uses a verb in the active voice. (B), (D), and (E) all use the passive.

27. (E) As soon as you see a sentence that begins, like this one, with a participle, look to see if it dangles. Who is carrying the warm water? Not the *sparrows*. Not the *groups*. The only possible right answer is (E).

28. (A) The original is the right version. The two complete sentences are separated by a semicolon, avoiding the run-on to be found in (B) and (E). (D) won't work because the *while* introduces a dependent clause, but the semicolon should introduce a complete sentence. (C) isn't wrong in its punctuation, but it alters the meaning of the original sentence.

29. (D) The original version of this sentence has no errors of grammar, but (D) is also correct and four words shorter. Choice (B) is a sentence fragment; it has no main verb. (C) is wordy, repeating the word *construction*. To avoid the illogical comparison of *construction* and *King Lear,* (E) should read *King Lear's*.

30. (C) The issue in this sentence is clarity rather than grammar. All five versions are grammatical, but (C) makes the point most clearly. The point is that though the capability has long been known, no one has made use of this knowledge until very recently (*just*). (C) rightly subordinates half of the sentence, using *although*.

31. (B) Like 25, this sentence has a pronoun (*which*) without a specific antecedent. (B) corrects this problem by adding the noun *schedule*. (C), (D), and (E) also lack a specific antecedent. What is it that will be *decreased* or *altered*?

32. (A) Though the original version is longer than the other choices, it is the only one that keeps the comparison logical. The unchangeable part of the sentence has *as important as enjoying,* so the first part must have an action parallel to *enjoying.* The nouns of (B), (C), (D), and (E) are not a similar activity.

33. (D) This sentence is testing for verbosity. All of the first four options are grammatical, but (D) alone avoids the unnecessary repetition of the word *mountains.*

34. (D) In the original sentence, and in (C), the *they* has no antecedent. Who is *they?* (D) is more concise than (B) (a passive) and (E).

35. (E) To be sure the reader does not think the mayor spent so much money on cosmetic surgery, (E) places the modifier *after a multimillion-dollar face-lift* next to what it modifies, the *Champs Elysées,* and changes *a* to *its.* The four other versions of the sentence place the modifier nearer to *Chirac.*

36. (A) The sentence is saying *completing . . . was as satisfying as.* The original version is the most concise and the most clearly parallel of the five choices.

37. (D) Both (B) and (C) can be eliminated, since the phrase which begins the sentence must modify the *Canadian motorists,* not the city in Florida. The problem with (A) and (E) is the idiom *descend into.* One can descend into a cave or a coal mine, but the correct idiom in this context is *descend on.*

38. (C) The series here uses two main verbs in the past tense (*stopped, ran*); the third verb in the series should also use the past tense.

39. (E) The problem with this sentence is the tense of the verb. The other two sentences in the paragraph that begin with *It is disproved* deal with situations in the past that continue to occur: dishonest politicians are still elected, and juries still make mistakes. For this reason, the use of the present tense is correct. Hitler, however, is no longer elected, so the verb should be in the past tense. Choice (E) corrects the tense and at the same time keeps the rhetorical balance of repeating *It . . . disproved.*

40. (D) Sentence 4 is an anticlimax. It is vague (what high school? what happened?) and more relevant to the next paragraph. The three other examples in this paragraph are more specific and more cogent.

41. (A) The deliberate repetition of the phrase *It is disproved* is an effective way of emphasizing how often the majority may be wrong. There are no instances of the other choices in the paragraph.

42. (B) Though several of these sentences aren't wrong, (B), with its subject-verb-object word order, is preferable to the wordier *there was* of (A) or the passive verb of (D). In (C) and (E), the *they* is a vague pronoun, with no specific antecedent.

43. (C) Unless there is a very good reason for repeating a word, try to get rid of repetitions when combining sentences. Here, choices (A), (D), and (E) needlessly repeat *majority* and *wrong.* (B) is better, but it loses the word play (*is . . . right, is wrong*) of the original. (C) keeps the play on words and, by using the plural *examples,* concludes the passage with a reference to both the first and second paragraphs, making the third unnecessary.

44. (B) There is no grammatical error in sentence 13. The revision can eliminate the undeveloped paragraph and the repetitions.

45. (D) There are two problems in these sentences. The phrase *the fastest way* is too far away from *trying to get,* which it modifies. The *this* in the second sentence is a vague pronoun. Choice (D) corrects both by moving *the fastest way* ahead of *using* and by eliminating *this.* In (E), the participle that begins the sentence dangles.

46. (C) The original version of sentence 2 uses a pronoun (*this*) with no specific antecedent. Choices (B), (D), and (E) may move the *this* to different parts of the sentence, but unless there is a specific noun for the pronoun to refer to, the error is still there. Add a word like *tendency, problem, attempt,* or *effort,* and the pronoun is no longer vague.

47. (C) The original version uses verbs for nouns in a series that lacks parallelism. The best choice must make all three elements parallel; here (C) uses three infinitives (*to earn, to get,* and *to live*).

48. (E) If you think only about today, you cannot be thinking about tomorrow, so to say so is redundant. The use of *but* is preferable to *and* in this context.

49. (A) Both sentences 3 and 13 shift pronouns. The passage usually uses the third person plural (*people, they, Americans*), but in sentences 3 and 13, the writer shifts to the second person *you.* In 13, the error is especially obvious because the sentence begins with *they.*

50. (C) The first and third paragraphs are about laziness and its relation to technological advances. The second paragraph, however, except for its last sentence, is about other matters, such as greed or the refusal to plan ahead.

51. (C) The error is in the verb form; it should be *may affect.*

52. (C) The phrase *last month* places the action in the past. The tense of the main verb should be past: *saved.*

53. (A) There is an idiom error in the opening phrase. It could be *Hoping to find* or *In hope of finding*.

54. (A) The error is the case of the pronoun *I*, the object of the preposition *like*. The correct form is *me*.

55. (B) The verb (*are*) comes before the subject (*claim*) in this sentence. But the two do not agree; *claim* should be the plural *claims*.

56. (C) The pronoun *he* is ambiguous in this sentence. From the context, a reader can't tell to which Willie *he* refers.

57. (E) There are no errors here. The singular verb *concludes* agrees with the singular *survey*, and the plural *are* with the plural *residents*.

58. (D) The *already* places the time of the meeting before the past tenses of *decided* and *learned*. Instead of the future *will meet*, the verb should be *had met*, the past perfect tense.

59. (C) The award is a thing, not a person, so the pronoun should be *which*.

60. (E) The sentence is correct. The opening phrase is properly parallel (*Carter's, Reagan's*), and the series of nouns is consistent.

PRACTICE TEST 4

PART A   Time—20 Minutes   ESSAY
1 Question

In twenty minutes, write an essay on the topic below. YOU MAY NOT WRITE ON ANOTHER TOPIC. AN ESSAY ON ANOTHER TOPIC WILL NOT BE SCORED.

The essay is intended to give you the chance to show your writing skills. Be sure to express your ideas on the topic clearly and effectively. The quality of your writing is much more important than the quantity, but to deal adequately with this topic you should probably write more than one paragraph. Be specific.

Think carefully about the following quotation and the assignment that follows. Then plan and write your essay according to the instructions.

"The way we speak—accent, choice of words, grammar—can say as much about us as the way we dress."

Do you agree? Write an essay using specific supporting detail in which you agree with or refute this idea.

WHEN THE TWENTY MINUTES HAVE PASSED, YOU MUST STOP WRITING AND GO ON TO THE MULTIPLE-CHOICE SECTION OF THE TEST. IF YOU FINISH YOUR ESSAY BEFORE THE TWENTY MINUTES HAVE PASSED, YOU MAY GO ON TO THE NEXT SECTION OF THE EXAM.

Directions: The following sentences may contain one error of grammar, usage, diction, or idiom. No sentence will contain more than one error, and some have no error. If there is an error, it will be underlined and have a letter beneath it. Sections of the sentence that are not underlined cannot be changed. In selecting your answer, observe the requirements of standard written English.

If there is an error, choose the one underlined part that must be changed to correct the sentence. If there is no error, choose (E).

EXAMPLE:

The film tell the story of a cavalry captain and his wife
       A   B

who try to rebuild their lives after the Civil War. No error
   C   D   E

Correct answer: A

1. Strange as it now seems, Japan and Italy once agreed to limit
         A   B

car imports because Japan fears competition from Italian cars.
                           C   D

No error
  E

2. In July 1991, there were darkness at noon in Mexico City as
          A   B

the moon passed between the sun and the earth. No error
           C   D   E

3. The advertisement for Neil Simon's play <u>Rumors</u> <u>features</u>
   A

   three <u>sets of mechanical false teeth</u> <u>who appear</u> <u>to be talking</u>
   B   C   D

   to each other. <u>No error</u>
   E

4. You can grow a number of spring-flowering bulbs <u>indoors, but</u>
   A

   if the plants <u>are to blossom,</u> <u>one must</u> carefully
   B   C

   <u>control the light.</u> <u>No error</u>
   D   E

5. <u>Despite lagging productivity</u> by <u>its work force,</u> the Cuban
   A   B

   government <u>has continued</u> to <u>provide</u> a first-rate health-care
   C   D

   program. <u>No error</u>
   E

6. <u>Nowadays, most medical authorities agree</u> that <u>huge doses</u> of
   A   B

   <u>just about any substance</u> <u>is likely to be dangerous.</u> <u>No error</u>
   C   D   E

7. As a <u>resulting of overgrazing,</u> firewood cutting, and
   A

   <u>increased cultivation,</u> the Sahara Desert has <u>steadily grown</u>
   B   C

   <u>larger</u> in this decade. <u>No error</u>
   D   E

8. <u>To safeguard wildlife,</u> the state of Florida will <u>line its highways</u>
   A   B

   with high fencing, <u>forcing</u> panthers <u>to scoot</u> beneath the roads
   C   D

   through specially designed animal underpasses. <u>No error</u>
   E

9. Hypnotism, chewing gum, and <u>nicotine-releasing skin patches</u>
                                              A
   are <u>probably</u> the <u>most used method</u> to break the
          B   C
   <u>cigarette smoking habit.</u> <u>No error</u>
               D   E

10. The <u>decline in</u> the industrial average was much <u>smaller than</u>
             A   B
    <u>the 1929 decline</u> because the Dow index <u>stands with</u> a much
              C   D
    higher level today. <u>No error</u>
                             E

11. <u>Missing the forehand volley,</u> a <u>relative easy shot,</u> Morea fell
                A   B
    behind <u>early in the match,</u> and <u>he never recovered.</u> <u>No error</u>
                   C   D   E

12. <u>In an area of</u> <u>the Pacific Ring of Fire</u> of <u>special interest to</u>
             A   B   C
    volcanologists <u>lie</u> the Siberian Kamchatka Peninsula. <u>No error</u>
                     D   E

13. Bears, mountain lions, beavers, <u>deer,</u> squirrels, and coyotes
                                       A
    <u>inhabit</u> Sequoia Park, and <u>they</u> may <u>prey upon</u> small rodents.
         B   C   D
    <u>No error</u>
         E

14. <u>No Latin American matador</u> <u>can become</u> famous
                  A   B
    without <u>he succeeds</u> in Spain, where bullfighting <u>was invented.</u>
                 C   D
    <u>No error</u>
         E

15. The discovery of the existence of a fifth force <u>could have</u>
                                                        A
    enormous <u>impact on</u> theoretical physicists who
                 B
    <u>are trying to develop</u> a unified theory
              C
    to explain the interactions of matter. <u>No error</u>
                D   E

16. When it is five o'clock in New York, <u>it is</u> <u>only four</u> in Texas,
                                           A   B
    and <u>it will be</u> two o'clock in California <u>or Oregon</u>. <u>No error</u>
             C   D   E

17. New Englanders seem to believe that <u>us Texans</u> talk <u>oddly</u>, but
                                          A   B
    we think <u>they are the ones</u> who <u>have strange ways of speaking</u>.
                  C   D
    <u>No error</u>
        E

18. <u>To encourage better reading skills</u>, teachers in the public
                    A
    schools <u>now requisite</u> students to submit weekly diaries
                 B
    <u>listing the books</u>, magazines, and newspapers <u>they have read</u>.
            C   D
    <u>No error</u>
        E

19. The <u>most delicious desserts</u> that can <u>be freshly made</u>
                 A   B
    <u>all the year round</u> <u>is probably</u> apple pie. <u>No error</u>
            C   D   E

20. Of all the plants <u>grown from tubers</u>, the begonias produce the
                              A

   <u>more spectacular flowers</u>, <u>wonderfully colored</u>, huge, and
                  B   C

   <u>easy to care for.</u> <u>No error</u>
            D   E

Directions: The following questions test correctness and effective expression. In selecting the answer, pay attention to grammar, diction, sentence structure, and punctuation.

In the following questions, part or all of each sentence is underlined. The (A) answer repeats the underlined portion of the original sentence, while the next four offer alternatives. Choose the answer that best expresses the meaning of the original sentence and at the same time is grammatically correct and stylistically superior. The correct choice should be clear, unambiguous, and concise.

EXAMPLE:

The forecaster predicted rain and the sky was clear.

(A) rain and the sky was clear
(B) rain but the sky was clear
(C) rain the sky was clear
(D) rain, but the sky was clear
(E) rain being as the sky was clear

Correct answer: D

21. The melting of Antarctic ice affects ocean currents, and the sunlight's penetration of the water and the growth of microorganisms are also affected.

(A) currents, and the sunlight's penetration of the water and the growth of microorganisms are also affected
(B) currents; also affected are the sunlight's penetration of the water and the growth of microorganisms
(C) currents, and it also affects the sunlight's penetration of the water and the growth of microorganisms
(D) currents, the sunlight's penetration of the water, and the growth of microorganisms
(E) currents, with the sunlight's penetration of the water and the growth of microorganisms also being affected

22. Coffee drinking may protect against cancer of the colon, <u>which</u> <u>is surprising, since coffee drinking increases</u> the risk of heart attack.

    (A) which is surprising, since coffee drinking increases
    (B) and this is surprising since coffee drinking increases
    (C) a surprising fact, since coffee drinking increases
    (D) and this surprises us because coffee drinking increases
    (E) which surprises, since coffee drinking increases

23. The excavations at Ceren reveal <u>the prosperity of the rural</u> <u>Mayans, the staples of their diet, and</u> the architecture of their homes.

    (A) the prosperity of the rural Mayans, the staples of their diet, and
    (B) the prosperity of the rural Mayan; the staples of their diets; and
    (C) the prosperity of the rural Mayans, and the staples of their diet, and
    (D) the rural Mayans, the prosperity and the diet they ate, as well as
    (E) how prosperous the rural Mayans were, what their diet was, and

24. Human cells grown in a test tube can reproduce as many as sixty <u>times then they die</u> from old age.

    (A) times then they die
    (B) times but then they die
    (C) times and then they die
    (D) times; then they die
    (E) times; before dying

25. In the official portrait of Richard III, it shows an attractive and healthy man and does not present the deformed demon of Shakespeare's play.

   (A) In the official portrait of Richard III, it shows an attractive and healthy man and does not present
   (B) In the official portrait of Richard III, an attractive, healthy man is shown; it does not present
   (C) The official portrait of Richard III shows an attractive and healthy man, not
   (D) The official portrait of Richard III shows a man who is attractive and healthy and does not present
   (E) Richard III, in the official portrait, is a man who is attractive and healthy, and he is not

26. George Eliot was an ardent and knowledgeable lover of music, and she had little skill in composing melodious verse.

   (A) George Eliot was an ardent and knowledgeable lover of music, and she had
   (B) George Eliot loved music ardently and knowledgeably, and she had
   (C) George Eliot was ardent and knowledgeable in her love of music, and she had
   (D) George Eliot was an ardent, knowledgeable music lover, having
   (E) Although George Eliot was an ardent, knowledgeable lover of music, she had

27. Nestled in the mountains of southwestern Colorado, the extinction of the town of Silverton is imminent with the closing of its silver mine.

   (A) the extinction of the town of Silverton is imminent
   (B) the extinction of Silverton as a town is imminent
   (C) the imminent extinction of the town of Silverton is likely
   (D) the town of Silverton faces imminent extinction
   (E) the town of Silverton will become extinct imminently

28. Alexander Frater was educated in Australia, <u>when he emi-grated to England</u>, and eventually became a correspondent for a London newspaper.

   (A) when he emigrated to England
   (B) emigrated to England
   (C) while he emigrated to England
   (D) emigrating to England
   (E) from whence he emigrated to England

29. In Hawaii, <u>they are emphasizing the Hawaiian language as a part of</u> a renaissance in the native culture, including music and dance.

   (A) they are emphasizing the Hawaiian language as a part of
   (B) the emphasis on the Hawaiian language is part of
   (C) they are putting emphasis on Hawaiian as a language as part of
   (D) by emphasizing the Hawaiian language, they are creating
   (E) the emphasis on the Hawaiian language is to them a part of

30. Women are starting small businesses <u>twice as often as men are; one of</u> twenty working women is now self-employed.

   (A) twice as often as men are; one of
   (B) twice as often as men are one of
   (C) twice as often as men are, one of
   (D) two times as often as men do, one of
   (E) two times as often as men do one of

31. Illiteracy costs more than five billion dollars in unemployment and welfare benefits yearly, affecting one fifth of the adult population.

    (A) Illiteracy costs more than five billion dollars in unemployment and welfare benefits yearly, affecting one fifth of the adult population.
    (B) Yearly, illiteracy costs more than five billion dollars in unemployment and welfare benefits, affecting one fifth of the adult population.
    (C) Affecting one fifth of the adult population, illiteracy costs more than five billion dollars in unemployment and welfare benefits yearly.
    (D) Yearly affecting one fifth of the adult population, illiteracy costs more than five billion dollars in unemployment and welfare benefits.
    (E) Costing more than five billion dollars in umemployment and welfare benefits, illiteracy affects one fifth of the adult population yearly.

32. Luis Jimenez's fiberglass sculpture *Fiesta Jarabe* depicting a traditional hat dance and placed just north of the Mexican border.

    (A) depicting a traditional hat dance and placed
    (B) depicting a traditional hat dance and is placed
    (C) depicting a traditional hat dance placed
    (D) depicts a traditional hat dance, placed
    (E) depicts a traditional hat dance and is placed

33. The developer plans to dismantle and move a fourteenth-century English church to Nevada which will give it the oldest church in the Western Hemisphere.

    (A) which will give it
    (B) and this will give it
    (C) which will give the state
    (D) and this will give the state
    (E) to give the state

34. Banking regulators have seized a Georgia savings bank and charged that the institution <u>both used deceptive lending and business practices and it misled</u> its stockholders.

   (A) both used deceptive lending and business practices and it misled
   (B) both used deceptive business lending practices and it misled
   (C) used deceptive lending and business practices and misled
   (D) both used lending and business practices that were deceptive, misleading
   (E) used both deceptive and misleading business and lending practices, and it misled

35. For three years, the group called White Flag <u>has virtually ignored Chicago, the city where they started in.</u>

   (A) has virtually ignored Chicago, the city where they started in
   (B) have virtually ignored Chicago, the city where they started in
   (C) has virtually ignored Chicago, the city where it started
   (D) has virtually ignored Chicago, where they started
   (E) have virtually ignored the city where they started, Chicago

36. Readers admire Margaret Fuller's <u>eagerness to succeed, that she is willing to work hard, and her refusal to give up.</u>

   (A) eagerness to succeed, that she is willing to work hard, and her refusal to give up
   (B) eagerness for success, willingness to work hard, and that she refuses to give up
   (C) being eager to succeed, willing to work hard, and her refusal to give up
   (D) eagerness to succeed, willingness to work hard, and refusal to give up
   (E) being eager to succeed, being willing to work hard, and refusal to give up

37. Understanding why a sentence or a paragraph is awkward is essentially no different <u>from when you see</u> why a mathematical proof is unconvincing.

    (A) from when you see
    (B) from if you see
    (C) from seeing
    (D) than when you see
    (E) than if you see

38. <u>Where the main purpose of the greenhouse is</u> to raise half-hardy plants for planting out in the garden or to grow flowering plants in pots for cut flowers and for bringing into the house.

    (A) Where the main purpose of the greenhouse is
    (B) When the main purpose of the greenhouse is
    (C) The main purpose of the greenhouse is
    (D) If the main purpose of the greenhouse were
    (E) While the main purpose of the greenhouse is

Directions: The following passages are early drafts of student essays. Some parts of them need to be revised.

Read the selections carefully and answer the questions that follow. There will be questions about sentence structure, diction, and usage in individual sentences or parts of sentences. Other questions will deal with the whole essay or paragraphs and ask you to decide about organization, development, and appropriate language. Choose the answer that follows the requirements of standard written English and most effectively expresses the intended meanings.

Questions 39–44 are based on the following passage.

The best things in life are free.

(1) I'm sure that many people wish that this statement would work for them. (2) I'm sure that they would like to have all the best things handed them on a silver plate. (3) But this is not how life works. (4) My father was not handed all of his possessions that he has now. (5) He worked hard to get them. (6) We didn't have them handed to us free of charge, and I am glad it went this way.

(7) People will respect others who work hard for a living versus people who get all of their success handed or given to them. (8) Hard work builds self-esteem. (9) Who are you if you do not even appreciate yourself? (10) People who never work lose the opportunity of learning about themselves, and do not know what self esteem is. (11) And they are not as happy as people who do know.

(12) So even if the money in this world could be yours free, it would be better to not take it. (13) In the long run you would be happier without it. (14) You might not be rich but you would have your self-respect and the respect of others. (15) And without self respect you will not be happy.

39. Which of the following is the best version of sentence 3 (reproduced below)?

   But this is not how life works.

   (A) (As it is now)
   (B) But life does not work this way.
   (C) And this is not how life works.
   (D) Life doesn't work like that.
   (E) Since life is not like this.

40. Which of the following is the best combined version of sentences 4 and 5 (reproduced below)?

   My father was not handed all of his possessions that he has now. He worked hard to get them.

   (A) My father was not handed all of the possessions he has now, but he worked hard for them.
   (B) My father was not handed, but worked hard for all of the possessions that he now has.
   (C) My father was not handed, but worked hard for all his possessions.
   (D) My father worked hard to obtain all his possessions.
   (E) My father worked hard for all the possessions that he has now.

41. Which of the following best describes the function of paragraphs one and two of this passage?

   (A) The first paragraph makes an assertion which the second paragraph explains.
   (B) Paragraph one makes an assertion which paragraph two contradicts.
   (C) Paragraph one raises a question which is answered in paragraph two.
   (D) Paragraph one offers an abstract idea which is supported by concrete examples in paragraph two.
   (E) Paragraph one presents generalizations which are supported by references to personal experience in the second paragraph.

42. Which of the following is the best version of sentence 7 (reproduced below)?

People will respect others who work hard for a living versus people who get all of their success handed or given to them.

(A) (As it is now)
(B) People will respect others that work hard for a living more than those who succeed because it was handed to them.
(C) People respect others working hard for a living more than those who get success handed or given to them.
(D) People will respect hard work versus those who get success handed to them.
(E) People respect those who work hard for a living more than those whose success is unearned.

43. The final paragraph of the passage differs from the first and second because it

(A) argues that unearned riches are not to be desired
(B) asks rhetorical questions
(C) is entirely directly addressed to the reader
(D) introduces a new topic for discussion
(E) uses examples from personal experience

44. The writer's purpose in the last paragraph is

(A) to summarize his or her position
(B) to summarize objections to his or her point of view
(C) to propose a solution to the question raised in the first two paragraphs
(D) to introduce a final example
(E) to allow readers to make up their own minds

Questions 45–50 are based on the following passage.

(1) I had not looked forward to going to my cousin's wedding in Idaho. (2) I did not want to go because it was on the last weekend of the summer, and I would rather have spent it with my friends at home. (3) I never had wanted to visit Idaho, even though my cousins lived there. (4) My family and I only had stand-by airline tickets, and we missed two flights, so we ended up waiting at the airport for three hours before we even left. (5) Finally having arrived there after nine at night, the weather was cold and rainy. (6) It made me feel like this would be the worst weekend of my life.

(7) When we woke up the next morning at the motel, I looked out the window, and it looked dismal, the sky was gray, and you could see small patches of rain falling. (8) My family and I eat a light breakfast and leave for the wedding. (9) It was a half hour drive to the wedding. (10) My cousin was getting married in a park. (11) By the time we got there it was starting to clear up. (12) The wedding was outdoors in the woods, and just when the bride came in, the sun came out. (13) You could feel everybodys spirits lift.

(14) After that everything seemed to go right. (15) The food at the wedding party was great. (16) There was a good band. (17) The friends of my cousin who were my age were fun. (18) When the time came to go home the next day, I was sorry to leave. (19) Next year I may go to college in Idaho.

45. Which of the following is the best version of the underlined part of sentence 5 (reproduced below)?

    Finally having arrived there after nine at night, the weather was cold and rainy.

    (A) (As it is now)
    (B) Having finally arrived there after nine at night, the weather
    (C) Arrived there finally, after nine at night, the weather
    (D) Not getting there until after nine at night, the weather
    (E) When we finally got there, after nine at night, the weather

46. Which of the following is the best version of sentence 6 (reproduced below)?

It made me feel like this would be the worst weekend of my life.

(A) (As it is now)
(B) I felt like this would be the worst weekend of my life.
(C) I thought that this would be the worst weekend of my life.
(D) It felt like this would be the worst weekend of my life.
(E) It seemed like this would be the worst weekend of my life.

47. Which of the following is the best version of the underlined portion of sentence 7 (reproduced below)?

When we woke up the next morning at the motel, I looked out the window, and it looked dismal, the sky was gray, and you could see small patches of rain falling.

(A) (As it is now)
(B) looked dismal; the sky was gray, and you could see
(C) looked dismal, the sky was gray; and you could see
(D) looked dismal, and the sky was gray, and you could see
(E) looked dismal. The sky was gray, you could see

48. Which of the following is the best version of sentence 8 (reproduced below)?

My family and I eat a light breakfast and leave for the wedding.

(A) My family and I eat a light breakfast before leaving for the wedding.
(B) Eating a light breakfast, my family and I leave for the wedding.
(C) Having eaten a light breakfast, my family and I leave for the wedding.
(D) My family and I ate a light breakfast and left for the wedding.
(E) My family and I leave for the wedding, after eating a light breakfast.

49. Which of the following is the best way to combine sentences 9 and 10 (reproduced below)?

It was a half hour drive to the wedding. My cousin was getting married in a park.

(A) It was a half hour drive to the wedding because my cousin was getting married in a park.
(B) Marrying in a park, the wedding was half an hour's drive away.
(C) It was half an hour's drive to the park where my cousin was being married.
(D) My cousin was being married in a park, and it was a half hour drive to the wedding.
(E) It was a half hour drive to the wedding; my cousin was getting married in a park.

50. All of the following strategies are used by the writer of the passage EXCEPT

(A) frequent reliance on figurative language
(B) chronological arrangement of events
(C) relating the first and last sentence of the passage
(D) use of a first person speaker
(E) use of details of weather to convey mood

Directions: The following sentences may contain one error of grammar, usage, diction, or idiom. No sentence will contain more than one error, and some have no error. If there is an error, it will be underlined and have a letter beneath it. Sections of the sentence that are not underlined cannot be changed. In selecting your answer, observe the requirements of standard written English.

If there is an error, choose the one underlined part that must be changed to correct the sentence. If there is no error, choose (E).

EXAMPLE:

The film <u>tell the story</u> of a cavalry captain and <u>his wife</u>
      A   B

who <u>try to</u> <u>rebuild their lives</u> after the Civil War. <u>No error</u>
    C   D   E

Correct answer: A

51. In four <u>densely printed pages</u> in <u>this week's</u> campus newspaper
             A   B

<u>are printed</u> the schedule of <u>all of next semester's classes.</u>
   C   D

<u>No error</u>
 E

52. A century ago José Martí <u>visits the United States</u> to
                          A

enlist <u>the support</u> of <u>exiled Cubans</u> in a war of
      B   C

<u>independence from Spain.</u> <u>No error</u>
      D   E

53. A worker <u>who suffers from</u> severe wrist pains <u>normally tries</u>
           A   B

treatments <u>like rest or splints,</u> or <u>you can undergo surgery.</u>
            C   D

<u>No error</u>
 E

54. Each year scientists <u>test their skills</u> against <u>a hostile nature</u> in
                                A   B

the <u>northernmost latitudes</u>
             C

by <u>performing a range of experiments.</u> <u>No error</u>
                   D   E

55. Neither the senator nor the president <u>were willing</u>
                                      A

<u>to compromise</u> <u>on the issue</u> of <u>reducing capital gains taxes.</u>
      B   C   D
<u>No error</u>
 E

56. <u>As part of the tribute</u> to Handel and Haydn, the chorus
            A

<u>included</u> four <u>of his works</u> in <u>its concerts</u> this year. <u>No error</u>
   B   C   D   E

57. <u>Like the Peace Corps,</u> the Korean Youth Volunteers
        A

<u>are well-trained</u> recruits <u>sent</u> <u>for assisting of</u> the Philippines
    B   C   D

and Indonesia. <u>No error</u>
           E

58. The writer of allegory <u>commonly invents</u> a world
                     A

<u>in order to talk</u> <u>about the world we live in;</u> the symbolist uses
    B   C

the real world to reveal a <u>world we cannot see.</u> <u>No error</u>
                         D   E

59. <u>Neither the violinist</u> nor the harpist <u>was accustomed to playing</u>
         A   B

modern music, <u>and so</u> the performance of the concerto was a
               C

<u>totally failure.</u> <u>No error</u>
   D   E

60. Since they <u>pay scarcely no taxes</u>, charitable foundations <u>have</u>
                        A   B
    more money <u>to disburse</u>, especially if they
                    C
    <u>can control administrative costs.</u> <u>No error</u>
                    D   E

ANSWER KEY FOR PRACTICE TEST 4

Identifying Sentence Errors

1. C	6. B	11. B	16. C
2. A	7. A	12. D	17. A
3. C	8. E	13. C	18. B
4. C	9. C	14. C	19. A
5. E	10. D	15. E	20. B

Improving Sentences

21. D	26. E	31. C	36. D
22. C	27. D	32. E	37. C
23. A	28. B	33. E	38. C
24. D	29. B	34. C	
25. C	30. A	35. C	

Improving Paragraphs

39. B	43. C	47. B
40. D	44. A	48. D
41. A	45. E	49. C
42. E	46. C	50. A

Identifying Sentence Errors

51. C	56. C
52. A	57. D
53. D	58. E
54. E	59. D
55. A	60. A

PRACTICE TEST 4 SCORING WORKSHEET

You can use the following worksheet to determine your scores. You will need two readers to score your essay. If they are not available, be objective and double the score you decide on yourself.

Part A: Essay

_____ + _____ = _____
first reader's score   second reader's score   essay raw score

Approximate essay scaled score (use the table on page 147) = ____

Part B: Multiple-Choice

_____ – _____ = _____
correct answers   wrong answers $\times$ .25   multiple-choice raw
score

Approximate multiple-choice scaled score (use the table on page 30) = ____

Composite Score

_____ + _____ = _____
essay raw score times 3   multiple-choice   composite
(or 3.02 for scores of 10–12)   raw score   raw score

Approximate composite scaled score (use the table on page 147) = ____

ANSWERS AND EXPLANATIONS FOR PRACTICE TEST 4

PART B

1. (C) The verb *agreed* and the opening phrase, *Strange as it now seems,* place the action of this sentence in the past. The verb *fears* ought to be *feared*, since the point of the sentence is that though Japan once feared Italian competition, it no longer does.

2. (A) The singular subject *darkness* does not agree with the plural verb *were;* the verb should be *was.*

3. (C) It is the pronoun *who,* not the verb *appear,* that is in error here. The pronoun refers to the sets of teeth, mechanisms, not human beings, so the correct pronoun is *which* or *that.*

4. (C) The sentence changes from a second person subject (*you*) to a third person (*one*). It should be either *you can . . . you must* or *one can . . . one must.*

5. (E) There is no error in this sentence.

6. (B) A subject and verb in this sentence are separated and do not agree. Since the singular verb *is* is not underlined and can't be changed, *huge doses* must be changed to *a huge dose* to correct the grammar.

7. (A) The opening phrase is not idiomatic. We say *as a result of* or *resulting from.*

8. (E) There is no error in the sentence.

9. (C) Since the first part of the sentence lists three, the singular *method* should be the plural *methods.*

10. (D) The error in this sentence is the unidiomatic use of the preposition *with*. The usual expression to denote the index level is *stands at*.

11. (B) The error is the confusion of an adjective and an adverb. The right word to modify the adjective *easy* is the adverb *relatively*.

12. (D) The subject of the sentence, the singular *Peninsula,* follows the verb, the plural *lie*. It should be *lies*.

13. (C) The *they* in this sentence is an ambiguous pronoun. It could refer to any of the animals, including the deer, beavers, and squirrels, which do not prey upon small rodents.

14. (C) The problem is the phrase *without he succeeds*. A better one would be *without success* or *without succeeding*.

15. (E) The sentence is grammatical and idiomatic.

16. (C) The sequence of tenses here is inconsistent. The first and second verbs use the present tense (*is, is*), but the third uses the future instead of another present.

17. (A) If you ignore the *Texans,* the error is easy to find: *that us . . . talk oddly*. It is an error of pronoun case, using the objective *us* rather than the subjective *we* as the subject of a clause.

18. (B) This is a diction error. The word *requisite* is a noun or an adjective but not the verb the context calls for. The right word is the verb *require*.

19. (A) There is an agreement problem here. The sentence gives only one example, apple pie. To be consistent, the sentence has to begin with *The most delicious dessert.*

20. (B) The error is a faulty comparative (*more spectacular*) where the context calls for a superlative (*most spectacular*), since the begonias surpass *all the plants grown from tubers.*

21. (D) The original version has faulty parallelism and is verbose. (B) isn't so wordy, but it shifts from the active verb (*affects*) to *affected are*. The *also being affected* of (E) is no better. The best choice is (D), which is the most concise of the five and has a parallel construction of the series.

22. (C) This is another of those sentences in which the pronouns have no specific antecedents but refer to a general idea or the entire first clause. Changing pronouns (from *which* to *this*) does no good. To repair a sentence like this, you can supply a specific antecedent (you might say *a fact which is surprising*) or get rid of the pronoun. Choice (C) adds a noun and eliminates the pronoun.

23. (A) Like 21, the sentence includes a series; the original version here is the best of the five—parallel, correctly punctuated with commas, and concise. The semicolons of (B) are incorrect; (C) has an extra *and*. (D) and (E) break up the parallel construction.

24. (D) This sentence runs on two sentences without any punctuation or connective between them. Here, the semicolon is the best choice with the two independent clauses. It won't work in (E) because the second clause is no longer independent; it is now a sentence fragment.

25. (C) Compare sentence (C) with (A) and you see that five words (*In, it, and, does,* and *present*) can be cut with no change of meaning. None of the four other versions of the sentence is as economical as (C), though they are all grammatical except (A), which has the vague pronoun *it*.

26. (E) The original sentence here is not really wrong, but it is less effective because it treats all the elements as equal, while the superior version (E) subordinates the first clause, making the meaning of the relation between parts of the sentence clearer. Here, choice (D) is a shorter sentence than (E), but the gain in clarity is worth more than the gain in economy, or conciseness.

27. (D) The phrase that begins this sentence begins with the past participle *Nestled,* and predictably, that opening phrase dangles. The town, not its extinction, nestles, so we can eliminate (A), (B), and (C). Choice (D) is more concise than (E).

28. (B) The sentence presents a series of three parts in chronological order. The first and third parts of the series use verbs in the past tense, but the second element is subordinated in (A), (C), (D), and (E). To keep the three parts parallel, there should be no *when, while,* or *whence,* and the verb should be in the past tense to maintain the parallel (*was educated, emigrated, became*).

29. (B) All four of the erring versions of this sentence have a vague pronoun (*they* or *them* in E). They who? (B) is the clearest and the briefest sentence.

30. (A) The original sentence is correct. The two independent clauses are separated by the semicolon. A period would also work here, but a comma or no punctuation at all will produce a comma splice or a run-on sentence.

31. (C) In this section of the exam, when all of a long sentence is underlined, there is a good chance that the problem being tested is the placement of a modifier. Here, the phrase *affecting one fifth of the adult population* modifies *illiteracy.* The good answer will find a way to keep the two together. (D) keeps the two together but misplaces *yearly* so that it appears to modify *affecting* rather than *costs.* (E) also misplaces *yearly.*

32. (E) This is a sentence fragment, with two participles but no main verb. (A), (B), and (C) retain the participle *depicting* and do not supply a main verb. (D) adds a verb, but the participle *placed* now modifies *dance.* (E) has the two required main verbs.

33. (E) Like 22, this sentence uses a pronoun with no specific antecedent and tries to correct the error by changing the pronoun; neither *which* nor *this* will work, but eliminating the pronoun eliminates the error.

34. (C) With the correlatives *both . . . and,* the same structure should follow each conjunction. Since (A) and (B) begin with *both used,* the *and* should be followed by a verb, not the pronoun *it.* (D) never completes the *both* with an *and.* (E) uses *both . . . and* correctly (to introduce adjectives that are parallel), but it is a very wordy sentence, four words longer than (C). (C) avoids a lot of trouble simply by not using *both . . . and.*

35. (C) The issues in this sentence are the agreement of the verb and pronoun with the subject *group* and the phrase *where . . . in.* Since *group* refers to a single unit, we should take it to be singular and use the singular *has ignored* and *it.* In the phrase *the city where . . . in,* the *in* is unnecessary.

36. (D) The sentence is testing parallel elements in a series. The series could use three nouns or three clauses beginning with *that* or three gerunds to keep the parallelism, though the *that* clauses would be wordy. None of the wrong answers uses all three consistently, but (D) uses three nouns (*eagerness, willingness,* and *refusal*).

37. (C) The phrase *is no different from* is another way of saying *is like.* Comparisons, whether negative (*not different*) or not should be kept as parallel as possible. Here, we need a parallel to the gerund *understanding.* The addition of subject (*you*) and verb (*see*) in (A), (B), (D), or (E) is unnecessary. The parallel of (C) is the most concise choice, the gerund *seeing.*

38. (C) This is a sentence fragment. Introduced by *Where,* it is a dependent clause. The change to *When,* or *If,* or *While* doesn't make the clause independent. (C) rightly drops the subordinating conjunction, and the sentence is now complete.

39. (B) The problem in this sentence is the pronoun *this*, which has no specific antecedent. Choices (A), (C), and (E) all keep the vague *this*, while in (D) the vague pronoun is *that*. Only (B) avoids the difficulty; *this* modifies *way*.

40. (D) These sentences are verbose, especially since *was not handed* in 4 is followed in 6 with the repetitive *We didn't have them handed to us.* This part of 4 should be eliminated in the revision. Another redundancy is following *possessions* with *that he has,* since possessions are what *he has.* Here, the shortest revision (D) is also the best.

41. (A) The first paragraph asserts that life doesn't hand us things free and that the writer is glad this is so. The second paragraph gives reasons to explain this view. Choice (E) is inaccurate, since the personal references are in the first paragraph, while the second is more general.

42. (E) The phrase *get all of their success handed or given to them* is awkward and verbose. There is no need for both *given* and *handed.* (B) has usage errors (*that* for *who*, the vague *it.*). The comparison in (C) is not parallel, and in (D) it is illogical, comparing work with people who work. (E) maintains a clear parallel and is not wordy.

43. (C) The final paragraph uses the pronoun *you.* Though *you* is used in one sentence in the second paragraph, all the other sentences use the third person.

44. (A) The last paragraph summarizes the writer's position—that unearned wealth will not bring happiness.

45. (E) The only version here that avoids a dangling participle is (E), which supplies a subject and a verb (*we . . . got*). In (A), (B), (C), and (D), it is the weather that arrives after nine, not the wedding guests.

46. (C) The trouble here is the use of *like* as a conjunction in the phrase *feel like this would be.* The error is minor, but given a chance to revise the sentence, you are better off with (C), which eliminates *like.* All the other choiccs use *like* as a conjunction, though the verbs are different.

47. (B) The issue here is the comma splice. Since *the sky was gray* is a complete sentence, it should be separated from *dismal* by either a semicolon or a period. (E) corrects the original error but introduces another comma splice after *gray.*

48. (D) In answering the questions in this section of the exam, you must keep in mind the paragraph as a whole, not just the sentence in the question. Here, though all of the answers are grammatically correct, you should choose (D), which has verbs in the past tense. The writer uses the past tense throughout the passage and should continue to do so here.

49. (C) Again, if you look at the paragraph, not just these sentences, you will see that sentence 8 uses the word *wedding,* and the word is repeated in sentence 9. Only choice (C) gets rid of this repetition. It subordinates the less important clause and is more concise than the other choices except (B), which is ungrammatical.

50. (A) The passage doesn't rely on figurative language (metaphor and simile). It does arrange events chronologically, connect the first and last sentence (by repeating *Idaho*), use a first person speaker (*I*), and use details of the weather to convey mood (sentences 5–7 and 12–13).

51. (C) The subject of this sentence is the singular *schedule.* The verb, which comes before the subject in this sentence, should also be singular, *is.*

52. (A) The phrase *A century ago* places the action in the past. The main verb, *visits,* should be in the past tense, *visited.*

53. (D) The subject of the first half of the sentence is *A worker,* but it shifts from the third to the second person, *you.* To be consistent, the conclusion should have *he can* or *he or she can.*

54. (E) This sentence has no error.

55. (A) The subject of the verb is singular, *the senator, the president,* but not both, so the verb should be *was.* Be watchful for agreement errors in sentences with *either . . . or* or *neither . . . nor.*

56. (C) The reference of the pronoun *his* is uncertain; it can be either *Handel* or *Haydn.* If it intends both, the sentence should use *their.*

57. (D) The idiom with *sent* is the infinitive *to assist* rather than the prepositional phrase *for assisting of.*

58. (E) There are no errors in this sentence.

59. (D) This sentence gets the agreement with *neither . . . nor* right, but it uses the adverb *totally* to modify the noun *failure.* The right word is the adjective *total.*

60. (A) The adverb *scarcely* counts as a negative, so this is a double negative. The right phrase is *scarcely any.*

PRACTICE TEST 5

| PART A | Time—20 Minutes
1 Question | ESSAY |

In twenty minutes, write an essay on the topic below. YOU MAY NOT WRITE ON ANOTHER TOPIC. AN ESSAY ON ANOTHER TOPIC WILL NOT BE SCORED.

The essay is intended to give you the chance to show your writing skills. Be sure to express your ideas on the topic clearly and effectively. The quality of your writing is much more important than the quantity, but to deal adequately with this topic you should probably write more than one paragraph. Be specific.

Think carefully about the following quotation and the assignment that follows. Then plan and write your essay according to the instructions.

"The more we know, the unhappier we are."

Write an essay in which you discuss what you think the author of this quotation means and whether or not you agree. Be specific and support your arguments.

WHEN THE TWENTY MINUTES HAVE PASSED, YOU MUST STOP WRITING AND GO ON TO THE MULTIPLE-CHOICE SECTION OF THE TEST. IF YOU FINISH YOUR ESSAY BEFORE THE TWENTY MINUTES HAVE PASSED, YOU MAY GO ON TO THE NEXT SECTION OF THE EXAM.

Directions: The following sentences may contain one error of grammar, usage, diction, or idiom. No sentence will contain more than one error, and some have no error. If there is an error, it will be underlined and have a letter beneath it. Sections of the sentence that are not underlined cannot be changed. In selecting your answer, observe the requirements of standard written English.

If there is an error, choose the one underlined part that must be changed to correct the sentence. If there is no error, choose (E).

EXAMPLE:

The film tell the story of a cavalry captain and his wife
      A   B

who try to rebuild their lives after the Civil War. No error
    C   D   E

Correct answer: A

1. Most university libraries now use an electronic system
                                   A

  that gives out a signal if a person leaves the library with a book
       B   C

  that you have not checked out. No error
        D   E

2. As Friedman warned in the early eighties, taxes and the cost of
                A

  living have risen steadily while the value of the dollar abroad
         B   C

  have steadily declined. No error
       D   E

3. Those musicians <u>having studied</u> under masters like Baker and
                          A
   Hess are the ones <u>who ought to become</u> teachers when
                          B
   <u>their performing careers</u> <u>have ended.</u> <u>No error</u>
            C   D   E

4. To complain about the death of the counterculture or <u>to insist</u>
                                                              A
   that <u>it still exists</u> is <u>to commit</u> the same error, <u>but a</u>
              B   C   D
   counterculture never really existed. <u>No error</u>
                                             E

5. <u>Though raised in conservative New Hampshire,</u> Miss Wade
                        A
   leads <u>a</u> <u>remarkably unconventional</u> life in an environment
         B   C
   <u>totally unlike that</u> of her childhood. <u>No error</u>
            D   E

6. Neither the British archaeologist nor the American, Miss

   Hopewell, <u>have discovered</u> anything <u>comparable in importance</u>
                    A   B
   to the artifacts <u>unearthed at Cuzco</u> <u>more than forty years ago.</u>
                          C   D
   <u>No error</u>
      E

7. <u>Using the inland roads,</u> the tourist will
            A
   <u>have fewer miles to travel,</u> but the scenery <u>is more inferior to</u>
              B   C
   what can <u>be seen on</u> the coastal routes. <u>No error</u>
                  D   E

8. One quarter of today's Spanish words have Arab origins,
                      A   B
   from the familiar bullfighting cheer *Olé* to the
                   C
   incongruously elegant word for sewer, *alcantarilla*. No error
                 D   E

9. Unable to depend on his brother, sister, or I, Mr. Owens
              A   B
   has hired a car at the airport and
       C
   has driven himself to Cleveland. No error
              D   E

10. If you want to get ahead in real estate, one must be ready to
                                              A
    make certain compromises, to have great patience, and at
                 B   C
    times, to tell half-truths. No error
           D   E

11. Between 1930 and 1950, musicians improvised on not only the
                          A
    songs of Gershwin, Porter, and Berlin, but also
           B
    less well-known writers like Wilder, Arlen, and Hunter.
                 C   D
    No error
    E

12. Michael Redgrave, Max Adrian, and Paul Rogers

    are scheduled to appear in *Uncle Vanya*, but he is unable to
         A   B   C
    make an appearance this week. No error
                 D   E

13. In parts of southeastern Europe, <u>such as Romania</u>, the end of
      A
    Communism <u>has only made</u> bad conditions <u>worse than</u> they
                  B   C
    <u>were.</u> <u>No error</u>
      D   E

14. The easiest way to reach Cnidus from Athens is not,

    <u>as would seem likely</u>, <u>in flying</u> to Istanbul, <u>but by taking</u> the
            A   B   C
    ship that <u>runs between Rhodes and the coast.</u> <u>No error</u>
                              D   E

15. <u>With scarcely no hesitation, in 1939 Hitler</u> <u>ignored the treaties</u>
                          A   B
    that Germany <u>had signed</u> and
                      C
    <u>massed his armies on the Polish border.</u> <u>No error</u>
                          D   E

16. The quarterback, <u>with the trainer</u> and two doctors,
                          A
    <u>were slowly walking</u> toward the sidelines, <u>while the crowd</u>
              B   C
    <u>groaned audibly.</u> <u>No error</u>
          D   E

17. The flight attendant <u>announced that</u> the plane <u>would leave</u> a
                              A   B
    little <u>more faster</u> if passengers <u>took their seats.</u> <u>No error</u>
              C   D   E

18. The walls of the prime minister's office are <u>eerily bare</u>, <u>as if</u>
                                                      A   B
    <u>he does not plan</u> to <u>stay there long.</u> <u>No error</u>
          C   D   E

19. After fourteen weeks of <u>complete inactivity</u>, the bear <u>raises up</u>,
                            A   B

    leaves his den, and <u>searches eagerly</u> for food of any kind.
         C   D

    <u>No error</u>
       E

20. The <u>last documented case</u> of polio in the Western Hemisphere
             A

    <u>was</u> a three-year-old boy <u>that</u> <u>contracted the disease</u> in Peru in
     B   C   D

    1991. <u>No error</u>
              E

Directions: The following questions test correctness and effective expression. In selecting the answer, pay attention to grammar, diction, sentence structure, and punctuation.

In the following questions, part or all of each sentence is underlined. The (A) answer repeats the underlined portion of the original sentence, while the next four offer alternatives. Choose the answer that best expresses the meaning of the original sentence and at the same time is grammatically correct and stylistically superior. The correct choice should be clear, unambiguous, and concise.

EXAMPLE:

The forecaster predicted <u>rain and the sky was clear</u>.

(A) rain and the sky was clear
(B) rain but the sky was clear
(C) rain the sky was clear
(D) rain, but the sky was clear
(E) rain being as the sky was clear

Correct answer: D

21. Manning's book on *Nicholas Nickleby* is the most dependable guide to this difficult novel, and it is also the wittiest account.

   (A) guide to this difficult novel, and it is also the wittiest account
   (B) guide, and it is also the wittiest account of this difficult novel
   (C) guide to this difficult novel, and the wittiest
   (D) guide and also the wittiest account of this difficult novel
   (E) and wittiest guide to this difficult novel

22. To lose weight rapidly, one should weigh every food portion carefully, exercise regularly, <u>and you should only drink</u> water, black coffee, or diet soda.

   (A) and you should only drink
   (B) and you should drink only
   (C) only drinking
   (D) and drink only
   (E) and one should drink only

23. <u>Different from any other designs in the show</u>, Orlando Fashions Company exhibited a collection made entirely of nylon.

   (A) Different from any other designs in the show
   (B) Different from any designs in the show
   (C) With designs different from any others in the show
   (D) Designed differently from others in the show
   (E) Different from other designs in the show

24. As Gordon's army advanced farther into the interior, <u>and its supply line from the coast became more and more vulnerable</u>.

   (A) and its supply line from the coast became more and more vulnerable
   (B) its supply line from the coast became more and more vulnerable
   (C) its supply line from the coast becoming more and more vulnerable
   (D) while its supply line from the coast became more and more vulnerable
   (E) and its supply line from the coast becoming more and more vulnerable

25. Ardmore has been cheated several times <u>because of his being of a trusting nature</u>.

   (A) because of his being of a trusting nature
   (B) because of his trustworthiness
   (C) because his nature is trusting
   (D) because he is trusting
   (E) being trusting by nature

26. A very old plant in our gardens, the cornflower appears in paintings made as early as the fourth century.

   (A) the cornflower appears in paintings made as early as the fourth century
   (B) cornflowers appear in paintings made as early as the fourth century
   (C) fourth-century-made paintings show cornflowers
   (D) paintings of cornflowers were made as early as the fourth century
   (E) paintings of cornflowers made as early as the fourth century

27. Tomoka Seki studied ballet in France for two years, and now she is studying Balinese dancing and Asian art.

   (A) Tomoka Seki studied ballet in France for two years, and now she is
   (B) Having studied ballet in France for two years, Tomoka Seki is now
   (C) Ballet was studied in France for two years by Tomoka Seki who is now
   (D) She studied ballet in France for two years, and now Tomoka Seki is
   (E) For two years, Tomoka Seki studies ballet in France now she is

28. If they are going to save the temples nearest the Nile, the floods will have to be controlled.

   (A) If they are going to save the temples nearest the Nile, the floods will have to be controlled.
   (B) If they are going to save the temples nearest the Nile, they will have to control the floods.
   (C) To save the temples nearest the Nile, they will have to control the floods.
   (D) The Egyptians must control the floods to save the temples nearest the Nile.
   (E) The floods must be controlled by the Egyptians, if the temples nearest the Nile are to be saved.

29. At one time, nearly all of Kuwait's 700 oil wells were on <u>fire the crippled</u> refineries were closed.

  (A) fire the crippled
  (B) fire but the crippled
  (C) fire, crippled, the
  (D) fire; the crippled
  (E) fire, crippled

30. The sky-diver compared his feelings to the elation <u>of winning a lottery, scoring a touchdown, or beating</u> the odds in Las Vegas.

  (A) of winning a lottery, scoring a touchdown, or beating
  (B) when one wins a lottery, scores a touchdown, or beating
  (C) of winning a lottery, of scoring a touchdown, to beating
  (D) of winning a lottery, of scoring a touchdown, or of beating
  (E) of a win in a lottery, scoring a touchdown, or beating

31. <u>In 1982, Arun Shourie exposed a multimillion-dollar scandal that involved the prime minister's son, and he</u> lost his job as a newspaper editor.

  (A) In 1982, Arun Shourie exposed a multimillion-dollar scandal that involved the prime minister's son, and he
  (B) Arun Shourie, exposing in 1982 a multimillion-dollar scandal that involved the prime minister's son,
  (C) In 1982, having exposed a multimillion-dollar scandal that involved the prime minister's son, Arun Shourie
  (D) It was 1982 when Arun Shourie exposed a multimillion-dollar scandal involving the prime minister's son, and he
  (E) In 1982, Arun Shourie exposed a multimillion-dollar scandal that involved the prime minister's son, and consequently he

32. The population of beluga whales in the Gulf of St. Lawrence has failed to <u>increase, and this</u> worries many marine biologists.

  (A) increase, and this
  (B) increase; and this
  (C) increase; this
  (D) increase, which
  (E) increase, a fact that

33. In the legend, the evil Ravana abducts the virtuous Sita, carries her off to Ceylon, and <u>he is defeated there by Rama in a final battle</u>.

   (A) he is defeated there by Rama in a final battle
   (B) there, in a final battle, he is defeated by Rama
   (C) falls to Rama there in a final battle
   (D) is defeated there, in a final battle, by Rama
   (E) it is there that he is defeated by Rama in a final battle

34. Yielding to the public demand for a happy ending, <u>the end of the film will be edited to reunite the lovers</u>.

   (A) the end of the film will be edited to reunite the lovers
   (B) the lovers will be reunited at the end of the film
   (C) the end of the film will reunite the lovers after being edited
   (D) after editing the film will reunite the lovers
   (E) the director will edit the end of the film to reunite the lovers

35. Some kind of expansion of the permanent five-member Security Council <u>is inevitable, it may come</u> in the very near future.

   (A) is inevitable, it may come
   (B) is inevitable, and it may come
   (C) is inevitable it may come
   (D) is inevitable, coming
   (E) is inevitable, maybe it will come

36. Late-night talk-radio programs that give the Chinese listener a chance to speak openly <u>have surprised and delighted a huge audience</u>.

   (A) have surprised and delighted a huge audience
   (B) have been a surprise and a delight to a huge audience
   (C) surprised a huge audience, also delighting it
   (D) surprised as well as delighting a huge audience
   (E) were surprising and a delight to a huge audience

37. The notion that human beings will usually act to benefit themselves is an idea that for even the most idealistic <u>is with easy comprehension</u>.

    (A) is with easy comprehension
    (B) is to comprehend easily
    (C) is easy to comprehend
    (D) is easy for comprehending
    (E) is with ease in comprehending

38. The increases in tourism and resort building <u>reflecting the health of the Chilean economy</u>, which has expanded by 12% this year.

    (A) reflecting the health of the Chilean economy
    (B) reflect the health of the Chilean economy
    (C) reflecting signs of the health of the Chilean economy
    (D) clear indications of the health of the Chilean economy
    (E) and the increasing health of the Chilean economy

<u>Directions:</u> The following passages are early drafts of student essays. Some parts of them need to be revised.

Read the selections carefully and answer the questions that follow. There will be questions about sentence structure, diction, and usage in individual sentences or parts of sentences. Other questions will deal with the whole essay or paragraphs and ask you to decide about organization, development, and appropriate language. Choose the answer that follows the requirements of standard written English and most effectively expresses the intended meanings.

<u>Questions 39–44</u> are based on the following passage.

(1) Obesity affects a large majority of the population. (2) I do not, however, consider obesity to be the last ten pounds that one must lose to look good in a bikini. (3) It is the fifty, sixty, even seventy pounds that one must lose to fit into their clothes. (4) In the most extreme cases, it can even be the hundreds of pounds that one must lose to stay healthy and alive.

(5) All who have suffered from obesity at one point or another of their lives share a special bond. (6) They belong to a special brother/ sisterhood due to all the alienation, humiliation, and ridicule they have felt throughout their lives. (7) Many people who have never had to deal with being obese look on in disgust. (8) They believe that these people just have no self control or discipline. (9) They do not realize that there is much more to it than that.

(10) Many obese people having a very low self-esteem. (11) This in turn can lead them into staying in abusive jobs or relationships in which they feel that they cannot achieve or deserve any better due to the way they look.

(12) The major cause of obesity is over-eating, but one must study that aspect much more carefully. (13) There is no single easy explanation for over-eating. (14) There are many reasons why a person over-eats. (15) Feelings of loneliness and insecurity may cause a person to turn to eating as a form of refuge. (16) They may in fact find solace with their next meal, or as means of dealing with problems. (17) One

may feel that since they do not have much control over their lives they can try to control what they eat. (18) Thus it becomes an issue of control. (19) From the scientific aspect there are also other things which must be considered such as: metabolism, body frame, and genetics.

39. In the first paragraph of the passage, the diction (word choice) of which of the following is probably in error?

    (A) *"large majority"* (sentence 1)
    (B) *"last ten pounds"* (sentence 2)
    (C) *"to look good"* (sentence 2)
    (D) *"extreme cases"* (sentence 4)
    (E) *"healthy and alive"* (sentence 4)

40. Which of the following is the best way to revise and combine sentences 5 and 6 (reproduced below)?

    All who have suffered from obesity at one point or another of their lives share a special bond. They belong to a special brother/sisterhood due to all the alienation, humiliation, and ridicule that they have felt throughout their lives.

    (A) Due to all the alienation, humiliation, and ridicule they have felt, all who have suffered from obesity at one point or another of their lives share a special bond of brother/sisterhood.
    (B) All who have suffered from obesity at any time share a special bond due to the alienation, humiliation, and ridicule they have experienced.
    (C) All people who have been obese share a special bond in a brother/sisterhood that the alilenation, humiliation, and ridicule that they have suffered has made.
    (D) Sharing a special bond of brother/sisterhood, all who have suffered from obesity at one time or another have felt alienation, humiliation, and ridicule throughout their lives.
    (E) Sharing the special bond of alienation, humiliation, and ridicule that they have felt all their lives are all who have suffered from obesity at some point or other in their lives.

41. Which of the following is the best version of sentence 10 (reproduced below)?

Many obese people having a very low self-esteem.

(A) (As it is now)
(B) Many people who are obese having very low self-esteem.
(C) Many people who suffer from being obese have a very low self-esteem.
(D) Many obese people had a very low self-esteem.
(E) Many obese people have very low self-esteem.

42. Which of the following is the best way to revise and combine sentences 12, 13, and 14 (reproduced below)?

The major cause of obesity is over-eating, but one must study that aspect much more carefully. There is no single, easy explanation for over-eating. There are many reasons why a person over-eats.

(A) One must study more carefully the major causes of obesity because, besides over-eating, there is no single easy explanation of why a person over-eats.
(B) The major causes of obesity, aside from over-eating, must be studied carefully because there are many causes, and none of them are simple or easy.
(C) The major cause of obesity is over-eating, but there is no single, easy way to explain why a person over-eats.
(D) The major cause of obesity is over-eating, and there are many reasons, and no single easy explanation of why people over-eat.
(E) There are many explanations, but none of them is simple or easy of why people over-eat, though over-eating is a major cause of obesity.

43. Which of the following revisions would improve the fourth paragraph of the passage?

   I. Clarify the reference of the pronoun *"One"* in sentence 17.
  II. Clarify the reference of the pronoun *"it"* in sentence 18.
 III. Make the references to the obese in the paragraph either singular or plural.

(A) II only
(B) I and II only
(C) I and III only
(D) II and III only
(E) I, II, and III

44. Of the four paragraphs in the passage, which, if any, is seriously undeveloped?

(A) none of the four
(B) paragraph one
(C) paragraph two
(D) paragraph three
(E) paragraph four

Questions 45–50: are based on the following passage.

(1) I think my violin is one of the most beautiful things that I have ever set my eyes on. (2) With a sleek coat of burnt amber, it has caught the eye of many people. (3) It wasn't only appearance that captured my attention, however, it has so much more to offer than good looks. (4) We are an inseparable couple, and we do just about everything together.

(5) This can be quite disconcerting to those that don't understand our relationship. (6) Our relationship is very special. (7) Because I chose my violin for myself makes our relationship all the more special to me. (8) A violin someone else chose for me would not mean as much to me.

(9) When I was in junior high school, my mother gave me one of her violins, and though I was pleased, it was not my own choice and one that I could really call my own. (10) Several years later, a friend who was a violin dealer called to say he had some new instruments which he

bought at an auction in New York. (11) I loved the appearance, look, and sound of my violin right away.

(12) Sound was the number one selling factor. (13) I was sure this was the instrument for me. (14) I tried it out in my house and in the big hall at the conservatory to see if the sound would carry in a big hall. (15) At last I had the violin I had always longed for. (16) Now we spend hours together each week.

45. Which of the following is the best version of sentence 3 (reproduced below)?

    It wasn't only appearance that captured my attention, however, it has so much more to offer than good looks.

    (A) It wasn't only appearance that captured my attention, however, it has so much more to offer.
    (B) Its appearance wasn't the only thing that captured my attention, it had more than good looks to offer.
    (C) It wasn't only the appearance that captured my attention, having more to offer than good looks.
    (D) Its good looking appearance wasn't all that captured my attention, it had more than good looks to offer.
    (E) It was, however, more than its good looks that captured my attention.

46. Which of the following is the best way to combine sentences 6, 7, and 8 (reproduced below)?

    Our relationship is very special. Because I chose my violin for myself makes our relationship all the more special to me. A violin someone else chose for me would not mean as much to me.

    (A) My violin would not mean so much to me if someone else had chosen it.
    (B) My special relation to my violin is because I chose it myself, not someone else.
    (C) My relationship with my violin is special because I chose it myself, and not someone else.
    (D) Because I chose my violin myself, and not someone else, our relationship is a very special one.
    (E) Choosing my violin for myself, our relationship is more special than if someone else had chosen for me.

47. One of the weaknesses of this prose, exemplified by such phrases as *"most beautiful I ever set my eyes on," "so much more to offer,"* and *"a very special relationship,"* is its heavy dependence on

   (A) parallel constructions
   (B) clichés
   (C) Latinate diction
   (D) slang
   (E) minor usage errors

48. Which of the following is the best way to combine sentences 11, 12, and 13 (reproduced below)?

   I loved the appearance, look, and sound of my violin right away. Sound was the number one selling factor. I was sure this was the instrument for me.

   (A) Loving the appearance, look, and the sound, which was the number one selling factor, I was sure this was the instrument for me.
   (B) Sure that this was the instrument for me, I loved the appearance, look and the sound was the number one selling factor.
   (C) Once I saw and heard my violin (the sound was more important), I knew this was the instrument for me.
   (D) The sound was the number one selling factor, and also I loved the look and appearance of this violin.
   (E) I loved its look, sound, and appearance (especially the sound), and so I knew that this was the instrument for me.

49. All of the following should be revised to reduce their wordiness EXCEPT

   (A) *We are an inseparable couple, and we do just about everything together.* (sentence 4)
   (B) *Because I chose my violin for myself makes our relationship all the more special to me. A violin someone else chose for me would not mean as much to me.* (sentences 7 and 8)
   (C) *. . . it was not my own choice and one that I could really call my own.* (sentence 9)
   (D) *Several years later, a friend who was a violin dealer called to say he had some new instruments which he bought at an auction in New York.* (sentence 10)
   (E) *I tried it out in my house and in the big hall at the conservatory to see if the sound would carry in a big hall.* (sentence 14)

50. Which of the following is the best paragraphing of the passage?

   (A) five paragraphs, ending with sentences 4, 8, 10, 13, and 16
   (B) four paragraphs, ending with sentences 4, 8, 11, and 16 (as it is now)
   (C) three paragraphs, ending with sentences 6, 10, and 16
   (D) two paragraphs ending with sentences 8 and 16
   (E) a single paragraph

Directions: The following sentences may contain one error of grammar, usage, diction, or idiom. No sentence will contain more than one error, and some have no error. If there is an error, it will be underlined and have a letter beneath it. Sections of the sentence that are not underlined cannot be changed. In selecting your answer, observe the requirements of standard written English.

If there is an error, choose the one underlined part that must be changed to correct the sentence. If there is no error, choose (E).

EXAMPLE:

The film tell the story of a cavalry captain and his wife
         A   B
who try to rebuild their lives after the Civil War. No error
    C   D   E

Correct answer: A

51. Promoted by relaxed social controls, a new liveliness
                  A
    is creeping into the Chinese press, though
       B   C
    with severely controls of the Communist party. No error
          D   E

52. In a sign of warming relations between Israel and Arab states,
                A   B
    Tunisia and Israel has agreed to exchange economic liaison
                       C   D
    officers. No error
             E

53. Adapted English words like *lonche* (lunch) are common among
    A   B
    Spanish speakers in border cities, and they show up even in
                                              C   D
    official police reports. No error
                            E

54. <u>In the first</u> scenes of the opera <u>are</u> the most difficult challenge
    　　　A　　　　　　　　　　　　　B
    to the soprano <u>singing the role</u> of Elvira. <u>No error</u>
    　　　C　　　　　　D　　　　　　　　　　E

55. Because they <u>had never swam</u> in a fresh-water pool,
    　　　　　　　A
    <u>several of the swimmers</u> from Pacific islands <u>had difficulty</u>
    　　　　　B　　　　　　　　　　　　　　　　　　C
    <u>in adjusting to</u> the chemicals in the water. <u>No error</u>
    　　　D　　　　　　　　　　　　　　　　　　E

56. The minister <u>expressed little confidence</u> in a <u>proposal for</u> a
    　　　　　　　　A　　　　　　　　　　　　B
    new proportional representation plan

    <u>intended for strengthening</u> the
    　　　　　C
    opposition voice in the legislature. <u>No error</u>
    　　　　　D　　　　　　　　　　　　E

57. After the Civil War, President Grant <u>made the acquisition</u> of
    　　　　　　　　　　　　　　　　　　　A
    <u>not only Cuba</u> but <u>also the Dominican Republic</u> a key,
    　　　B　　　　　　　　C
    <u>though doomed</u>, part of his foreign policy. <u>No error</u>
    　　　D　　　　　　　　　　　　　　　　E

58. The Academic Decathlon team has decided <u>to increase</u> its
    　　　　　　　　　　　　　　　　　　　　A
    practice time <u>to four hours a day</u>, and so <u>they are meeting</u> at
    　　　　　　　B　　　　　　　　　　　　C
    the <u>coach's house each evening</u>. <u>No error</u>
    　　　　D　　　　　　　　　　　E

59. For the Cajun dinner, the caterer featured red beans and
    _____
          A
    popcorn shrimp <u>as appetizers</u> and <u>serves</u> blackened red fish
                        B   C
    <u>as the main course.</u> <u>No error</u>
              D   E

60. Either Dallas or San Francisco <u>are strongly favored</u> to
                                                A
    <u>represent</u> the conference and <u>to win</u> this
         B   C
    <u>year's national championship.</u> <u>No error</u>
                    D   E

ANSWER KEY FOR PRACTICE TEST 5

Identifying Sentence Errors

1. D	6. A	11. C	16. B
2. D	7. C	12. C	17. C
3. A	8. E	13. E	18. E
4. D	9. B	14. B	19. B
5. E	10. A	15. A	20. C

Improving Sentences

21. E	26. A	31. C	36. A
22. D	27. B	32. E	37. C
23. C	28. D	33. C	38. B
24. B	29. D	34. E	
25. D	30. A	35. B	

Improving Paragraphs

39. A	43. E	47. B
40. B	44. D	48. C
41. E	45. E	49. D
42. C	46. A	50. D

Identifying Sentence Errors

51. D	56. C
52. C	57. E
53. E	58. C
54. B	59. C
55. A	60. A

PRACTICE TEST 5 SCORING WORKSHEET

You can use the following worksheet to determine your scores. You will need two readers to score your essay. If they are not available, be objective and double the score you decide on yourself.

Part A: Essay

_____ + _____ = _____

first reader's score   second reader's score   essay raw score

Approximate essay scaled score (use the table on page 147) = _____

Part B: Multiple-Choice

_____ – _____ = _____

correct answers   wrong answers × .25   multiple-choice raw score

Approximate multiple-choice scaled score (use the table on page 30) = _____

Composite Score

_____ + _____ = _____

essay raw score times 3   multiple-choice   composite
(or 3.02 for scores of 10–12)   raw score   raw score

Approximate composite scaled score (use the table on page 147) = _____

ANSWERS AND EXPLANATIONS FOR PRACTICE TEST 5

PART B

1. (D) There is a shift in the clause that concludes the sentence from *a person* (a third person subject) to *you* (a second person subject). It should be either *if you leave* or *a book that he or she has not checked out.*

2. (D) The subject and verb in the second half of the sentence do not agree. The subject *value* is a singular, so the verb should be *has . . . declined.*

3. (A) The phrase *having studied* is not idiomatic here. A phrase like *who have studied* would be parallel to *who ought to become* later in the sentence.

4. (D) The problem in this sentence is the use of the conjunction *but.* The sense of the sentence as a whole calls for a connective like *because,* or *for,* or *since.*

5. (E) There are no errors here. The participial phrase at the beginning does not dangle, and the verb and the adverbs are used correctly.

6. (A) With two singular subjects joined by *either . . . or* or *neither . . . nor,* the verb is singular. Here, *have discovered* should be *has discovered.*

7. (C) By itself, the word *inferior* means *lower in quality,* so there is no need to use the intensifier *more* in this context.

8. (E) There are no errors in this sentence. The *today's* apostrophe is correct, and the adverb *incongruously* correctly modifies the adjective *elegant.*

9. (B) The pronoun *I* should be *me*. Though it is separated from the preposition *on,* it is still its object and should be in the objective case.

10. (A) There is a shift of pronoun here. The sentence begins with *you* but switches to *one*. It should read *you must be ready*.

11. (C) The sentence begins with *improvised on . . . songs* but moves from *songs* to songwriters. To be consistent, the second term should be something like *the songs of . . . writers like* or *the works of.*

12. (C) The reference of the pronoun *he* is unclear. It can refer to any of the three actors listed at the beginning of the sentence.

13. (E) There are no errors in this sentence.

14. (B) The phrase *in flying* is unidiomatic in this context. It should read *by flying* and parallels *by taking* later in the sentence.

15. (A) Since *scarcely* is a negative, this is a double negative. It should be *scarcely any*.

16. (B) The phrase *with the trainer and two doctors* is parenthetical. The subject is the singular *quarterback*. To agree, the verb should be *was walking*.

17. (C) Since *faster* is the comparative form of *fast (fast, faster, fastest)*, the use of *more* is redundant.

18. (E) This sentence is correct. The adverb *eerily* modifies the adjective *bare,* and the verbs are correct.

19. (B) There is a diction error in *raises,* misused here for *rises*. The verb *raise* takes an object and means *to lift up* (I raise the window shade), while *rise* is intransitive. A bear could rise, or a bear could raise himself up.

20. (C) The correct pronoun to refer to a boy is *who* rather than *that.*

21. (E) All of these sentences are grammatical, but (E) is the most concise in normal word order. (C) uses the same words, but the word order is unconventional, making *wittiest* an afterthought.

22. (D) We can eliminate (A) and (B) because they use *you,* but the sentence began with the pronoun *one* (the third, not the second, person) as the subject. (E) corrects this error, but the repetition of the *one should* breaks the parallel verbs without a repeated subject. (D) keeps the parallel use of active verbs, while (C) replaces the verb with a participle.

23. (C) Choices (A), (B), (D), and (E) are adjectival phrases that modify the *designs* or *collections,* not the company. The designs, not the company, are *different.* With the *With designs* phrase, the phrase now logically refers to *Orlando Fashions Company,* which follows it.

24. (B) The sentence is a fragment in all four versions except (B). Here, the first clause is dependent, and the main clause has a subject (*supply line*) and a main verb (*became*). Though both (A) and (D) also use *became,* the clauses are still dependent because the conjunctions (*and, while*) join them to the initial dependent clause. The *becoming* is a participle, not a verb.

25. (D) The problem of the original sentence is its verbosity. The phrase *of a . . . nature* is always verbose; the adjective by itself will say the same. The trouble with (B) is that *trusting* and *trustworthy* have very different meanings. A trusting person may be trustworthy or devious, and a trustworthy person may be trusting or skeptical.

26. (A) The original is the best version. Since the sentence begins with the phrase *A very old plant,* the first words after this introductory phrase should refer to a plant, singular, not to plants such as *cornflowers* (B). (C), (D), and (E) misplace the modifier by following the initial phrase with *paintings,* not a *plant.*

27. (B) Though the original sentence is not wrong, it treats the two clauses as equal. Choice (B), by subordinating the past to the present, establishes a more meaningful relationship between the parts. (C) shifts from passive to active, while (E) uses the present tense to describe action in the past.

28. (D) The *they* in the dependent clause is a pronoun without an antecedent. Who are they? Choices (B) and (C) revise without solving the problem. Both (D) and (E) substitute a noun for the vague pronoun. (D) is preferable because it uses two active verbs and fewer words.

29. (D) There are two complete sentences here, run together with no punctuation between them. They should be punctuated as two sentences with a period after *fire* or with a semicolon, as in choice (D).

30. (A) The three elements of the series here should be kept parallel. Choice (A) uses three gerunds. (B), (C), and (E) are not parallel; (D) is wordier than (A).

31. (C) In choices (A), (D), and (E), the pronoun *he* could refer to either Arun Shourie or the prime minister's son. (B) and (C) avoid this ambiguity. The sequence of verb tenses is clearer in (C), showing that the exposure caused the job loss.

32. (E) The pronouns (*this* and *which*) in (A), (B), (C), and (D) have no specific antecedent; (E) avoids this vagueness by adding the noun *fact.*

33. (C) The first two verbs in this sentence (*abducts* and *carries*) are active, but the third verb is passive in (A), (B), (D), and (E). Choice (C) keeps all three verbs in the active voice. (C) is also the most economical of the five options.

34. (E) Seeing the participle at the beginning of the sentence, the wise test-taker will check to see if the participle dangles. Who yields to public demand? Not the *end* of a film or the *lovers* in a film. Only (E) supplies a human agent which the participial phrase could logically modify.

35. (B) Without a conjunction, (A) and (E) are comma splices. (C) is a run-on sentence. (D) changes the meaning by leaving out the *may*. By adding the conjunction *and,* (B) corrects the comma splice.

36. (A) The original sentence is better than the four alternatives. It uses two parallel active verbs in the perfect tense. Choices (C), (D), and (E) use one verb and a participle or noun. (B) has a parallel structure but a wordier one than in (A), using eleven words instead of seven.

37. (C) If you focus on the phrase *an idea that . . .* , you should hear the idiomatic rightness of *is easy to comprehend.* The adjective *easy* modifies the noun *idea.* (D) also has the adjective *easy,* but the idiom with *easy* is the infinitive rather than the preposition and gerund.

38. (B) The sentence is a fragment, lacking a main verb. Only (B) supplies the verb needed to make the sentence complete.

39. (A) The phrase *large majority* is an overstatement. If it were true, the obese would be the *large majority* and only a small minority would not be overweight. If the obese really were a large majority, would they suffer from discrimination? A better word choice would be something like *large segment* or *large part* or *large section.*

40. (B) The original version repeats the word *special* and uses the wordy phrase *at one point or another of their lives* (one word, *sometimes,* or a phrase like *at any time* says the same thing). The *special bond* and the *special brother/sisterhood* can easily be combined, using one or the other. In the second sentence, both *all* and *throughout their lives* can be deleted without any loss of meaning. Though several of the choices are grammatical, (B) is the most concise sentence, without changing the emphasis of the original.

41. (E) The original is a sentence fragment, with a participle (*having*) rather than a main verb. The easy solution is (E), changing *having* to *have.* (D) is a complete sentence, but the change of tense is inconsistent in this context. (C) is also a complete sentence, but it is wordier than (E).

42. (C) The chief difficulty in the original is the vague phrase *but one must study that aspect much more carefully.* What does *aspect* refer to? *Cause, obesity,* or *over-eating.*? Choice (C) is clear, grammatical, and concise.

43. (E) The reference of *One* is not immediately clear. Is it an observer of the obese or an obese person? The *it* in sentence 18 is also vague, having no specific antecedent. The paragraph changes from the singular (*a person*) in 14 and 15 to the plural (*they*) in 16 and 17.

44. (D) The third paragraph of only two sentences is not developed. It would logically form the conclusion of the second paragraph with some sort of connective.

45. (E) The incomplete use of *so* (*so much*) is awkward; *appearance* and *good looks* denote the same thing; and the sentence has a comma splice. Several of the choices also have errors of grammar: a comma splice in (B) and (D), a dangling participle in (C). Choice (E) is concise and grammatical.

46. (A) There are several obvious redundancies in these three sentences: the repetition of *relationship* and *special,* the restating in sentence 8 of what 7 has already said. Choice (A) eliminates the repetitions.

47. (B) The phrases are clichés. They are not parallel constructions, Latinate, slang, or ungrammatical.

48. (C) The *appearance* and *look* are the same. Choices (A), (B), (D), and (E) fail to eliminate this tautology (saying the same thing twice).

49. (D) Choice (D) is not verbose. In (A), *We are an inseparable couple* says the same thing as *we do just about everything together.* In (B), sentence 7 is not very different from sentence 8. The two halves of this part of sentence 9 in (C) are almost the same. In (E), *big hall* is literally repeated.

50. (D) The best division is into two paragraphs, with the first ending after sentence 8.

51. (D) The adverb *severely* should be replaced by the adjective *severe,* which modifies the noun *controls.*

52. (C) This is an error of agreement. The subject of the verb is plural (*Tunisia and Israel*), so the verb should be *have agreed.*

53. (E) There are no errors in this sentence.

54. (B) This is also an error of agreement. This sentence places the verb before the subject, but the subject is the singular *challenge,* so the verb should be the singular *is.*

55. (A) The verb form is incorrect here; the verb is *swim, swam, swum.* In the past perfect tense (with *had*), the correct form is *had swum.*

56. (C) The idiom error here uses a prepositional phrase with a gerund (*for strengthening*). The more idiomatic phrase would use the infinitive, *intended to strengthen.*

57. (E) The sentence correctly handles the parallelism with the *not only . . . but also* construction.

58. (C) Though *team* can be a plural, the first part of this sentence uses a singular verb (*has*) and a singular pronoun (*its*), so *they are meeting* should be *it is meeting.*

59. (C) Since the sentence begins with the past tense verb *featured,* to maintain consistency, the second verb should be *served.*

60. (A) The subject of the sentence is singular, either *Dallas* or *San Francisco,* not both.